T0365903

WITH A
Foreign
Accent

FRANK WEINMAN

authorHOUSE®

AuthorHouse™
1663 Liberty Drive
Bloomington, IN 47403
www.authorhouse.com
Phone: 1 (800) 839-8640

Published by AuthorHouse 07/10/2017

ISBN: 978-1-5049-7273-4 (sc)
ISBN: 978-1-5049-7274-1 (e)

Print information available on the last page.

TABLE OF CONTENTS

PREFACE

Frank Weinman always like to write. In his later years, retired and living in California, he took writing classes to improve his skills in a language that was not native to him. Over the years, he wrote monographs on various aspects and periods of his life. Eventually, he combined these writings into a master volume he entitled, *With a Foreign Accent*. It is an account of his life growing up in Austria, his family life, his marriage to Teri Vidor, their harrowing escape from the Nazis in late 1941, and their new life in America, with their daughters Francie and Linda.

Frank...Grandpa Frank...passed away on the day after his 95th birthday, July 10, 2009. Over the next few years his daughters, now including Judy Lichterman, the daughter of Frank's second wife, Frances Alt, kept his manuscript in a bound loose-leaf booklet.

In the summer of 2015, I decided to edit Frank's manuscript into a book that would include other writings of his, mostly addendums to his life story: his reflections on turning 45; his account of a journey he took with his family back to his home town of Vienna, Austria, and to the home of his first wife Teri in Slovakia; and his account of his 90th birthday cruise in 2004. There are also his reflections on family members who had passed away, such as his aunt Kamilla, his older brother Charles, and his sister-in-law Magda, who, with her parents and much of Teri's family, perished in the Holocaust. Also included are translated letters sent to and from Teri's family in what was then Kassa, Hungary (now Kosice, Slovakia) during the years 1941 to 1944, after Frank and Teri had settled in their new home, Chicago, Illinois.

What follows is a fascinating and at times dramatic tale of a man who lived through both good times and frightfully horrible times. It is dedicated to his grandchildren, great-grandchildren and any future generations who may want to look back and see what life was like for a proud Austrian Jew, who became a proud American citizen, during some of the most momentous days of the 20th century.

June 2017
Stuart Schwartz
Frank Weinman's son-in-law

INTRODUCTION

There is a game we play sometime. We wonder what is more important. What shapes us more?

The genes we inherited from our ancestors, or circumstances we encounter after we are born, such as the love our parents show us, our place within the family, formal or informal education, how the world treats us.

Or finally, luck, just plain luck. It was mostly luck that kept me alive during the horrible years from 1938 through 1941. And it was most certainly my luck to find a wonderful wife, my children's mother, who allowed us to find some happiness even during those years, and later, until her death in 1975. More luck to find a second wife, good and patient enough to live with me now; luck to have children and stepchildren who turned out well and grandchildren who promise the same.

I remember so well my father's advice to me when, after apologizing for one of my frequent misdeeds, I tried to belittle myself.

DO NOT MAKE YOURSELF TOO SMALL. YOU ARE NOT THAT GREAT!

He was right. Modesty is becoming to Moses or to Einstein. I cannot afford that luxury; I must write my story myself.

Knowing that these pages are not concerned with a very important life or with events that have not already been told, I must ask myself: why am I writing this document? Except for a few personal observations, I cannot add much to already existing stories about my time, nor can I find a burning desire from my children for more information. They do and should live their own lives. Furthermore, much of what I have to say is painful. I managed to survive under very difficult circumstances. This very survival might be the key to my writing, not just the necessity to fill my time, though that is important for me, but more so the hope that some of the facts I'll describe may not be known and some of the ideas prove interesting.

I was an 18-year-old boy in Vienna, Austria when I finished high school with an examination called "Matura." While the word means "becoming mature," this examination marks the end of all general or liberal arts education. Further learning would be of a specialized nature. But finishing high school, called more modestly and more accurately "middle school" in German-speaking countries, was an even more important milestone for me. Until then, the summer of 1932, I thought I had the right always to be treated fairly. When I performed well in school I felt entitled to good marks. When I did poorly I expected to be found out. At home, too, my parents were predictable. In short, until the summer of 1932 I lived a normal life, whatever that means.

My position within the family was clear. As the younger brother, I was frequently teased. Being three years my senior and therefore wise, my brother would sometimes take advantage of me. Once, when my parents were not at home, there was an important telephone call; it was absolutely mandatory for my parents to call back as soon as they returned. My brother had taken the call but he asked me if I felt smart enough to remember the message. Being already ten years old, I promised not only to remember but also to deliver it. I forgot, of course.

Half an hour after our parents had come home, my brother innocently inquired if they had called their friends, as promised by me. I was scolded for not delivering the message, my brother praised for reminding them. Not until an hour later did I realize that I had been set up, that it might have been easier for my brother to deliver the message himself. But my parents did not see it that way.

My brother may have been fifteen years old and I twelve when we played a lot of table tennis.

He was better than I was, of course, but wanted to assure himself a good sparring partner. In order to do this, he promised me he would tell all of our friends that it was I who was the better player, if I only won a single game against him, but I never did. He would have kept his promise!

My beautiful mother, who probably preferred me to my brother because as a child I looked more like her, was to be pampered; this was established by my father, 11 years her senior. He, on the other hand, certainly favored my brother, who looked more like him. After every meal our family took together, my father would remind us boys to thank mother for the good food.

"Why should we?" I once asked my father. "She did not cook it, our maid did; and you are the only one of our family who makes money."

As always, my father had a good answer.

"Your mother plans all meals; she plans everything; she is the most important member of our household; the best and most beautiful mother anybody ever had! Don't you ever forget this!"

Of course, I had the best and most beautiful mother; I knew that. But the most important member of our household was my father. Nobody else. Only he had all the answers; only he would always tell me what to do, not only what I did wrong but also what I did right. He would often accomplish that with a Latin proverb which he carefully translated and analyzed for me.

I remember a game my father used to play with us boys. He would stand in the middle, pretending to be the sun, but always turning to us. My brother was supposed to be the earth, walking in a circle around my father. I, the smallest, was playing the moon. While my brother walked around my father, I had to run around my brother. After a while I got quite good at this game.

My mother was a very wise person, but I recognized that only many years later.

During any emergency, and only then, would she take over! In 1939 and 1940 when my father and I were about to lose all hope, she kept our family functioning. And she was a peacemaker! Both my father and I suffered a bad temper then, but my mother knew how to handle us. It was she, before my father, who welcomed Teri, my first wife, into our family and thus assured an excellent relationship between my wife and my parents.

I was not until 1932 or 1933 that bad things started to happen to me. My world changed for the worse, and it wasn't my fault! A bad case of polio almost killed me. Though I recovered completely after a few months, too much time had been lost for me to pursue my plans to study law as well as commerce (we might call it "business administration" now). Even more important, the Great Depression hit Europe and especially Austria, where I grew up, with tremendous force. I still studied law at the University of Vienna but without attending any lectures after January 1933. I would take concentrated courses later to enable me to pass my first examination.

In the meantime, my father could use me in his factory in Czechoslovakia until my brother finished his Ph.D. in chemistry a year later. This might sound like a sacrifice on my part now, but it was, without any doubt, the right decision and turned out to be of great benefit for our family and probably mostly for myself.

When the world as we knew it came to an end in March, 1938 (Hitler's Germany invaded and annexed Austria) my brother emigrated to America, quickly found an excellent position in Chicago, no doubt aided by his high university degree, and his subsequently-acquired experience in my father's factory. He managed to bring first my wife and me and then my parents to America. Once here it was thanks to him that I not only immediately had a job, but also advanced rapidly.

Starting with my nineteenth year, and through very bad, good and very good times, there has been a unifying factor in my life, ever since I put the age of comparative innocence, high school, behind me: A FOREIGN ACCENT.

Only up to my eighteenth year was I allowed the luxury of expressing myself in my native language, German. I spoke and wrote it well, if my high school grades meant anything. But afterwards my surroundings were Slovakian, Czech, Hungarian, French, and for half a century now, English.

True, with the exception of Hungarian, I understand all these languages; but most certainly I am not perfect in any one; even my German is rusty now. I think or write or dream only in English. But while my grammar is fairly good, my spelling middling, my word power poor, my foreign accent is strong enough to make me suffer when I hear myself on a tape recording. During my working career this hurt me but little, and may even have helped me sometimes because as a technical advisor, I was assumed to have great knowledge in my field. What other reason could there be to send a fellow whose English is less than perfect to see important customers. Only in America! In any other country known to me, a foreign accent leads to being ridiculed or even shunned.

But more than any experience I had with business acquaintances or friends, it is myself who has made me feel inadequate. While I am a reader of English novels and enjoy English theater, English poetry does not appeal to me very much. Also, I often feel bad because I have not expressed myself as well as I should have, although I am certainly not afraid to speak up, be it in small or large groups. Self-confidence—some may well call it arrogance—is not missing. I believe this is due to positive reinforcement I was lucky enough to get as a child: a happy life both at home and in school. Perhaps it was also important to have among my ancestors, on both sides, many with good intelligence; also a few eccentrics. Some of them might have been just a little crazy.

Now, with more than half of my eighth decade behind me, I can probably call my life a moderate success. A success because I managed to survive; because of two excellent marriages; because in spite of coming to America with one suit, six shirts, a change of underwear and a $300 debt, I never lacked for anything really important. I was always able to support my family well by any reasonable standard. On the other hand, I feel I did not live up to my potential. I should have done better.

Financially better perhaps (I was never interested in comparing myself to those who have more money than I) but much more importantly by not trying to achieve goals that probably were within my reach. For instance, during my working career in this country, which lasted 39 years, all of which was spent with the same company, I should have contributed more by working more diligently and getting along better with my co-workers. I am even convinced that I got as high as I did (production manager) only because my brother was a key employee of the company. However, more important I think than failure to make just more money or to rise higher in the business, is that I did not dare to change jobs in order to do what I really wanted to do. For instance, run a big travel agency. I might have done that well because of my knowledge of languages; being able to spot trends early, having traveled quite a bit myself, and liking it. Or else, I might have become an international buyer for large companies.

Finally, perhaps my greatest love might have been teaching.

My greatest regret, as far as not fulfilling my potential is concerned, must be that I did not do much better in mastering the English language, which I already spoke reasonably well in Vienna, at age seventeen. My writing certainly does not satisfy me; my accent should be better; I do not have enough words at my command.

But it is rather late in my day; better to use whatever word power I have right now and go on with the job of writing about my life, most of which was lived speaking with a foreign accent.

I

ROOTS AND RELATIVES

I was born in 1914, in Vienna, Austria, in the GOOD OLD DAYS. This was a few weeks before World War I started, when Vienna was the capital of the Austro-Hungarian Empire. It is true that the immediate cause of the war, the assassination of the old Emperor Franz Josef's nephew, who was supposed to succeed him, had already happened. Still, as a boy I was proud to have been born in the GOOD OLD DAYS. My country was big and important and Vienna, my hometown, still amounted to more than memories of a glorious past. My Vienna of the 1920's, I actually remember, was a wretched place. Most people were poor.

Much more important, nobody could imagine that it could ever be different. World War I had long ended but when we referred to "peacetime," we understood this to mean the year, or decades, or centuries, before 1914.

Yet I loved Vienna and felt sorry for anybody who was not fortunate enough to be Viennese. I cannot tell where this fascination with my home town came from. It certainly ended a long time ago. But perhaps I really relived the old songs telling us how Vienna would always be "the city of my dreams."

It may well be that all human beings have a tendency toward local patriotism; or perhaps the beauty of the Viennese Woods or of many of the magnificent old buildings really impressed me. But why? I had as yet no opportunity for comparison. Moreover, none of my parents or grandparents had been born in Vienna. This was true for most, if not all my friends. As old as the city may have been, it really only grew rapidly during the last decades of the 19th and the first decade of the 20th century. But in spite of coming from "the provinces," my relatives considered themselves true Viennese. There was, for instance, a brother of my maternal grandmother who told me once when I visited him:

"You must know, of course, that the mayor of Vienna is an idiot."

I had always been told that our mayor, a Social Democrat, was a great guy.

"Why, uncle?" I wondered.

"He is so ignorant he does not even answer my letters. Every week I explain to him how he should run our city. It does not have to be poor, you understand. Look at me: I came from Bohemia as a boy with not a cent to my name. But I worked hard and became rich.

But nowadays, people don't want to work. Socialism, they call it. Laziness, which is what it is really. I am a liberal, which means everybody that works hard can make it and no government can take away what is mine. And I want no aristocracy, either. Before the war, I explained to Emperor Franz Josef that God does not want any noblemen. I proved it to him in a letter: if God Almighty had wanted aristocrats, then every child born to their families would have a golden stamp on its behind. But nobody has such a golden stamp, which proves that we are all alike."

My great uncle Adolf had many such stories. One day, he explained to me that every human being should walk around naked for at least half an hour every day. If we all did that, God would know that we want to go back to the Garden of Eden where we were naked.

"Don't believe the lie that Adam and Eve first sinned and afterwards put some clothes on. It was the other way around."

"How do you know, uncle?"

"I know, boy. How do you think I made all my money? Some fifty years ago, when I was a young man, I invented a knitting machine and had it patented. Now people can have inexpensive underwear. But nothing that's cheap is good for us. Had I invented something else, people would still go around naked and not sin."

There was no use telling my great-uncle that human beings wore clothes before he was born. He saw the world his own way, but I loved the old man and his stories. I did not know then, of course, that he told the same stories to anybody who would listen.

"His wife is a saint, otherwise she could not live with this old fool," my mother explained to me once. "Someday he'll get himself in trouble with his letters. Luckily, nobody takes him seriously. But it's true, he was a brilliant man in his youth."

God must have loved this brilliant man turned a little foolish. When he died he was close to 100 years old, just a year of two before Hitler came to Vienna.

My maternal grandparents had come to Vienna shortly after 1900 from Bohemia, now the westernmost part of Czechoslovakia. The Jews from that province were heavily inbred. Perhaps that helps to explain why so many of them were brilliant, like the writer Franz Kafka, but also a little crazy. Until 1848 (thus not long before my grandparents were born) there had been a local law in that province that only the eldest son of any Jewish family was allowed to marry. This may have led to many cousin-marriages because the parents of daughters wanted to secure them a partner as early as possible and looked no further than their extended family. Actually, some of the younger sons married too, but because the ceremony, though performed by a rabbi, was not recognized by the government, their children were considered to be born out of wedlock and carried the mother's name only; thus, the children of brothers could have different last names.

After 1848, the Jews of Bohemia (the name of that province in the language of the land is "Czechy") did rather well. Having been peddlers before, they often became shopkeepers or owners of taverns. In the middle of the 19th century many railroads were built in Bohemia, probably the most prosperous province in the whole Austrian Empire. The Jews had one advantage over their immediate neighbors: there were bilingual, speaking not only Czech but also German.

There is a strange reason for this: the government, probably as early as the late 18th century, allowed the Jews to run their own schools, but under the condition that instructions were conducted in German, while their neighbors' schools were in Czech, the native tongue.

Three important consequences followed: first, the Bohemian Jews forgot the Yiddish language, as they never did in Poland. Second, they became better educated since they knew Czech anyway but, also knowing German had access to both cultures. Finally, a wedge was driven between the Czechs and the Jews because the Czechs resented the fact that Jews spoke the language of the Emperors. "A Jew is not a Czech," was a common saying before World War I. (By the way, the relationship between Czechs and Jews between the wars was excellent. The younger Jews, born after 1918, spoke Czech much better than German.)

My maternal grandfather, Fritz Neumann, would often tell me how his parents met; this must have been around 1850.

"My father Aron was a peddler when he was young, but not very successful. You see, another young woman was a better peddler; she gave him too much competition. But he was a smart man. He went to her and asked her to marry him. She did, and became my mother."

I don't know who was responsible for their common success, but they became quite well- to-do. They opened a store, later added a saloon, and also bought several small farms and ran them. In 1885, my grandfather's elder brother, Ignaz, who had just married Babette Hasterlik, was supposed to take over the business, but he refused.

"Let Fritz be a shopkeeper. I don't want to stay here. My new wife has a brother in America, in a city called 'Chicago.' He is doing very well there and we want to try our luck there too."

The two brothers agreed that Ignaz would get all available cash in lieu of his future inheritance. In Chicago, he started a small brewery. After all, the Bohemians know how to make beer. It is interesting he gave his brewery the name "Hapsburg." What loyalty to his emperor!

That's how I happened to have relatives in America!

After the Nazis came to Austria, in 1938, these relatives brought my brother to America and he, in turn, made it possible for us to come. But more about that later.

My grandfather, Fritz Neumann, was already married to Paula, nee Engel, when he took the store over from his father, Aron. But Aron, who according to old photos looked every inch a patriarch, didn't trust his younger son.

"I'll keep the farms, for the time being. When I see that you do a good job at the store and the saloon, I'll give one farm after the other, not to you, but to the children you will have. So, go to work, both you and Paula."

My grandfather reported this conversation to me. He added:

"We showed him, all right. Not only did the store do well, but the children came, one every other year. And my father lived up to his promise and gave every child a farm. But after the fourth child he asked your grandmother to be more careful; he had no more farms."

I found it interesting that it was my grandmother who was given the burden to be "more careful" (indeed there were no more children) because as far as I can remember, it was always she who was in charge. It was at her insistence that the family moved to Vienna around 1905. And when my grandparents celebrated their golden wedding anniversary in 1935, my grandfather stood up to his full height—about five feet two—and gave us the following speech:

Now listen, my children, grandchildren, all you relatives and friends: my wife and I have had an excellent marriage; all the fifty years were happy. You know why? Because I always did what she wanted. And tonight will be just like 50 years ago, only I won't be so excited."

My grandmother was a very good-looking woman in her youth, and a very strong one. Too strong, perhaps. She absolutely dominated her three younger children, all girls; only her oldest was a boy, my uncle Joseph, called "Pepa." Somehow, my grandmother had the idea that only boys mattered; she insisted the three girls were to wait on their brother and later on their husbands. When my uncle developed a touch of tuberculosis at age 17, my mother, a year and a half younger and the oldest of the three girls, was charged with taking care of her brother. She had to quit school for half a year in order to move with her brother to a spa some 100 miles from Vienna. Her duties included making sure that he ate well, also sewing any buttons that might come loose. I asked my mother if she did not object to this arrangement:

"No," she said, "how could I? My mother wanted me to do it. There was no room for any argument."

"But didn't you resent the fact that you had to wait on your older brother when you were 16?"

"I certainly did not resent him. Anyway, he improved after a few months and we moved back to Vienna. I always loved him."

"But," my mother added, "when his TB came back a year later, and it was decided to send him to an expensive sanatorium in Switzerland by himself, I was a little unhappy, especially since I too had developed a persistent cough by that time. But your grandmother said it was not right to spend a lot of money on girls."

I have no idea whether or not my uncle really had TB; a few years later the war (World War I) broke out and he served four years on the Italian front without any apparent harm. He died in 1988, in New York, just a little over 100 years old. My mother's cough, however, turned into asthma. She suffered from this disease most of her life.

According to the best doctors of Vienna and later Chicago, this asthma was of the "nervous" kind and could possibly have been cured by psychoanalysis when she was still young. She died at age 64, 30 younger than her two sisters or her brother.

My maternal grandparents spoke German with a Czech accent. I was curious why they had moved to Vienna; were they not happy in their Czech village?

"Quite the contrary," my grandfather explained. "Those were the best years!"

"Well, why didn't you stay there?"

"That's not easy to explain, my child." (My grandfather always called me "my child" because "I love you," he said). "Perhaps we wanted our children to grow up in Vienna, the big city, because my three girls might find better husbands there. And we wanted our son to go to the best high school. Most likely, we moved because so many others moved to Vienna, the Emperor's town!"

"Could it be that you preferred the German culture of Vienna to Czech?"

"No. Certainly not. The Czech farmers were well-educated. Most villages had a little library! And the Czech music! This was the time of Dvorak and Smetana! You know, *The Bartered Bride!* There is nothing like it!"

He started to sing a few tunes from this opera.

"But you see, we got a lot of money for our store, and your grandmother suggested we should invest it in her brother's business in Vienna. He could use the money. Of course, I became a partner." So again, it was my grandmother's decision!

I asked my mother if she was happy growing up as a teenager in the big city, after having lived in a village for the first twelve years of her life. Did it not bother her to attend school in a different language?

"The language did not bother me. As a matter of fact, a year or two of my grammar school had been in Germany anyway; we Jews were all bilingual. And we did have fun in Vienna, right from the start! Me or your uncle Pepa played the piano and he often invited a few of his high school friends over.

"We danced! But while he was playing the piano, he would watch that none of his friends danced too close. He would scream: "Stop it!" when he thought his sisters were in danger of getting seduced by the boys or by the waltzes. Of course, we watched him. When he looked down at the piano keys, we danced close again! And I loved school and my teacher, she loved me too. I did not attend public school; your grandparents insisted I should go to a private school called "Miss Frankle's Academy for Girls." We studied French, piano, literature, and history. You name it. But most of all, good Viennese cooking."

Sometime in the 1930s, I learned more about my mother's youth as a teenager. My parents used to keep an ancient large folder on the desk in the living room; bills to be paid or other important letters were temporarily kept there. Whenever we were searching for something, "large folder" was the place to look! I was doing just that one day when I noticed that this folder had an extra pocket stuffed with soft tissue.

Being curious, I removed the tissue and found in it an old newspaper clipping from the year 1905. Looking closer, I saw that it was a review of Lehar's operetta, *The Merry Widow.* I showed it to my mother and saw her blush! My mother, the old lady in her forties, blushed with excitement!

"I've been looking for this clipping for some twenty years!" she screamed. "I must have stuffed it into a secret pocket of the folder! I brought it with me when I married."

"Was this piece of paper important to you?"

"But of course! I was at the premiere of *Ibe Merry Widow!* It was one of the most important days of my life! I was about your age. We had come to Vienna just a little earlier and my father took us all to the theater. You cannot imagine the excitement; even the Kaiser was there! And the melodies…" She hummed *The Merry Widow Waltz* and she sang *Vilya's Song*.

"Have you seen the opera since?"

"Oh, no! It couldn't be as nice again, I wouldn't spoil my memories."

My parents went to the theater fairly often. Both would dress very carefully, my mother always being in charge of judging my father's appearance. Somehow she was supposed to have perfect taste; she came from a well-to-do family! My father's family had been poor. My paternal grandfather, his name was Hermann, was born in Misslitz, a small town in southern Moravia.

Misslitz was then a German-speaking, so-called "Autonomous Jewish Community." Until 1848, this was of great legal importance. The Jews were allowed to run their own affairs. Unlike in neighboring Bohemia, all sons could legally marry. However, there was one very important restriction: no Jew was allowed to move away from the town. As a matter of fact, the Jews were not even supposed to spend the night anywhere else but in "their" town without special permission. Obviously, it was not good for a peddler to have to come home every evening. Therefore, shortly after 1848, when all Jews in Austria (Moravia as well as Bohemia were among the many provinces of the Hapsburg Empire) were given equal rights, my great- grandfather Elkan and his family moved from Moravia across the border to the province of Lower Austria. This was a journey of six miles. My grandfather was about 10 years old.

I find the names interesting: both on my mother's and on my father's side, the great-grandfathers have Hebrew, biblical names. The grandfathers, however, have German names. In Central Europe, Yiddish ceased to be spoken around 1830, probably because 40 or 50 years earlier (under Emperor Joseph II), the Jews of the western provinces of the Empire were asked, or forced, to have all schooling in German.

I know little about my great-grandfather Elkan except his name and the fact that he died young and had at least two sons and one daughter. Even about my grandfather, Hermann, who died around 1908, I am not well informed.

My father, who was otherwise very family-oriented, rarely mentioned him. All he would say about his father was: "He did the best he could."

Knowing that my father never said anything bad about anybody, least of all about his family, I must assume Hermann Weinmann was not a very great person. He certainly never made more than a bare living. I heard rumors that he was a little too fond of the bottle. Around 1905 my father brought his parents to Vienna and supported them until their deaths.

By far the most interesting person among my immediate ancestors must have been my paternal grandmother, Augusta (called "Gusti") nee Bauer. She came from a little town in southern Moravia, also an "Autonomous Jewish Community." Judging from her brother and many nephews and nieces I still meet, the Bauers must've been a notch above the Weinmanns. Born around 1850, she had at least a fair education, knew quite a bit about contemporary German literature, and played the "zither," a string instrument which was like a poor man's piano.

When I was a teenager my father took my brother and me to see Braunsdorf, the village in lower Austria where he was born and raised. I thought I had never seen a smaller place! And when he showed us the house of his parents I was really appalled. A miserable hut, I thought.

"Father, you told us you grew up in a decent place!" my brother said. "This house has no more than two rooms and no bathroom."

"Well," my father answered, "it looked bigger to me then. Also, I remember there was a little shack attached for the goat. We had to have fresh milk!"

"But where did you sleep, your parents, your three brothers, your sister?"

"The parents slept in the kitchen, the larger of the two rooms. My sister, the baby, slept with them.

Of course, we ate in the kitchen too. The other room was ours, the boys. We had a table where we did our homework, four chairs and four cots. We washed in the kitchen. An outhouse was next to the goat's shack."

"But father, you told us so much about your mother reading poetry to you," I said. "How could she do that in this place?"

"We had a petroleum lamp; it was always warm in the kitchen, I remember. Of course, we had a chest of drawers for our clothes, and a large shelf for the books. I guess my mother must have brought several volumes with her when she married; mostly Goethe and of course, Heinrich Heine."

II

MY PARENTS

Most likely, my paternal grandmother named my father (her second son who was born on February 25, 1878) Heinrich, after her favorite poet Heinrich Heine, her idol. She wrote a few poems herself, much in Heine's style.

To this day, I find it hard to understand how my father, who I remember as a sophisticated, well-read man, could have grown up in a miserable hut in a village of probably fewer than 200 people. The closest grammar school was at least an hour's walk away. The Weinmanns were the only Jews in the village; no possibility for religious affiliation existed within any reasonable distance. To make matters worse, the family was not only desperately poor but my grandfather Hermann never amounted to anything and my grandmother Augusta had five surviving children to bring up! Luckily, I was always interested in family history and had enough opportunity to talk not only to my father, but also to two of his brothers (the third was a victim of World War I) and his only sister, my aunt Sophie, who lived to be ninety years old.

Her son, my cousin, Professor Daniel Brunner of Tel Aviv, Israel, is the only one of my extended family with a claim to fame. A cardiologist, he was one of the first physicians to stress the importance of jogging and did important research on the importance of diet on heart disease; he is still lecturing in America, Europe and Asia. *(Editor's note: Dr. Daniel (Dolfe) Brunner died in 2009.)*

"Your father was always a great guy," Aunt Sophie told me, "definitely my favorite brother. I remember him as the leader from way back. He is six years older than I and maybe that's why I came to him with my problems. Our mother often said: "Always turn to Heinrich when you need help. As you know, I am not exactly beautiful, to put it mildly, but your father always said I was."

"But Aunt Sophie, you are still good-looking. I bet as a young girl you must have been really pretty."

"You are a flatterer, just like your father! No, I probably look better now than when I was young."

"You know, I have the Weinmann features! Your father had them too, of course: a good size nose, deep-seated and narrow eyes, kind of Chinese, and bushy eyebrows. But you know how it is with a man: 'he looks so interesting.' That's what all the women said about him; that's why he could marry the most beautiful woman, your mother."

"You did not do so badly either; you certainly have a handsome husband."

"Oh yes. And it was your father who gave me a handsome dowry."

My uncle Alfred, my father's oldest brother, was the only very good-looking one of the Weinmann siblings. He was also soft-spoken. A real gentleman and a successful salesman. I asked him how come my father was sent away to high school, to a distant town? Why was my father, rather than Alfred, the first-born son, so favored?

"As the oldest boy, I was apprenticed to a tailor when I was still quite young. You won't believe it, but I am a fully trained tailor, although I haven't had a needle in my hands for decades. Anyway, your father was always the smartest in school. I think our mother, your grandmother, always had in mind that Heinrich should be the educated one of our family."

"But uncle, didn't you resent that just a little bit?"

"No, really not at all. Your grandmother was a very smart woman. She asked for my opinion. She told me that your father would face very difficult years; because from the moment he entered high school he would have to be on his own. The family certainly had no money to support him. All we could do for him was to find a distant relative who would let him live with their family. From the second year of high school on, your father made money by tutoring some of his fellow students, enough to buy clothes."

I also tried to interview my Uncle Julius, my father's youngest brother, but he was not very easy to talk to. He was the only one of the Weinmann siblings who spoke the broad peasant's dialect; my father could do that too whenever he wanted. It was sometimes good for business, but usually his German was perfect. Actually, my father and Julius had very similar features when they were young. It was difficult for me to tell them apart on a photo taken when they were in their 20s, before Julius got rather fat. One day I succeeded in asking him what kind of a boy my father was.

"Always a smart ass, your father Heinrich. I had a hard time in school because the teacher wanted to know why I was not as good as he. But let me tell you, and you better believe it, your father was always a good guy. I'd have been in a bad fix if he had not been there when my business went kaput."

My uncle Julius died soon after this conversation, his business still not very prosperous. But his oldest son Walter, a carbon-copy of his father, with a good sense of humor but utterly uncouth, would take over. The second son, Dr. Otto Weinmann, living in Vienna, was in medical school at that time. *(Editor's note: Otto Weinmann died in Vienna in 2010.)* It was utterly impossible for a young man, especially a Jew, to find a job in Vienna during the Depression. Therefore, most of my friends studied at the university until they graduated (tuition was practically free), in order to have something to do. This proved to be a blessing later when Hitler got to Austria and all Jews had to flee.

But there was a third child, my cousin Hertha, a very intelligent girl who had just graduated from a college specializing in the design of ladies' fashionwear. When her father died, it was a forgone conclusion that she would turn to her uncle, my father, to find her a job. Her older brothers could not possibly support her.

Both my brother and I liked Hertha very much and asked my father to do something, just anything.

My father agonized. "I have no doubt that she's a very capable girl, but what can I do for her? Nobody is hiring; so many women in Hertha's line are getting laid off."

It was only natural that my mother got involved. Her father and her uncle were partners in a business that manufactured ladies' blouses. So my mother tried to intervene for Hertha but was flatly turned down. No openings! But my father did not give up. It was the time of the Jewish High Holidays; he asked his father-in-law, my grandfather Fritz:

"Are you going to temple again this year?"

"Of course, Heinrich. You know that."

"But won't you and your brother-in-law feel just a little bit bad when you pray? You just turned down an orphan, my niece Hertha. Her father just died and…"

I don't know what happened afterwards, except that my cousin Hertha went to work for my grandfather and was an instant success. Later, my grandfather and especially his brother-in-law, often thanked my father because his son, who also worked in their business, would marry the girl!

No wonder that I remember my father as the one everybody turned to for advice, and also for money. Since I later worked in my father's factory, I came to know that he was never really wealthy. He never deserved his reputation as the "rich uncle." He just considered it his duty to help.

Although my father was born in the small village of Braunsdorf, Lower Austria, his birth certificate was written by the "Jewish Community of Misslitz, Moravia" (*Editor's note: the town is now called Miroslav in Moravy, The Czech Republic).* His family had left this town almost thirty years earlier, but the fact that he "belonged" to a town that would become part of Czechoslovakia from 1918 on, was to be of enormous importance for me later. When my father was eight or nine years old, the family moved to nearby Eggenburg, a town of about five thousand inhabitants.

"Your grandfather had rented a horse-drawn wagon; he was the driver and my mother was sitting next to him, holding the youngest child, your Aunt Sophie," my father told us.

"We boys had to walk, of course. The wagon was loaded sky-high with all our belongings; I was impressed to see how much we had! The trip took about three hours and when we arrived at Eggenburg I could hardly believe that such a huge town really existed.

It had real streets, and some were even paved! What really impressed me most was to see a house being built on the edge of the town. I had never realized that there could be such a thing as a new house. In Braunsdorf all buildings were old; they had always been there."

"Did you have a bigger house in Eggenburg?" I wondered.

"Not much. And we could not have the goat anymore. Our family probably moved for business reasons. In other words, Eggenburg was a better place for my father to peddle from, and perhaps because the school was close by."

"But you didn't stay there long."

"For a couple of years only, but my younger brothers and my sister had all their schooling there, until they were 14 years old. As you know, I was the only one to be sent away to high school at age 11." I must explain here that in Europe of the 19th as well as the early 20th century there was a double track of schooling.

Most of the children, perhaps ninety percent, stayed in grammar school until age 14. Only a small minority, supposedly the most gifted, were sent to high school after the fifth, and later the fourth year of grammar school. There were eight years of high school, called "gymnasiums." This school had nothing to do with gymnastics. Just the opposite. The students received a classical education, Latin from the first year on, Greek from the third grade up, and history was stressed a great deal, but also a lot of mathematics.

As far as the knowledge was concerned, a high school graduate was at least equivalent to a student who had gone to or three years of college in the United States. This meant a lot of work; to flunk a grade was quite common. For those students who were a little slow, the parents often hired a tutor, and that was the lucky break my father got! Since he was a poor boy and doing quite well in school, the teachers recommended him as an inexpensive tutor for some of his fellow students.

"I had room and board with distant relatives," my father told us. "Although there was not much 'board,' I never got enough to eat. But I made enough money to buy clothes and also for my hobby."

"Your hobby? Didn't you have enough to do?"

"It didn't take much time. I was writing letters to nonexistent people, just to prove that the earth was really round, as our geography teacher claimed. I would send a stamped envelope with nothing in it to Mr. Josef Weinmann at a fictitious address in Paris. Should this gentleman not be there, forward to San Francisco, then to Tokyo, then return to sender."

"Did it work? Were your letters really returned to you?" I wondered.

"Yes, two of them came back to me, with pretty notes indicating in French, English and in Japanese that Mr. Josef Weinmann was not there. One of my teachers had helped me find addresses in Paris, San Francisco and Tokyo."

I don't know why the high school (the German word is "Mittelschule" which translates to middle school; high school in the German-speaking countries usually means university) in the rather small county seat of Horn, Lower Austria, was so much better than comparable schools in America.

As a matter of fact, I wonder if the schools really were better, or was it just the student body? But there is no doubt that my father, who had no university or college education, would have been considered an extremely well-educated man in the U.S. He knew Latin and classical Greek, had several years of French, and a good understanding of math. He had a better than fair knowledge of world history and geography. He spoke and wrote excellent German, and had read not only the German classics, but also Shakespeare and Moliere in translation. All of that, coming from a very poor family with only his mother as a role model.

"Did you work very hard as a student? I mean, did you study day and night?" I once asked my father after he displayed some knowledge of advanced algebra.

"I can't remember any extraordinary work load. I certainly slept all night! Perhaps the tutoring I did during most of my student years helped; also, the fact that I had a good memory for the spoken word. All teachers were required to lecture on their subjects; only after listening to the lectures, never before, were we encouraged to read up on the lessons."

Being a high school graduate entitled a young man to a very important privilege in Austro-Hungary. He did not have to serve in the army for three years, but rather just for one. This one year consisted of an officer's training school; thus, my father became a "second lieutenant of the reserve" at age 20.

Both my brother and I would question my father about his experiences during that year of army duty, but he absolutely refused to talk about it.

"It was the worst year of my life." This was all he would say.

Shortly after his year in the army my father caught a severe cold while swimming in the river Danube. Somehow this cold led to an inflammation of the cardiac muscle and almost to his death. His heart suffered permanent damage, which proved to be a blessing in disguise a few years later. When the war broke out in 1914, he was rejected for military service.

Coming out of the army in 1898, he needed a job. Just like many other young men at this time, he wanted to go to Vienna, the capital of the empire and the most important city in the world as far as he was concerned. His mother, my grandmother Augusta, remembered some distant relatives lived in Vienna and had some kind of business there. She wrote to them, and so it came to be that my father entered the office of a small paint factory. And that's how my father, as well as my brother and I, would always be connected with paints, as long as our working careers lasted.

My father told me: "We worked seven days a week at that time, but on Sundays we had the afternoon off. The work was sheer drudgery for me. All I was supposed to do was to copy the incoming orders into a ledger book, then make additional copies for the production department."

"Couldn't you use carbon paper?"

"We didn't have that yet. And certainly no typewriters! That's why my bosses almost fired me. You see, my mother's relative complained to her that I was absolutely useless because of my bad handwriting. But this was my lucky break."

"You're telling me that your terrible handwriting, which I unfortunately inherited, helped you?"

"Yes. My mother received a letter complaining about me and threatening to fire me. But she answered with the suggestion to perhaps give me a different job, where my handwriting would not be such an impediment. That's how I became a salesman! You see, having copied orders for half a year, I was already familiar with pricing all of our items. I knew that our company accepted a great deal of flexibility. In other words, while lower-priced orders were accepted, better prices were, of course, preferred and carried a higher commission.

When I was given my 'last chance to prove myself or be fired' and asked to sell, I knew what kind of customers were more ready to pay higher prices and what kind of paints they were most likely to buy. I wrote what we would call "jingles" today, extolling the virtues of some specific paints, to which I gave fancy names: aluminum paint became "ALUMINAX." I called white glossy paint "GRANITIN" because it dried to such a hard surface.

Then there was a paint additive, already around for many years, which I called "NUMBER 4712." You see, a perfume had just been introduced by a French or German manufacturer under the name of "Number 471 V" together with a lot of advertising for this product. So, my name, Number 4712, had instant recognition."

All this happened sometime during the first years of the new century. I often wonder what would have happened to my father's career had he come to America as a young man. I think he'd have done well. Only a few years ago a letter fell into my hands, written in 1905 by my father's boss and addressed to my grandmother. It was a long letter, but one paragraph read as follows:

"I love you like a sister, but your son Heinrich shows no gratitude to me. Just because he is my best salesman, he refuses to have his commission reduced. Has this young fellow no shame? Does he not know how bad his handwriting is?"

"Just what made you go into business for yourself?" I once asked my father.

"I realized that sooner or later the factory would fail. The owners could not adjust to the new century. Even more important, I was ready to start a family, but I wanted to be sure I was financially able and secure enough to give my future wife what she needed."

"So you did not know mother yet?"

"No. I also wanted to bring my parents to Vienna and see my sister married first.

Then I was lucky enough to find a partner who was a chemist. I only knew how to sell, so I needed somebody who could manufacture our products. We were fortunate to make money from the start."

"Well, how did you meet mother? Did you like her right away?"

"I fell in love with her immediately. She was, and still is, the most beautiful woman I've ever seen. But that's a long story. Better ask her." So I did.

"Mother, how did you and father get together?"

"I was ready to get married. You see, I was almost 21 years old. You know that I love my parents very much, but my mother, your grandmother, is a very strong-willed woman. I thought it might be nice to be the lady of the house. Anyway, your father and I were introduced by my uncle."

"So, just to get out of the house, you married the first fellow you got introduced to?"

"No, it was not as simple as that. About half a year earlier my parents had taken my brother, my sisters and me to a dance. It was a Sunday afternoon, I remember. These affairs could be deadly boring because all we girls could do was sit and wait until somebody asked us to dance. Anyway, this pale young man with a huge mustache came to our table, bowed low to my parents first, then looked at me and asked me to dance. He was so much fun!"

"But I thought you were introduced by your uncle?"

"That came later. After we had danced once or twice and told me how beautiful I was (really, I was not bad looking at that time), he brought me back to my parent's table and that was all. But I did not forget him. He had such an interesting face, not exactly handsome but somehow easy to remember. You know that he is still the darling of all the ladies."

"Did he introduce himself, did he ask for your name?"

"Of course. But you see, nowadays when you meet a girl you like you simply ask for her phone number and call her up. I guess you could not do that in 1910. Anyway, your father was too shy, though that's not one of his faults now, and I thought I would never see him again."

"Until you were formally introduced?"

"Exactly. A few months later my uncle put an ad in the newspaper, a blind ad of course, stating that his niece might consider getting married."

"And father answered?"

"No, there were several answers. Of course, it was said in the ad that I had a handsome dowry besides being good-looking and all that. But your father didn't answer. It was his mother, my future mother-in-law, your grandmother, who answered! Anyway, she and my uncle met, my uncle gave her my photo, which she showed to your father, and he recognized the girl from the dance. He wanted to see me immediately, but that's not how it was done! First, he had to meet my parents, who asked him all kinds of questions about his business; then my uncle took me to see your father's mother. His father had already died. I already had heard lots of mother-in-law stories. I was scared. But when I first met her I was sure that I would not marry anybody else but her son. She showed me his picture, I recognized it, of course. But believe me, I also practically fell in love with this lady, my future husband's mother. Obviously, she liked me too. Your father and I were married late the same year."

III

CHILDHOOD

Looking back more than three-quarters of a century, I feel my life has consisted of three distinct portions. First, from my birthday on July 9, 1914 until 1938, when the world as I had known it came to an end. Second, the dramatic years until 1941. And finally, America. But this is hindsight!

It's difficult to know the difference between actual memories of events and about stories heard later, but it seems to me that I remember an awful lot of excitement when I was two years old: the death of Kaiser Franz Josef. An important event: he had reigned since before some of my grandparents were born! Of course, there was a war on, but that did not mean much to me because my father was at home. He had been rejected for active duty because of his bad heart.

My brother, three years my senior, and I had a nanny by the name of Hermine. She lived with us and was considered, at least by myself, very much a part of our family. Of course, my mother was there too, but her main purpose in life, as far as I was concerned, was to love me and be loved in return. When we moved to what is now

Bratislava, Czechoslovakia, in the fall of 1916, nothing changed as far as I was concerned. Hermine, our nanny, came along and the five of us were still together.

I learned only much later that the move was for business reasons. My father and his partner had started a second paint factory in that town which needed supervision.

"Actually, why did you need that other plant?" I asked my father much later. "Was it not all one country, Austro-Hungary?"

"Politics, you know," he said. "The Hungarians didn't like to buy from the Austrians! Of course, Czechoslovakia did not exist in 1916 and Bratislava was then called either by its German name, Pressburg, or preferably Poszony, the Hungarian name. Most important for me, it was only 35 miles from Vienna."

"Were the Hungarians such chauvinists?"

"Definitely. That's why I had to send your brother to a Hungarian grammar school although he did not know a word of Hungarian. It's true that the Hungarians were not treated well by the German-speaking Austrians until 1867. But when they, in turn, became the rulers of their half of the Austro-Hungarian Empire, they certainly oppressed their own minorities. And when Czechoslovakia was given many Hungarian-speaking citizens after 1918, they were made to suffer. I guess that's how it is in Europe."

That conversation took place much later of course but I remember that my father always liked to explain. Rarely did I get a short answer to a question. But looking back to earlier memories, I remember the porcelain jars, closed on top except for a small opening. One was shaped like the Emperor Franz Josef's head, the other one like his successor, Karl.

Every week we boys were given a few coins which we had to throw into the openings, I guess for the war effort. Of course, I preferred Franz Josef because my name was Franz and my brother, whose name is Charles (Karl in German) only donated his offerings into the head of the new emperor because he carried his name. Actually, I wondered already at an early age just why we boys were named Karl and Franz? These names had not been in our family before. There may be a fancy explanation: both my parents were very much enamored with the German classical writers. There's a play by Schiller, second only to Goethe in the pantheon of dramatists. The play is call *Die Raeuber* (The Robbers). The three main characters are the father Henry, the older brother Karl, and the young brother Franz. Just like us! But Franz, in Schiller's play, was a bad person. I resented that.

The earliest event I remember with certainty is the armistice of November, 1918.

Everybody was shouting with joy and so was I, jumping up and down, saying the word "Waffenstillstand," the German word for armistice, and quite a mouthful for a four-year-old boy to say over and over again.

I remember distinctly that everybody was happy. Either people didn't know that the war had been lost or they just didn't care. But a few weeks later, in January 1919, it was quite different. There was a military concert in the town square and our parents took us to witness the great event: the military orchestra played taps.

Everybody cried. The next morning the Czechs marched into Bratislava. It was the end of the Austro-Hungarian Empire. Our nanny wanted us to crawl under the beds. Being Austrian herself, she thought the Czech soldiers would kill all children and possibly also rape all women.

My mother, on the other hand, as a Czech by birth, remembered that the Czech soldiers were actually very nice people. She was sure they would not do anything bad. But just to be safe, our nanny prevailed and we were made to hide under blankets. My father definitely saw the funny side of the event.

"There is a rumor the Czechs will take hostages among the leaders of the town when they march in, to make sure that all the people behave themselves. Now, some of my best friends are sure to be important enough to be considered leaders and are saying goodbye to their families. What nonsense!"

My father was right, of course. Not only were there no hostages, but also the takeover was quite peaceful and we children could come out from under the blankets.

"As a matter of fact," my father said, "it will be good for business that our town belongs now to Czechoslovakia. The Hungarians are losers; the Czechs are the winners. It's always better to be on the winning side. Now Bohemia, Moravia and Slovakia will be a whole new country, a good country, I believe."

But as far as our family was concerned, my parents decided to move back to Vienna. We stayed in Bratislava only until the end of the school year. My brother, however, was taken out of the Hungarian school and given private tutoring in German because he was to enter the third grade of grammar school in the fall.

I have a pretty good recollection of our summer vacation in 1919: our family spent it in Marienbad, now Marianske Lazne, Bohemia. Just recently I visited this spa again. The old hotels look rather seedy now. There are few beautifully dressed ladies to be seen and yet, many old memories came back to me. There is still the balcony of the Grand Hotel Excelsior, on which we stood while a friend of my father serenaded my mother with his flute, playing Mozart's *A Little Night Music*. We all laughed because he had trouble with his instrument. And I visited the forest where my father took us boys in order to show us the exact spot where Goethe wrote the poem, *Ueber allen Gipfein ist Ruh* (It's Quiet Over All the Treetops). Unfortunately, the forest does not look quite as I remembered it because acid rain has taken its toll. I even found the little brook (it had been a mighty river in my memories) where my brother almost drowned after falling from a bridge.

In the fall of 1919, our family moved back to Vienna. The war had been over for a year now and my father was forced to make a decision, which was to affect us for more than two decades: he had to choose between Austrian or Czechoslovakian citizenship. Because his father, my grandfather Hermann Weinmann, had been born in a town that became Czechoslovakian territory in 1918, my father could claim Czechoslovakian citizenship. But on the other hand, he had maintained his legal residence in Vienna and he himself had been born in Austria and definitely was an Austrian, and that's what he chose to be.

I feel, somehow, that my father's decision was based more on cultural than on financial consideration. He wanted his sons to grow up, and be part of the German cultural environment.

The city of Vienna was a dismal place in the early 1920s. I remember beggars on every street corner, mostly war veterans with one leg missing. There was very little food, practically no fruit, and no coffee except a brew made from acorns. What few eggs available were not fresh, but rather swimming in a liquid of calcified water. More often than not they would stink when opened. But what I remember most vividly were the long lines in front of hot dog stands. Not that many people wanted to buy the sausages: they were much too expensive. What the Viennese poor of 1920 wanted was the water in which the hot dogs had been boiled. Twice a day, this greasy liquid would be given away free and eaten as soup.

Much food came from the United States. There were soup kitchens called "Amerikanische Ausspeisung," a particularly ugly word in German meaning "feeding, given away free." The only meat available also came from the U.S. It came in tins with a picture of cattle on them and was called, in German, "Xomett Peef" (corned beef). But it was so salty as to be barely edible. More important was the canned milk, rather freely available and called "Amerikanische Kondenzmilch." It was thick and overly sweet.

Since there was actual starvation among the poor, many children were sent away for several months or even years to be cared for abroad. The countries that most frequently volunteered to take children were Holland and Denmark. Both countries had been neutral during the war and were therefore rather well-to-do. The youngsters came back well-nourished, ruddy, looking so different from the pale Viennese children!

On the playground, they would show off some of the foreign language they had learned from their foster parents.

And therein lies a story, a very ugly story few Americans know about. Almost 20 years later, the children, now being close to 30 years old, with their knowledge of Dutch or Danish, would have their language exploited by the Nazis. Having been exposed to the foreign language when they were very young, these one-time foster children had no German accent and could now be used as spies. During World War II, unlike World War I, the Germans invaded both Holland and Denmark. Holland, especially, paid dearly for the feeding of Austrian and German children 20 years earlier.

In the fall of 1920, I entered grammar school (the city of Vienna was much too poor to have kindergarten) and thus my formal education started in an old, ugly building, smelling of urine. Other than dirty desks and benches, the school provided only a blackboard and chalk; no books, paper or pencils. We were asked to bring cardboard, scissors and a little flour from home.

Working with these utensils, we spent the first few months making a box with many partitions to contain the letters of the alphabet. Under the supervision of the teacher, we cut the cardboard into strips and glued them together with a paste made from flour and water. Somehow this really worked and we could now proceed to cut out of the paper the capital letters of the alphabet and put them into the partitions. Then we were shown how to form words, using our letters, copying what the teacher wrote on the blackboard. I find it hard to believe now, but by the end of the year we all knew how to read! Not that the teacher was particularly good; he was a bitter man who never smiled; during the war, he had become somewhat crippled. Wrongdoers were beaten mercilessly with a cane.

However, I noticed soon that only poorly-dressed children were so abused, never my friends nor I who came from "better families." Most likely my parents gave money or food to the teacher, both strictly forbidden in Socialist Vienna.

There were two more subjects in first grade: the multiplication table up to 10×10, which we repeated endlessly in unison, and singing. Two of the songs I remember to this day, as well as the multiplication tables. My parents had promised me a different school for the next year that would be brighter and "more fun." But they were very careful to praise the new school without denigrating the old one. I believe now that both my mother and father purposely avoided saying bad words about anybody, especially about anybody in authority at the moment. This gave me a sense of security and made me feel that this world is a good place to live in. However, I remember an event that upset me greatly. One day my mother asked me:

"Of course you love both of us and we both love you. But tell me, whom do you love more, your father or your mother?"

Feeling uncomfortable, I tried to get out of this situation.

"Of course I love you, I love you both alike!" But my mother would not let me off so easily.

"There must be a difference, only a slight difference. Just tell me: whom do you love a little more?" I didn't like this at all.

"Why do you want to know?"

"Just do me a favor and tell me, please."

Actually, there was no doubt in my mind and probably not in hers: my father had always preferred my brother; not only was he the first-born but also he looked like my father, everybody said so. And everybody also said that I should have been a girl because my features were so much like my mother's. I knew, or at least I thought I knew, that I was her favorite but at this moment I was mad at her. Why didn't she leave me alone?

I promised myself that if I ever had children I would never ask them such a stupid question.

"Well, if you really want to know, I probably love father a little more." I have no idea what happened afterwards, only that she looked hurt.

Our family spent the summer between my first and second grade of grammar school in a little village in southern Moravia. There was a small, lazy river, just shallow enough for me to wade across. Reeds were growing near it and I was shown how to make a life preserver out of them. I remember how wonderful it felt to lay on these reeds tied together with a string, paddling with my hands and pretending I was a big ship. But I was not always allowed to be lazy.

Often I was asked to help with the harvest and that I enjoyed most of all. The work was done by hand, the wagons were drawn by horses, no different than it had been done for hundreds of years. Everybody was working and sweating and having a good time, at least that's how I remember it. My job was to pick up sheaves of wheat, which had been left in the field, and bring them to one of the wagons. Being a city boy who always lived in large towns and suburbs, I look back to this summer of 1921 as the only time I ever spent in the rural surroundings. I liked it.

In the fall of 1921, my parents transferred me to a different grammar school, a new one that had just reopened as a public school. It had been a private institution, but in socialist Vienna private schools were not desirable and it was forced to close. However, when I attended it the tradition of a more liberal institution was still very much alive. There was definitely no corporal punishment. As a matter of fact, not much punishment at all. Whomever did something very good received a "stroke of praise" which the teacher, with much ado, entered into a large book. "Evildoers" were given a "stroke of punishment" which was entered into the same book.

Actually, this book was never referred to again, but as far as we were concerned these strokes were a big event. The teacher was a pretty young lady in her 30s who stayed with us from the second to the fourth grade. I loved her, of course. I had the impression that she also liked me very much, as a matter of fact probably more than any of the other students. But I soon found out that every one of the other children also felt that they were the preferred ones! I can think of no higher praise for a teacher.

We had books now, plenty of paper to write on, even colored pencils, but only one set for the whole class. First thing in the morning, we had to report on the weather as we experienced it. There were four possibilities: clear, partly cloudy, cloudy and rain. The teacher took a vote and whatever weather received the most votes was solemnly pronounced to exist for the morning. We had received the first lesson in democracy.

There was no doubt in anybody's mind about the fact that at the end of second grade every student was expected to read fluently. There were no exceptions. As far as the other subjects were concerned, by the end of the fourth grade we had mastered simple fractions and elementary geometry. We were pretty good in spelling (much easier in German than in English) and had learned a lot of history of our native Vienna, which we considered the center of the universe.

There was one sour note in my grammar school days. Every Wednesday morning the girls would make fun of us boys, usually singing a little song telling us how stupid we were. Therein lies a story. On Tuesday afternoon there was a separation of the sexes. The boys, by a male teacher, were taught how to do simple tasks with our hands such as making baskets, or using hammers and screwdrivers. At the same time, the girls had sewing lessons given by our regular teacher. It was at this time that the girls rehearsed how to make fun of the boys the next day, I suspect with the help of the teacher. I wonder why she did that? Did she, perhaps, want to overcome a possible inferiority complex of the girls? We boys tried to reciprocate, of course, but were never able to get together on how to do it, and beating up the girls was prohibited.

At the end of the fourth or fifth grade, we and our parents had to make a big decision, important for the remainder of our lives. Should we stay in the same school until we finished eighth grade at age 14, when we were ready to start an apprenticeship in one of the trades, or should we transfer to middle school, which consisted of eight grades, thus taking us to age 18 or 19 and, if successfully completed, would give us the right to enter a university. The vast majority, I'd guess 85 percent, took the shorter and easier school. Only a select few went to "middle school," but they first had to pass a rather difficult examination, which many flunked. You were allowed to take this examination twice: after fourth and after fifth grade.

My parents had no doubt that I should go to middle school, as my father had done. Also, my brother had passed the examination after his fourth grade, and so had I. At the same time, our family moved to a much larger apartment in a rather exclusive part of Vienna. My father's business must have been good, and I felt that, upon entering a new school, I was no longer a small child.

IV

NOT QUITE A TEENAGER

One does not always become very popular in school by giving only the right answers, or even worse, by volunteering these answers too often. The school system in Vienna did not encourage competition. The idea of "class rank" did not exist. As a matter of fact, a student who always excelled was not very well-read. It was "nice" to be good, but not all that good. If there was a suspicion that any student spent an excessive amount of time with homework, the whole class condemned him.

To be smart, to be fast, was not nearly that bad but still did not contribute to one's popularity. It got you the reputation of being arrogant: don't raise your hand too quickly or too often. Give others a chance. On the other hand, when the teacher asked the whole class a question, which seemed to be difficult and nobody volunteered an answer for a while, then the one who, after some hesitation, raised his or her hand, was called on. If they gave the right answer, they became a hero and loudly congratulated. Obviously, there is a thin line between being merely too quick and being the only one who knows. As I look back through my school years I can see now that I often did wrong, though never on purpose. I never tried to show off.

Nevertheless, I seemed to have had the reputation of being a smart kid who needed to be stepped on once in a while. I was never elected to be class leader, though I was by no means unpopular. I had many good friends. All this, together with the fact that I was never very good in sports and really somewhat lazy, lead to a certain arrogance. I thought that while I could not run as fast or catch a ball as well as many of my schoolmates, when it came to thinking, I was as good as anybody and better than most. And should I get into a tight situation, I could probably talk my way out of it.

My middle school class during the 1920s and 30s was a rather close unit. It lasted for eight years and ended with a final examination called "matura," which qualified the student for any university in Austria or Germany, though most, for financial reasons, stayed in Vienna. From the first to the eighth grade of middle school the same students stayed together; there were no choices as far as the curriculum was concerned. Obviously, by the time we were in the higher grades, we knew each other well, for better or worse. Since admission to the university did not depend on the final grades as long as the student passed the final "matura," there was no reason for competition. Friendships, started at age ten, sometimes lasted until eighteen.

Even during non-school hours, I usually associated mostly with my schoolmates; we were in the same Boy Scout group, but more about that later.

It is more than a half-century since I attended grammar school, "middle school" (the last four years would coincide with American high school) and university. Somehow I always managed to pass as a rather well-educated fellow, but I must wonder why. Am I self-educated perhaps? With the exception of reading quite a bit about Judaica, I could not say that I qualify. No, I think it's because my high school education (Austrian "middle school") was different from the American equivalent, and probably much better.

A comparison is at least partially unfair because we in Austria were a select group, only perhaps ten or fifteen percent of grammar school students went on to "middle school." But there are other differences as well. Most important, I believe, was the curriculum. The student or his parents knew what courses to take once the decision was made on the kind of school to attend. I do not believe that a youngster of 13 or 15 or even 17 is qualified to make a good decision on which courses to take.

The Austrian curriculum lead to a certain skeleton of knowledge that stayed with the student and could be fleshed out later, rather than a few patches of specialized knowledge superimposed on a wall of general ignorance. This applies to history, physics, geography, mathematics, philosophy, understanding of grammar and composition and ease of expression, just to name a few subjects in no particular order. I can think of no European-educated people who are afraid to speak up in a crowd. We were taught to do that. But there might be an additional reason for the comparably better result of Austrian education: from the first to the eighth grade of middle school it was quite easy and not shameful to flunk a grade, which had to be repeated. You had to pass every subject in order to be promoted to the next higher grade.

Could it be that our teachers worked better? I don't think so, although each "professor" had to be a specialist in the discipline he taught. A Latin teacher would not teach chemistry. A biology teacher would not teach philosophy. Moreover, our professors had to lecture and only after hearing them was the student encouraged to do his own reading on the subject matter. (This made it easier for somewhat lazy fellows, such as me, who had a good memory for the spoken word. We were supposed to take notes during the lectures but I didn't do that: better to listen, I thought, and later consult the textbook at home.)

But the personal qualities of our middle school professors weren't all that good. I believe that, on the whole, my children's high school teachers in Illinois were probably more caring, more dedicated than the teachers I had in Vienna.

This type of "middle school" I attended from my 10th to my 18th year was called "Realgymnasium," which meant that we had not quite as much emphasis on drawing and living languages as in the "Realschule." Nor did we study as much Latin, and no ancient Greek at all.

From the first grade of realgymnasium (corresponding to the fifth grade of American school) we had French as a foreign language, freehand drawing (which essentially consisted of making pictures with watercolors), German, history, geography, mathematics, zoology, gym and "religion." By no means was every subject taught every day. For instance, history, geography, zoology or "religion" was given only twice a week. French and math probably five times weekly. School hours were daily, including Saturday, from eight until one or sometimes two o'clock. Each subject was taught for 50 minutes, followed by a ten-minute break

With the exception of gym and "religion," the teachers came to our room rather than students changing locations.

The study of religion was absolutely obligatory. If the parents of the student claimed they did not believe in any of the established religions, they had to choose one for their child anyway for the purpose of school instruction. There was no way to get out of this. Vienna, being called a "red" (socialist) city, many parents tried. But the Austrian courts run by the Catholic state of Austria that was perpetually fighting with the socialist city of Vienna always ruled against them. There were three religions: Catholic, by far the dominant faith; Protestant, which included all Christians not Catholic, and Jewish. In our class, there may have been 20 Catholics, 3 Protestants and 10 Jews. The number of Jews attending middle school greatly exceeded their ten percent share of the Viennese population, because most Jewish parents expected their children to have an opportunity to attend a university later. This was impossible for students with no more than grammar school and some secondary school leading to an apprenticeship in a trade. When the time for religious instruction came, the Catholic children stayed in the classroom, the Jewish and the Protestant children were sent to other rooms.

Our instructions in the Jewish (or as it was most often called, "Mosaic") religion was a farce most of the time. Many teachers did not even pretend to do any work with us, at least not in the higher grades. As I remember it now, there were aimless discussions, or else we did our homework for mathematics or Latin with the teacher reading the newspaper. However, there was one important exception: in one of the higher grades, I may have been 16 or 17 years old, our teacher was a retired officer who had been a Jewish chaplain in the Austro-Hungarian army during World War I. He told us of many anti-Semitic incidents that had occurred then (he was much too careful to talk about any anti-Semitism during the present time around 1930) and always ended the hour with a call to Zionism. He managed to let us know, without ever telling us so directly, that there was not much of a future for a Jew in Austria.

This was not at all the message I had received heretofore from either my parents or from school.

I was brought up to believe that justice will prevail. Maybe not immediately, maybe not always. After all, we were Austrians and Austrians do not believe in absolutes; there was always sloppiness. But in the long run we would receive what we deserved. Be a good citizen, don't hurt your fellow man and all, well almost all, will be well with you. Anyway, our country was Austria. Had we not studied her history and geography with much diligence? But here was this man: tall, impressive, well-spoken; a person to be respected because he was our "professor."

He told us about a faraway land called Palestine, which we should consider to be our home, either to go there or at least to know it well; to love it and help it to become an independent Jewish state. Why? The most important reason: there is a lot of anti-Semitism in Austria. "They" don't want "us" here, and it isn't going to become any better. And why Palestine? Because of our history, our sentimental attachment. Anyway, our Eastern European brothers wouldn't consider any other place.

I had several teachers during my high school years who influenced me profoundly. First was our homeroom teacher, Dr. Dengler (more about him much later). I use the words "homeroom teacher" as the nearest translation of the German "Klassenvorstand." The word means something like "standing before the class." Indeed, this man was much more important than a homeroom teacher. It was he who set the tone of our relationship to the school and to all learning.

His most important message to us: life is fair. Try to excel, but cooperate. Do not belittle anyone. Be curious but respect authority. Dr. Dengler taught German and French. In the highest grade, he also taught philosophy, and without any doubt he was an excellent teacher. In German, he insisted that every one of us learn to express himself well, both in writing and orally. From the time we were 13 or 14 years old, we had to stand in front of the class at least once a month and "give a speech." The subject was up to each student, at least until the higher grades when the teacher assigned a theme. We had to speak for 10 minutes or so, and then we were critiqued, first by our fellow students, then by the teacher, both for the content and the form of our speech. It was strictly forbidden to use "negative criticism," which meant that we could never say, for instance, that the speech did not make any sense. Rather, we had to say that we could not quite understand it. When the speaker slurred his words, or spoke too fast, the correct criticism was, "I might have enjoyed the speech more if spoken more distinctly or more slowly." But within this framework, and as long as the speaker was not attacked personally, the critics were merciless. As a result of these exercises, which went on for many years, none of us students were afraid to stand up before any crowd and speak up and we also learned to mind our manners when debating.

I also have much to thank for our teacher of mathematics. He was demanding and insisted on quite a bit of homework. But before starting on any new concept, he explained and encouraged questions and answered them patiently.

It was this man, I believe, who encouraged me to listen, listen carefully, rather than to distract myself taking notes.

"Whatever I say is also in your book," he would emphasize. "Look it up at home, but while I am explaining, listen to me and tell me right away if you don't understand."

I enjoyed school and usually did rather well, especially in the higher grades. Very early in my career as a student, I found out that a "good reputation" is very important. For instance, when it came to translating a paragraph from French or Latin, I would not be called by the teacher if we had done the translation at home. Of course, so the teacher thought, I had done my homework. On the other hand, if we had to wrestle with a text we had never seen before, if "new" work had to be done in class, I was likely to be the one who had to show the class (helped by the teacher of course) how to interpret. This was a "no lose" situation.

If I did well, I showed my knowledge; if not, the teacher assumed that whatever I had to do was probably very difficult. It must have been in the higher grades of school that I discovered a peculiar gift: I performed much better under pressure than without it. For instance, every month or so we would have a written test in Latin. Using our dictionary, we had to translate a passage from an author we had never studied before. Not only was understanding required, but also speed, since we were supposed to finish quickly.

I usually performed well on these tests but when I tried to repeat for my classmates afterwards what I had just done, I often failed. Not being under pressure anymore seemed to reduce my abilities.

One of my favorite subjects was history. Twice a week, from the fifth to the twelfth grade, we studied history: essentially Western Civilization with a special emphasis on Germany and Austria. All history was taught to us twice, beginning with the Stone Age and the Ancient Egyptians until the present. During the first year of middle school we covered Antiquity, the next year the

Middle Ages, then the period from the Renaissance to the French Revolution, and finally modern times.

Then, in the fifth year of middle school, corresponding to our ninth grade, we started all over again.

The second time around, we had a teacher who would present the material in a more sophisticated way, again covering the same periods of time. We finished with the present time at the end of our school. Always, the teacher would lecture first; only then were we encouraged to cover the same material by reading our text book and any other source. Every other week or so there were oral examinations. One of us was called upon to tell the class whatever he remembered about the specific occurrence. If the teacher did not like it he would call on another student. Debates, while not encouraged, often did take place and would become quite lively. Never, however, were "exchanges of ignorance" permitted. If you interrupted either the teacher or a fellow student, you'd better know what you were talking about or you were mercilessly put in your place. In the higher grades, an examination would often be as follows:

Teacher: "You know, of course, that the American Revolution started in 1776. Why? Who can tell me what happened in England approximately at the same time? In France? Germany? Any other country?"

This kind of examination encouraged thinking, of course, which is fair, but it also emphasized speed, since whoever raised his hand first was called on for an answer. It was at that time, I believe, when I first noticed that many Jewish students, I among them, seemed to be a little quicker than the rest of the class. Not necessarily did we know more or even pretend to be better, more thorough thinkers, it's just that we "caught on" a little faster. I wondered if we Jews did not seem to be pushy to our Gentile friends.

For friends we were. There was not much of a split among us along religious or racial lines. One or two of my classmates call themselves "National Socialists" (this was in 1930 or 1931, later they were known as Nazis), but nobody paid much attention. It was just their private opinion anyway. They were not among the smarter students, nor remarkable in any other way. As a matter of fact, I was quite friendly with one of them. We went on an extended trip together in the summer of 1932, after our final high school examinations.

There were four of us on the trip: the third was a baptized Jew, a rather disagreeable fellow; the fourth, whom I liked best, was the son of a grammar school teacher (not Jewish) who called himself a Social Democrat.

Shortly before Christmas of 1924, when I was a little more than 10 years old and in my first year of middle school, there was an event which would forever change our family. We were supposed to go on a little trip, a winter vacation. My mother was packing a suitcase in the living room while my brother and I kept ourselves busy in our room. Suddenly we heard a scream as we had never heard before. It sounded inhuman, piercing and monotonous. We rushed into the living room and found our mother, then 35 years old, lying on the floor.

"I fell," she screamed, "it hurts so much I can't stand it. Help me."

Our father was not home from work yet, so we called our doctor, who had my mother immediately transported to a hospital! The same evening our family heard the verdict of the prominent surgeon who had just operated on my mother:

"Mrs. Weinmann had a very unfortunate fall and fractured the top of her right femur. I did my best to line up the bone in such a way that it might heal properly. Frankly, I'm not sure it will. She will have to lie still for several months; the leg will be immobilized from the toe to the hip."

My father tried to press the surgeon for more information. "Is she still in great pain? Will she ever walk again?"

"The operation was done under general anesthesia, of course. When she wakes up she won't be in pain, which must've been terrible after the fall. I hope she'll walk again but with the aid of a cane, because her right leg will be a little shorter. It is most important that she keep herself as still as possible for the next four or five months, then I'll remove the gypsum bandage and we'll see."

The method of nailing bones together for better and faster healing had not yet been developed. So, my poor mother had to stay in bed, always lying on her back, until May of the following year. Even after the cast was taken off, progress was slow. Only in late summer of 1925 could my mother walk, and until the end of her life only slowly and with the aid of a cane.

My mother's suffering during that time must have had a profound influence on my father, and for several reasons. First, to see his wife, whom he loved, suffer so much, hurt him too. But he also suffered financially. The load of caring for my mother was enormous. Not only did we have two servants, a cook and a housemaid, but also a nurse came during the day to look after my mother. My father's business may have been profitable at that time, but it was never big enough, I believe, to support such an expensive household. Moreover, we had moved from a small apartment to a huge one just a few months before my mother's fall. Very expensive furniture, including a grand piano, had been bought. A painter, then in vogue, had done my mother's portrait.

I remember my father saying that his financial reserves had been used up. He complained especially about the high fees of an interior decorator who had been hired to advise with the purchases of furniture and wallpaper. All that was before my mother's accident. Did my father feel bad about taking too much money out of his business? I think so, although he never quite said it.

"Remember, always remember," he often said to my brother and me during that time. "Even if the three of us will eat nothing but dry bread, mother has to be properly cared for!"

I may have been 11 or 12 years old when I first became aware of discussions between my parents about money, always behind closed doors. My father obviously felt that we were spending too much money. My mother would answer, often tearfully, that she needed even more to keep our household running. My sympathies were with my mother, of course, because I did not want her to cry. But it was not many years later that I realized what was to blame: our apartment was too big, too expensive. We did not need so many rooms nor furniture that fancy. Two huge rooms, both beautifully furnished, were hardly ever used. One was a formal dining room, the other room, which was called a "salon," contained the grand piano, several upholstered chairs covered with a fabric so expensive that we children were discouraged from ever sitting on them, small tables and armoires made of dark, glossy wood with inlaid patterns. A huge tiled oven was supposed to heat both rooms (our building had no central heating), but it took so long to warm up and was probably so expensive to operate that it was seldom used.

I must have found invoices for the furnishings of these two rooms and of the interior decorator's fees somewhere, because I figured out just how much it was costing us every time we entered the salon. Given its rare use and a reasonable life expectancy for our family, how much more enjoyment we could have had by using the money elsewhere. I promised myself never to live in a place too expensive for my income.

My brother and I shared a large room; I could not have imagined it differently. It contained two brass beds, a big rectangular table with drawers, several chairs, a huge commode for our clothes, a shelf for our books (built-in closets did not yet exist) and of course, a tile oven. We two boys lived rather peacefully together; my brother's main complaint was my tendency to mess up the room. We did our homework on the large table. When one of us wanted privacy (usually for reading), he went into the living room next door. This was the room where our family ate, but it also contained several very comfortable leather chairs and a huge cabinet with shelves filled with books, although the fancy bound "classics" were kept in the "salon."

Homework for school did not occupy me too much. It seems I always knew how to avoid what I considered "busy work." From my seventh or eighth year on I spent most of my time reading. Children's books at first, then Greek or German myths and fables by the Brothers Grimm. Soon however, I read any book I found in the book cabinet. I did not realize at the time that my father saw to it that I found just the right books. I cried with Eliza in *Uncle Tom's Cabin* (and decided right then that Americans were barbarians), a children's edition of *Gulliver's Travels*, as well as *Don Quixote* and *David Copperfield* read over and over. I was most impressed with Mr. Macawber's saying: "You spend one penny less than you make, you are happy; one penny more, unhappy."

My favorite book was *Jan and Sam in the Forest* by Ernest Thompson Seton: two carefree teenage boys who have lots of adventures. I believe what impressed me most about this book was the life with nature it described. I had not known one could exist except in a big city.

All these books I read, of course, in German translation. I was not even aware that Dickens wrote in English, only that some of the proper names were hard to pronounce. My favorite book by a German author was *The Bee Maia* by Bonsels. A bee has lots of adventures with spiders, bugs and hornets.

V

TEENAGER: THE BOY SCOUTS

My brother had loved being a member of the Boy Scouts, but only for a short while. The singing was fine with him, even the Sunday outings; but when the leader of his group explained that a Boy Scout must be self-sufficient, even be able to sew, and asked Charles to sew a little bag, he quit.

"I do not want to sew," he explained. "I do not have to sew. Furthermore, I don't want to be ordered to do anything!"

So, when I was asked by my cousin Herrmann to join his Boy Scout group, I refused at first. Since big brother did not like it, why should I? But my cousin persisted with his invitation. As the son of my father's older brother, he once explained to me, only half joking:

"If we Weinmanns were a royal house, I would be the heir presumptive; I could give you orders! But I only ask you, not order you, to come to my Boy Scout group; so please, please."

The truth is that I had always patronized my cousin Herrmann. Not only was I a year older than he, but also smarter, I thought. When we played together, as we often did, he would always do what I asked him to do. I'm afraid he admired me. Despite this patronizing attitude, I felt I should give in to his wishes, just for once, and go with him to the Boy Scout meeting. There was one every Tuesday.

A bunch of boys about my age greeted me. "So you are Bubi's big cousin?"

"My name is Franz Weinmann," I said, "but who is Bubi?"

Herrmann blushed. "You know, they call me 'Bubi' (little boy in German) here," he admitted to me.

"When I first came to the group, the leader asked me for my name. 'Weinmann,' I said. But he probably wanted to know my first name. 'How does your mother call you?' 'Bubi,' I answered. My name stuck to me."

Herrmann/Bubi must have given me quite a buildup; I could see why he insisted on me showing up at the meeting. He had promised to bring me. And that's how my involvement with the Austrian Boy Scouts began. I was not quite 13 years old at the time, a little fat and a little too smart for my own good, and very much in love with myself.

Everything I saw at the Boy Scouts fascinated me. Almost all the boys, with the exception of my cousin Bubi, were a little older than myself. I felt challenged. There was much singing and I liked that. Games were played which allowed me to excel; the leader read stories to us in the darkness of a room we called "home."

It was all very romantic. On Sundays, and almost any kind of weather, we would go on an outing, which lasted from 9 o'clock in the morning until late in the evening. I usually came home after dark.

I believe now that what fascinated me most about the Boy Scouts was the fact that there were no "grownups" around. Our group consisted of about 30 or 40 boys; the teacher was no more than 18 years old. Then there were three troop (a smaller unit) leaders, about 16 years of age. The majority of us boys were therefore 13 to 15 years old. There was absolutely no supervision, at least in our group, by anybody older than a teenager.

On Sundays, we met at the last stop of one of the streetcar lines leading towards the Vienna Woods. From there we walked to a meadow where we played soccer or volleyball. I soon discovered that I was quite poor at these games. At volleyball, I often dropped even easy balls. At soccer, I would more often than not miss the ball altogether. In retrospect, I wonder why I was so poorly coordinated. Quite likely, there was a very good reason other than an utter lack of self-confidence when it came to sports. For instance, I did not realize that, in order to catch a ball, one must constantly have his eye on it.

I was somehow afraid of the ball because I knew I would fail. In all other physical activities, I was pretty good, like erecting tents or building "houses" from branches, or hiking (I did not tire easily), or reading maps. I made friends easily. Soon, I brought some of my school friends into the group.

What I remember best about my Boy Scout days are the summer camps I attended. Four of them, in consecutive summers from 1927 to 1930. Summer camp was by far the most important activity. The rest of the year was essentially a preparation for it. During summer camp we had no restrictions imposed by schoolwork or by our parents. For six weeks, 30 or 40 boys lived their own idyllic life. The camp was always in a beautiful spot in the Austrian Alps, sometimes in a converted barn, sometimes in a small hut, usually near a lake. We would do our own cooking, of course, in a kitchen which was often constructed by us and therefore quite primitive: essentially a wood-burning stove, a table and shelves for pots and pans. Usually we had no running water; it had to be brought in from a pump or even from a brook flowing near the camp. For the purpose of cooking, we divided ourselves into groups of four, one being the leader, another his assistant, the remaining two just helpers. The leaders and assistants were required to attend "cooking classes" for three or four sessions in the nearest village, often several miles away. As far away as possible from the kitchen we had three or four "latrines," essentially big holes filled with lime.

"How can you possibly want to spend your summer vacation in such a primitive place?" my parents would ask me every time before I registered for camp. "You are used to decent food at home; you'll get sick from eating what you cook."

I protested. "You don't understand. I couldn't care less for the stupid summer vacations I had to take with you. Camp! That's the real life!"

Looking back from the safe distance of more than half a century, I find it hard to understand why my parents permitted me to go to camp. There is no question that the sanitary conditions were absolutely inadequate. As a matter of fact, many boys did get sick and I was one of them. The food was terrible, of course, and often there wasn't enough. Nor were the activities all that great. We played a *lot* of ball or other games that I actually didn't enjoy all that much, and after lunch we usually had "free time," which meant that there was nothing to do and I was bored. I must ask myself now just why I insisted, year after year, on attending summer camp, always against the advice of my parents?

The answer is, I believe, that we were brainwashed. Actually, that we brainwashed each other. All year long we told each other how much we were looking forward to camp. Everybody who had already attended camp, including myself, after the first year, would tell the new boys how wonderful it had been. On second thought, I actually have quite a few outstanding memories. About one week after camp started, there was always a "fire drill." In the early hours of the morning, around two or three o'clock, the leader would wake us up, screaming:

"Up everybody! Get dressed, quick! Fire! There is a terrible fire!"

Sure enough, not far from our camp, we would see burning timber and high flames. It looked as if the whole forest was on fire. Within a few seconds, everybody was outside, but when we came closer, we saw a couple of our older boys throwing dry straw on the fire. It looked really scary. But right afterwards, when everybody had seen the "terrible forest fire," they extinguished it with water they had prepared in a few buckets.

"I just wanted to know how long it would take you to get up from your straw sacks. Fifty seconds, not bad! Last year it took a whole minute! Anyway, the village fire department was notified of our fire drill and they won't come. Now that we are all up and excited, we can't go back to sleep. We'll go for a walk into the forest. Don't get lost! Walk single file, follow me!"

I guess you have to be a teenage boy to enjoy a walk through a forest in almost complete darkness. I could barely make out the boy in front of me. Only when coming to a clearing could we see stars. They looked so bright.

After an hour or so we came to a meadow, just in time for sunrise. Surprise! A few boys had breakfast prepared for us, only the usual breakfast: milk and bread with a little jam, but it tasted divine.

The high point of summer camp was always "the tour." For 10 days or two weeks we would leave the camp, get our backpacks full, very full, with clothing. We would take a train only far enough to get to a village in the Austrian or Swiss Alps where we could start our wandering: up and down mountains, across streams and brooks, always far from any important spas or any place where our parents might have taken us.

In Austria, we bought milk, bread and cheese or sausages in small village stores. In Switzerland, we could not even afford that luxury because we Austrians were only permitted to buy very small amounts of Swiss currency. So, we carried bread and salami with us. After a week in our backpacks, the food got rather ripe, but we boys were always so hungry, we'd eat anything. We never paid for a night's lodging. A little before dark we would go to a farmer and ask for permission to stay overnight in one of his barns, sleeping in the straw or hay. Permission was usually granted, but we had to promise not to make a fire. Once, in Switzerland, a farmer would not trust our word and asked us to give him all the matches we carried. Unfortunately for us, we could not give him any because we had none (nobody smoked, of course) and when the farmer insisted, we were just about to leave when the leader suddenly said:

"Just a moment! I remember I have matches! Please wait a minute!"

He started to empty his pockets, then his backpack, and sure enough on the bottom of it was a matchbox that he gave to the farmer who now permitted us to sleep in his hay. Our leader later explained to us:

"It happened before that we'd been asked to turn in our matches. So, just to be prepared like a good Boy Scout should, I always carry a box with me."

There was an International Boy Scout camp near the village of Kandersteg in one of the most beautiful valleys of Switzerland. We had made reservations to stay there, but before we got to the camp, our leader stopped at a little mountain stream and told us:

"I have some good news and some bad news. Last night when I called the camp, I was informed that they are looking forward to greeting us. We will be the first Austrian Boy Scouts for years and we can stay there overnight. We'll even get a good dinner and breakfast. That's the good news, but now comes the bad, bad news: they have only room for 25, and we are 33. So, as much as it hurts me to tell you, eight of us can't go to the camp. I can't make up my mind how to select the eight unfortunate chaps who have to stay out and sleep on some farmer's hay.

Now, as you know, there are four groups of eight boys each. One troop will be unfortunate. So, just to be fair, we will all pretend to go to the camp and get ready, wash really well at this brook here, clean our shoes, brush our hair, and then the troop leaders and I will vote on which of the troop is the least clean. You'll be very sorry for them because the camp is so beautiful and the Swiss dinner will be marvelous, but they can't come."

So, of course, we all washed and scrubbed and, within each troop, inspected each other for any dirty ears or shoes, at least the younger boys did. Anyway, half an hour later, the troop leaders went through a big show of inspection and decided that all of us looked just fine: the older boys had never believed the story of "not enough room!" Anyway, they knew it was just a good way to make everybody wash.

Without question, the food we ate, whether on tour or in the camp, was inadequate. Bad and too little. We had meat once a week, but the "meat" consisted of a little sausage. Otherwise we had potatoes, potatoes and for a change, sometimes macaroni. Whatever vegetables we consumed were cooked into a soup. Actually, only milk, usually mixed with cocoa powder, as well as bread and jam, was plentiful. We all lost weight with such a diet but did not seem to mind that too much. Once in a while, one of us got a box with cookies from home but had to share

Frank Weinman

it with the rest of the troop, a celebration. And yet, after summer, I was in better shape than before!

In the fall, when we had our first gym class in school, we always lined up in front of the ropes which were hanging from the ceiling.

"Up, boys!" my gym teacher yelled. "Show me what you can do!"

Most of us at least tried to climb up the dangling ropes. Some made it only to the middle, others to the top. But a few other boys and I just stood there, unhappy because we knew we could never do it.

"Don't give up," the teacher turned to us. "Try, just try."

I might as well pretend, I said to myself, and got hold of my rope. Surprise! I had no difficulty whatsoever in climbing to the ceiling, then looking down at my classmates, grinning with pride. I could do it! Not just math and French and history, but also "the rope." A little more muscle on my arms and legs acquired during summer camp, as well as much fat lost from my behind, had helped a lot.

During my second year in summer camp, I had a horrible experience. I got sick with a bad sore throat, and our group leader checked me in at a local hospital, a wise move because he didn't want to be responsible for sick boys. But because I ran a high fever and could hardly talk, he asked for somebody to stay with me. One of the bigger boys, actually one with whom I never had been very friendly, volunteered. At night, I suddenly woke up from my sleep: I felt that my penis was being fondled.

"Stop that! What are you doing?" I tried to shout, but I could hardly make a sound.

"Why, don't you like that?" The boy who slept in the same bed with me laughed. "We always do that. Don't you know why I volunteered to stay with you? Only to have you for myself." And, being much stronger than me, he proceeded to "play" with me, as he called it.

I scratched, bit, used every means at my command to get rid of him and finally managed to scare him enough to leave me alone. I had never had such an experience before, of course. I only knew very vaguely that there were such people as homosexuals.

By next day, a physician lanced an abscess in my throat. I felt better and returned to the camp with the other boy. He never spoke another word to me; I didn't mention the incident to anybody, thinking that this boy was crazy. Only much later, when I was a better observer, did I find out that homosexuality among Boy Scouts was not all that unusual. Some of the older boys would look for a very young, pretty one. Actually, this fact should not be too surprising: why would an 18-year-old young man forego all company of girls and take the extremely time-consuming, unpaid task of leading a group of younger boys? Of course, this looking for homosexual relationships was by no means the rule. A completely different motive for older boys to "stay on" and become leaders was a sense of duty, as one of the most capable leaders once explained to me:

"I enjoyed being a Boy Scout so much; it's only fair that I give others a chance. And there is something else. There is a strong sense, when you are a Boy Scout, that this is a good world, and you are to make it even better. There is very little fighting among us; competition is only encouraged in sports. You are educated to love nature and to look for some very high, possibly a little elusive, ideals."

Well, all this may be true. There is no doubt that I profited much from my Boy Scout experience. To this day I am a good hiker, sure-footed, and I do not tire easily. When I had to get along on very little food, but still had to work hard, I could do it. And a strong urge to see only the good side in people, plus an absolute fear of hurting others, may well have come from my Boy Scout experience.

But I am convinced that another side to this movement existed, at least as it could be found in Central Europe. Besides the obvious homosexual "invitation" to some of the younger boys, there was an exclusion of all female company, together with the overly romantic picture one gets from many of the songs. They describe a longing for the ideal love, which seems to be forever elusive. We were made to imagine girls as creatures utterly different from us boys, girls wishing to be left alone, to be adored from afar, not liking us boys very much. (I was already eighteen years old when a girl convinced me that my Boy Scout image had been wrong; I'll forever thank her!)

There can be no doubt that a teenager should not have the heavy responsibility that comes from being an uncontested leader. Four instance, the burden of administering the funds needed for establishing a summer camp and keeping it going should not fall on so young a man. As a matter of fact, I remember that in one of the camps, we ran completely out of money. We had to call our parents to wire us money for food, while we pawned a few cameras. Furthermore, an adversarial relationship was often encouraged between us Boy Scouts and our parents. We asked for no interference, no questions, and no help, except for money. Parents were people to be avoided.

No, the Boy Scout movement, as I remember it, educated us to be not quite for this world. We were striving for some very high ideals, to be sure, but we did not quite know what they were. A friend, a little wiser than I, once told me:

"You Boy Scouts have no idea what you want, but you want it very badly."

There was no direction to our idealism. Other youth movements, connected to Socialism or Nationalism, had positive goals, which we utterly lacked. We imagined this world as a much better place than it actually was. It never entered our minds that some human beings may not be very good or even trustworthy.

Sometimes I have been asked for advice about having boys join the Scout movement. I am of two minds. Yes, it's a good thing, it will help you physically, and you'll have some lasting, wonderful memories. But do not stay too long, and always keep your eyes open.

VI

MY LAST HIGH SCHOOL YEARS

Finally, in the fall of 1930, I severed all connections with the Boy Scouts. The last summer camp had come to an unpleasant end. The leader, not yet a senior in high school, was either quite inexperienced in monetary matters or even a little crooked. We ran out of money. There were desperate telephone calls to parents. Anyway, the camp was over prematurely, and I joined my parents and my brother in Bad Gastein, a beautiful spa in the Austrian Alps. I felt much closer now to my family than I had in years, especially to my brother. He had come to Bad Gastein after tramping through Switzerland and France; he and two friends, schoolmates, stopped cars on the road and asked for rides going west. No doubt, a special bond of friendship is established on such trips; to this day, the three men, all residing in the U.S. since 1938, still see each other.

Bad Gastein was, and still is, not only a beautiful spa with an enormous waterfall right above the town, but also a very expensive one. My parents stayed at the Hotel Europe, one of the best, while my brother and I in a more modest place, though still very good, a 15-minute walk away. Why? Was it to save money? It seems to me the obvious reason then, but now I don't think so. It is quite possible that they wanted to be alone, a kind of second honeymoon. My mother had gone through a bad bout of asthma, which plagued her through most of her life. But she felt temporarily better. After all, she was 41 at that time, and my father a very young 52. Why shouldn't they have a chance to be by themselves, away from home?

I had become somewhat estranged from my brother Charles. Not only was he three years older than me, but also his interests were quite different from mine. While I still lived in the "never-never land" of the Boy Scouts, he had already finished his first year of university, studying chemistry. That was an obvious choice since our father's paint factories were essentially chemical enterprises and my father himself had no chemical background at all; he depended on his partner, Dr. Winter, who had a PhD in chemistry.

But as Charles and I wandered through the forest telling each other about our experiences, we became much closer.

"I guess you did the right thing leaving the Boy Scouts earlier," I would say. "Now I have so much to catch up."

"I can help you, I believe," Charles said. "Your last two years of high school will be as easy for you as they were for me. We Weinmann boys have no problems with school. University is something else, though. Everybody else is just as smart as you. Anyway, now, since you have lots of free time, study things you really want to know; go out in the evening; there are so many theaters in walking distance from us; and for God's sake, don't be afraid of girls!"

"I'm not afraid of them, I just never know what to say; actually, I don't know any girls; I don't even know how to dance."

"That you should learn right away. Our parents wanted to send you to dancing school last year, but with your stupid Boy Scouts, you had no time! You'll meet girls there and they might even like you. And I'll introduce you in the "Kette" (Chain). You'll find lots of interesting people there."

"I thought I have to be a university student to become a member," I said.

"True, but you can attend our meetings if I bring you. After all, the 'Kette' is an association of children of Freemasons, and you are the son of a Freemason, just as I am. As long as you don't get father into trouble."

Freemasons in Central Europe were quite different from what they are in the U.S.

First, and foremost, they were a truly secret organization; when my brother asked me not to get our father into trouble, he meant that I should not talk to outsiders. While not exactly prohibited, the Masons were not welcome in very Catholic Austria. No Freemason would, for instance, wear his emblem in public. There was certainly no noisy "Shriner" (the highest order of the Masons) parades. Although the only prerequisite for being a Mason was "to be a good man of good reputation," it was not easy to become a member. Before even being introduced to a lodge, the prospect has to be sponsored by two members, and was investigated and voted on. Only two blackballs were allowed, out of a vote of several dozen. But once you belonged to a lodge, the Freemason gained a family of friends, real friends. Although there were many Catholics among them, quite a few Catholics hated the Freemasons, who were much more liberal than the general population. For practical purposes the membership consisted mostly of lawyers, doctors, university professors and industrialists. There were hardly any government employees or trades people among them. Quite possibly, with all the stress on "all men being equal," the Masons in Central Europe considered themselves a little superior to everybody else, as indeed they were.

On a Tuesday, in the fall of 1930, my brother brought me to the old, shabby-looking building which housed all the lodges of the Freemasons. Not being members, but only children of a member, we were not allowed to enter the inside of the building. Our room was immediately to the left of the huge entrance door; this was ours, the youth organization's home. I was to be connected with the "Kette" for many years, but I never saw more of the building, which had no identification, only a house number. Never did I go through the outside door without a feeling of awe.

I was introduced to 30 or 40 young men and women, almost all a few years older than me. My brother explained that, although I could not become a full member for two years, I was sufficiently mature to attend the meetings. Then he introduced me especially to the only "old" person present, a man of about 50, much honored by us, who was acting as a kind of chaperone.

I can't help thinking now, 60 years later, that I left one group – the Boy Scouts – only to become a member of another equally tight-knit group, the youth organization of the Freemasons. Both went on outings on Sundays, both consisted of young people. But, what a difference, and not only in age! My new friends were mature, intelligent adolescents of both sexes, most of them students, but also some "working" people. Our activities on Tuesdays consisted essentially of lectures and discussions. Many of these presentations were given to us by Freemasons, men much older and always very knowledgeable, often famous in their professional fields. But quite a few times, our own members gave lectures on topics they were familiar with – always very well-prepared because they knew that afterwards, during the discussions, they'd be mercilessly grilled and would have to defend their opinions. I remember that, much later, when it was my turn to "lecture," I had a little stage fright, probably the only time in my life.

We took ourselves rather seriously, perhaps a little too much so. Once, after a lecture on the philosophic notion called Determinism, we debated endlessly. Some thought that we were creatures with our own free will, others were sure that everything was pre-ordained. Always a little arrogant, I was with the "free-willers," of course, only I alone was the captain of my ship.

There were lectures on every possible subject: politics, of course, local and global; music, architecture, literature, science, psychoanalysis (Freud) and, preferred in Vienna, individual psychology (Adler).

In Vienna, any group of young people, however organized, would spend Sundays outdoors, and we were no exception. Our Sundays were to be for fun only, no intellectual discussions, no lectures. In summer we rented a large cabin on a beach at the Danube, at Klostemeuburg; there was swimming, boating, ball playing and plain lying in the sun. And flirting, of course. Unlike Tuesdays, when only daughters and sons of Freemasons were allowed, on

Sundays we could bring friends, and these friends would often bring their own friends. I often wondered how these outsiders felt who knew, of course, of our formal Tuesday meetings, which they could not attend. Somehow, there were no problems. As a matter of fact, two of my girlfriends came from this "outsiders" group.

I must have been able to organize my time well in 1930 when I was 16 years old. Just as my brother did at that age, I started to take private lessons in two foreign languages: one was English, which I found easy. My teacher was a British lady, a good teacher who made me love the language. Within a few months, I was able to speak a little; the first book we read together was Oscar Wilde's *The Happy Prince*, a collection of fairy tales, written in especially simple language. The other language I started to study, simultaneously, was Czech. Since my father owned a paint factory in Czechoslovakia, which I was to inherit someday, the knowledge of this language was advisable. There were quite a few Czechs living in Vienna, holdovers from the time when Vienna was the capital of the Austro-Hungarian Empire.

Many retired Czech soldiers had also settled in Vienna. My teacher was one of those; a retired colonel, who augmented his pension giving lessons in his native language. He may well have been a good teacher, but Czech is as difficult to learn for German-speakers as English is easy. In English, practically all words have Germanic or French/Latin roots and therefore always looked familiar to me, at least in print. On the other hand, there were no associations at all possible with the Czech language. Every word was a struggle to memorize and often even harder to pronounce. But the most difficult thing was grammar! Every noun has seven cases (Latin has six, German four, most of them not used; English or French have just one). For instance, the endings of the same noun are different in Czech depending on whether you go to it, live in it, work with it, speak about it, or call it. Unfortunately, my teacher was a perfectionist, and I guess, so was I. Every time I started a sentence, I was already worried about the correct ending of the noun soon to follow.

"Speak Czech with your mother!" My father often said. "She knows the language since she was a child in the Czech village!"

But my mother refused. "I remember only the peasants' language. I can't even read a Czech newspaper; I don't know all these fancy new words."

As if two foreign languages were not enough, I also studied Italian during the latter part of the year. The Italian government gave the classes free of charge; even the books were free. The only "price" the student had to pay was to listen once in a while to indoctrinations that the fascist Italian government gave us in an ever so subtle way.

Not all my activities during these happy last two years of high school were connected with the young Freemason organization, school, or foreign languages. Like so many other children of the Viennese middle-class, I had to take piano lessons. Unfortunately, I was too lazy to practice, and after several years of wasting my parents' money, I finally got their permission to stop. Still, I was interested in music; during my Boy Scout days, I had played the guitar but was not particularly good at it. All I was able to do was to accompany the songs we sang.

It would have been redundant to teach "music appreciation" in Vienna—everybody appreciated music anyway. I went to the State Opera frequently—standing-room of course. Sometimes we went as a "claque." This was a barbaric institution for the privilege of entering without paying. We hired ourselves out to a "claque chief" who told us when to applaud, whom to applaud and even sometimes when to hiss.

Feeling sure that I was not very gifted to perform music but still liking to be involved with it, I became interested in music theory. With a few friends, I spent several hours a week, late evenings, attending lectures at the "Volkshochschule" (College for the People) and learned quite a bit about triads, scales and musical moods. I can hardly imagine any American youngsters having such interest, or any American city that was as broke as Vienna was, sponsoring such courses free of charge.

Between my junior and senior year of high school, I enjoyed quite a remarkable summer. First, Italy, but not as a tourist! Rather, as an unpaid (but also not paying) helper to my brother, who had gotten himself a summer job as a guide for a group of some twenty girls attending a trade school, together with their teacher. All my brother and I had to do was to make sure that all arrangements were in order: take care of complaints, keep everybody happy. The main function was to go shopping with the girls and act as their interpreter. I was supposed to know Italian; after all, I had studied it for several months! Strangely enough, I could speak it a little. Having just the most basic knowledge of a foreign language, the most important thing is not to be afraid to speak it. And being 17 years old, I was afraid of nothing, except girls! My brother, who had no such problems with the girls, always found himself surrounded by them; I was the only boy besides him. The girls were a little older than I and, being not bad-looking, I got plenty of overtures. All I could do was to blush. Not even my brother's encouragement helped. But, anyway, I got to see Venice, Verona, and a little more of northern Italy free of charge.

It was only the middle of July when the Italy trip was to be over. My brother had to stay with the class until they safely reached Vienna, but I was under no such obligation. Just after we crossed the Alps and reached southern Austria, I left the train and joined a Zionist camp where my cousin Adolf (that was his real name; as soon as he got to Israel, what was then called "Palestine," he changed it to Daniel) was one of their leaders. We had exchanged impressions about our youth movements for years. He had been as enthusiastic about his Zionist group as I was about the Boy Scouts. But a whole year had gone by since I quit, so I accepted his invitation. I was curious what I might find.

"Finally, you are seeing the light!" He greeted me. "Shalom! You will be happy to know that we are not aimless drifters like your Boy Scouts. We know what we want."

"You are not going to tell me that you all want to go to Palestine?"

"We certainly do."

"And leave all your friends, your parents…"

"I don't think so. They will come too! They'll have to. Look, this is 1931. Within a year or two Hitler will come to power in Germany. How long can it be until the Nazis get to Austria, too?"

We had many discussions while I was in the Zionist youth camp, which on the surface, was not so different from the Boy Scouts. If anything, their conditions were even rougher than ours had been. They played ball, they hiked, just as we had done. Enjoying better leadership, their food was better prepared but just as Spartan. But otherwise, what a difference! There was endless indoctrination. They put on plays with Zionist themes. But the most striking difference was their singing. Never, ever would they sing German songs. Mostly the language was Hebrew, which few understood, but also some French or even Dutch, which nobody understood either.

"Why are you doing this?" I asked my cousin. "I can see why you like Hebrew songs. But Dutch?"

"We are singing in Hebrew, not only because we like the songs, but also because it's a good way to learn a little of the language. And Dutch? No good reason except that we don't want to sing in German.

"Unfortunately, we can't help speaking it for the moment because we know no other language. But as soon as possible, we want to forget all about German culture!"

(Well, let's see. I visited my cousin just a few months ago, almost 60 years after this conversation. He has been living in Israel since 1939, long before it became a state. He is a famous physician, still working as a scientist, but what did I find on his bookshelves? Goethe, Heine, Kafka, Schnitzler, even Shakespeare in German translation.)

Not long after my arrival, the whole camp went for a few days on a tour into the high mountains surrounding the camp. Since I had no heavy shoes with me, I was afraid

I'd be left behind, but there was a girl who happened to have an extra pair she was willing to lend me. Her shoes were a little tight, but I could wear them – and we quickly became good friends. As a matter of fact, I thought she was very pretty, and I told her so.

"I'd really like to be your girlfriend when we get back to Vienna," she said to me. "I like you, but I must tell you that I'm 'making Aliyah' (emigrating to Palestine) in two months from now."

"What?" I interrupted. "You? A pretty girl? What are you going to do in Palestine? Grow oranges all your life? How can you leave Vienna?"

"I'm afraid you don't understand. Eretz Israel will be my whole life."

I guess I cried a little that night. For the first time I met a girl I really liked, but I'd never see her again because she'd waste her life in such an impossible country.

("What became of the pretty girl who lent me her shoes?" I asked my Israeli cousin recently. "Did she really leave Vienna soon after I met her?"

"Oh yes," he assured me. "She's living in Haifa, has many children, at least two dozen grandchildren, quite a lady, but not so pretty anymore.")

I spent only two weeks in the Zionist youth camp. While I could not believe my cousin's dire predictions about Hitler coming to power in Germany and Austria, the absolute dedication of all the young people I met there, and the sound arguments I'd heard that Austria was certainly not a good place for a young Jew to be, was enough to make a Zionist of me. I understood that the leadership of the young Zionists was turning children against their parents, who not only felt comfortable with Austro-German culture but also did not want to lose their children. But maybe the parents were wrong! (Seven or eight years later, the lives of these same parents were often saved because they could join their children in Palestine.)

I was to spend the second half of the summer of 1931 in a Czech village with relatives of my mother. My father insisted on that. I should become as fluent as possible in the Czech language. But just before I left southern Austria, I had an adventure.

In order to catch a train to Vienna, I had to cross a lake in one of the local steamboats. I noticed two ladies from England were causing a little commotion; one was a girl of my age, the other one a little older. I soon learned that they had asked for some information, but in English and nobody understood them. Just trying to be helpful, I acted as an interpreter. I guess they wanted to know about hotels, but I was not prepared for the reaction.

"Thank you ever so much," said the older of the two ladies. "We were hoping to find somebody like you who might help us; we don't speak one word of German, you see."

"It was entirely my pleasure," I interrupted. "For me, any occasion to practice my poor English is a real joy."

"Your English is marvelous!" the younger of the two chimed in. "Do you think…"

I saw her throw a pleading glance to her friend, who nodded.

"Well…do you think you could stay with us for a week while we are in Austria? We'd be ever so happy."

"We would pay you, of course," added the older one, who seemed to be in charge.

"Of course, you would have your own room in any hotel where we'd stay. You see, this trip to Austria is a present to my sister. She got such excellent marks in school. To have you with us would make it perfect!"

Not only was my vanity touched, but "sister" was a very pretty girl; I really wanted to accept, but probably because I was too shy to be with two young ladies, I refused politely, explaining that I had to be in Vienna that very evening. Much, much later I could not help reflecting what would have happened had I accepted, which of course I could have done. We might have corresponded afterwards; in 1938, they might have assisted me in getting to England. The British were always helpful to those they knew personally. My whole life would have been changed.

I cannot remember ever feeling under pressure during the last years I spent in high school. I was a good student.

I did homework "selectively," in other words if, in my own opinion, it was worthwhile. I never took notes during classes; being a strictly auditory type and having, in my late teens, an excellent memory. All I had to do was listen carefully to the lectures of my teachers.

"First, listen to me because I prepared the lesson for you," the teachers would say. "Then do your own reading, on your own time."

This is exactly what I did, and it worked for me. Whenever I had reason to believe that the teachers view might have been slanted, such as in history, I was especially careful to read sources that differed from the teacher's opinion, and presented this material when he called upon me. I never got into trouble because I also repeated the teacher's views.

As I've noted, the climax of high school was the examination called the "matura." We had to pass this after our senior year. Four subjects had to be done in writing, in class: Math, Latin, French and German. But as a kind of dissertation, we had to compose a long (at least 30 pages) paper on any subject we chose. This was a lot of work that could be avoided only by an oral examination in a subject other than the four mentioned above. Almost nobody chose that option. A representative from the school board would be present, too much excitement. But being much too lazy to write a long paper, I figured that the teacher wouldn't mind showing off a good student in front of the "man from the board." So, I "volunteered."

I chose geography. There were to be two questions: one about Austria, our homeland, and the other one about a non-European continent of the student's choice. North America (was I prescient?) in my case. I diligently prepared myself; I knew the capitals, as well as the most important city of every state in the U.S., including its economic strength, rivers, mountains, etc. I considered it less likely to be asked about Canada. But just to be sure, I familiarized myself a little with that country too.

The day of the examination came. Not only a mean-looking school board member, but also the principal of our school was present. I was the only one who had chosen geography. Maps of Austria and North America were on the wall. But there was also what we called "blind" maps, with only the outlines of the states or provinces on them. Unidentified little rings in black for cities, rivers in blue and mountains in brown. Whatever the "Austrian" question was, I had no difficulty with it.

"Very good," the teacher said. "Now, go to the map of North America and tell us what you know about Mexico!" I had a terrible feeling in my stomach. I had not studied Mexico, knew next to nothing about it except the story of Juarez and Maximilian, the Austrian prince who came to a bad end there. But with the unlimited self-confidence only an 18-year-old boy who has not yet tasted defeat can have, I kept my cool. There was a lot of brown on the Mexican map. The rings for the cities were almost all in that brown color. No big rivers. I knew, from U.S. history that there had been wars with Mexico. I started to talk.

"When we speak about North America, we might often think only about the two giants: The U. S. and Canada, where only English and some French is spoken. But the third nation on that continent is Mexico, a proud, Spanish-speaking country, that would not tolerate European intervention! Most of Mexico is situated in the tropics. The climate in the low-lying sections is unhealthy, especially on the Gulf. It must be, so I thought. There were very few rings for cities. But in the higher altitudes, on the interior plateau, many good-size cities are prospering thanks to the arid climate. Most important, Mexico, being washed by the Pacific on the west and the Gulf on the east, is a true bridge between the U.S. to the north and the smaller Central American countries."

"Thank you," the teacher interrupted me. "You seem to have a very good knowledge of Mexico."

My bluff worked. Since I had also done well on all written examinations, I received excellent grades on my final high school report and felt on top of the world. In that summer of 1932, I thought there was nothing I couldn't do. But soon, very soon, I would know better. Not long after my 18th birthday, the carefree days of my life came to an end.

VII

AFTER HIGH SCHOOL— UNHAPPY YEARS

Do we ever know how happy we are? Probably not. Anyway, when are we really happy?

Or, for that matter, unhappy?

I believe there is more to it than just "having a good or bad time." For instance, during the terrible years of 1939 to 1941, when I often didn't know if I would live another month or sometimes even another day, I was seldom unhappy because I always knew things would change, one way or another. But after the summer of 1932, when I had finished high school, I often felt desperate, trapped.

I had made such good plans for the fall of 1932. I would start with my studies at the University of Vienna, taking not just one but two subjects: law (there was no such thing as an undergraduate curriculum) and also, simultaneously, business administration (called "world trade"). I felt sure I could do it; my self-confidence was enormous at that time. My parents approved. But first, in August of that year, I was to go on a trip with three of my high school colleagues. We would tramp our way through Austria, Northern Italy and Yugoslavia.

All went well for a while although I soon found out that my fellow travelers and I didn't have much to say to each other, we really had not been very good friends before. But one morning, in a small town in Yugoslavia where we were paying guests at relatives of one of the fellows, I woke up with a terrible headache. We decided that I would not join in our activities planned for this day; but in the evening, I felt I had a high fever. The next day I felt terrible pains in all my bones, pains much worse than I had ever experienced before or since.

The other fellows were nice enough about it, they'd wait for me to get well, they said, but after a couple of days they left me in the care of our host. I would take a train back to Vienna when able to do so. But soon I noticed that I could hardly swallow anymore and had lost control of my bowels. When I tried to get up, I found my right leg paralyzed. I could still walk but only with a cane, dragging my leg. A few days later I felt my fever subside, although the pain continued. I thanked my host, who was glad to see me leave, somehow made it to the railroad station and wired my parents to pick me up.

My father was out of town; my mother screamed when she saw me: "What happened? I hardly recognize you."

Well, it turned out that I had contracted poliomyelitis, and a bad case at that. I was taken to a specialist, who shook his head.

"Had I been able to see you right after you came down with the disease, I could have helped, put your leg between splints, ordered complete rest. But now..." He shrugged his shoulders.

(Only many years later was I to learn how lucky I had been. Complete rest was the worst treatment possible; immediate exercise is best.)

Anyway, I slowly recovered, helped by some electrical treatment my brother was trained to give me. I regained control of my esophagus and bowel muscles and after a few months, started to walk more normally. Having lost over 50 pounds, I was much too weak to attend the university, although I registered for the required courses at law school. Only in December was I able to go to classes but felt, for the first time in my life, that I could not concentrate; I hardly knew what was going on.

(Hitler had become Chancellor of Germany early in 1933, but we, in Austria, didn't feel involved.) We had a family conference. By that time, I had regained some of my weight; I felt healthy again. Only a slight limp remained which would stay with me for another year.

"I feel so useless," I complained. "Too much time was lost; I can't study business administration anymore, examinations in law school don't start until the third semester, I wish I could get some kind of job, maybe work in our factory in Vienna."

My father interrupted. "I'm so glad you said that. At this time, I could not possibly fit you into the Viennese business. As a matter of fact, my partner, Dr. Winter, is running it more than I do, and we are not always seeing everything eye to eye. What I could use here in Vienna is a chemist who would understand more about the manufacturing end."

"I can certainly interrupt my studies for a while," my brother said. "All I am doing now is my thesis, but that could wait if you need me."

Father would not hear of this. "In only one year you will get your doctorate in chemistry. You should finish! But," he turned to me, "if you want to work now, I'd be very, very happy to have you with me in our factory in Bratislava. I want to spend more time traveling, get more business; it would help me to have someone whom I can really trust."

"But this is unfair to Frank," my brother said. "You let me go to college for over three years now; why should he not have his chance."

My father prevailed; nothing else would have made sense. But ever since, to this day, my brother Charles seems to feel that he owes me something because he finished his studies while I did not. Anyway, my career started in Bratislava, Czechoslovakia, in February, 1933 and ended there only when we lost our factory to the Nazis in the fall of 1938. There was only a short interruption in 1934 when I studied for and then passed my first examination in law school in Vienna.

My father saw to it that I got the best possible training. At first, I worked only in the office. I entered the incoming orders and that gave me a little knowledge of who our customers were and which salesmen were the best. I soon discovered that all of our biggest customers bought from us only because my father personally contacted them. Then I was in charge of petty cash as well as distributing the worker's wages (in cash, no checks), a good way to get in touch with reality.

"Whatever your activities are now," my father often told me, "they are only an introduction. Soon you will be doing what really counts: selling. Selling! This is what started my career, and you are better off than I because you speak Czech. You'll do very well."

I doubted that; I knew that I did not have his relaxed, but at the same time calculating way of doing things. I was not that good at handling people. But I was always good with numbers. It did not take me long to realize that our business was doing poorly, our cash flow was barely adequate to pay our bills and not sufficient to buy new machinery when the old would wear out. When I pointed this out to my father, he replied:

"I know that. But why are you such a pessimist? These are the hard times; the Depression won't last forever. In just a few years, with your help, we'll do fine. You think this company hasn't got enough capital. Wrong! My greatest resources are my two sons, your brother and you!"

I could not help but feeling terrible when I heard that. What could I, the inexperienced 19-year-old, do? Why did my father trust me so much? My arrogant self-confidence of high school years was gone. But what hurt me most during the first few years I spent in Bratislava was loneliness.

I could not spend every evening with my father, and anyway he traveled a lot. I had no friends, and did not know what to do with myself after work. I only lived for the weekends when I could return to Vienna, only 35 miles away from Bratislava, where I could see my friends from the "Kette," the association of Freemason's children.

"You should stay in Bratislava over the weekend sometimes," my father advised.

"How can you make friends when you are not here? Get yourself a girlfriend, if possible one with whom you can speak Czech!"

I had no idea how to go about that, although I felt sure that my brother could have done it. My Boy Scout experience did not qualify me for seeking out the female gender; all I could do was dream about girls. A little later, in early summer, I acquired a "girlfriend," but in Vienna where I still spent every weekend. But it was not my doing! One nice Sunday, while we were on the usual outing in the Vienna Woods, the president of the Kette, a man in his early 20s, two heads taller than me and fifty pounds heavier, took me aside.

"Frank, you are an idiot," he explained. "As the president of this organization, I feel responsible for everybody having a good time. Don't you see that pretty girl over there looking at you? Talk to her. If you don't, I'll beat you up." Just to illustrate his point, he stepped on my foot. I didn't dare to wince.

Well, Lisa and I became good friends. We went on endless walks. I really felt flattered to be seen with her. She had an excellent figure, was good-looking, fun to be with and, I believe, really liked me. But, in my 19th year, I could not muster the courage to do more than talk! I never dared to kiss her although I wanted to so badly.

Our friendship lasted the better part of a year. She introduced me to her family, which made me feel a little uncomfortable. (Why was I so respectable?) Finally, she got tired of me, letting me down easy.

"Frank dear," she explained, studying the floor while talking. "I'll be extremely busy next weekend, also the weekend thereafter. Would you mind very much not calling me?"

I understood and tried to take my father's advice to spend my weekends in Bratislava rather than to hurry off to Vienna.

In the meantime, in the spring of 1934, I had passed my first examination at the law school of the University of Vienna, after three months of concentrated study. By attending a special class for three hours in the morning, then studying until midnight every day, I could do three semester's work in that many months. I liked the subjects very much, also the challenge. It gave me pleasure to realize that my mental faculties were as good as before my bout with polio. Physically, I had completely recovered even earlier, regained all lost weight, and had gone skiing. But how was I to overcome my loneliness? Saturday evenings I roamed the streets of Bratislava, thought for a while of getting involved with one of the hundreds of prostitutes who walked the same streets. But I could not get myself to do it. Then I placed an ad in a local paper looking for female company, but that did not work out either.

My father could not quite understand my problem. He had so many friends, and he was not even good-looking; shorter than me, and a little fat, with very small eyes but a big nose. His only good feature was his long, white hair. Of course, he was witty, never at a loss for words, never timid, a little pompous, I thought. But the ladies loved him, and their husbands liked him too. When he entered a room, everybody knew he was there.

"I'll introduce you to the sons of two friends of mine," he said to me one day. "They are a little older than you, have a little too much money, but that shouldn't make you feel inferior; you are my son."

Well, I met Mr. A., age 26, and Mr. K., 23 years old. We never got around to calling each other by our first names. But soon we started a weekly card game, the classical game of Central Europe: Tarock.

It is played with special cards containing 21 trumps, the lowest of which is number one. The goal of the game is to make many tricks and if at all possible, to make the last trick with the lowest trump! It's a fun game; two of the players always gang up against the third.

One evening, Mr. A., who was in love with the most beautiful woman of Bratislava, but who was unfortunately already married, said to me:

"Mr. Weinmann, I have some excellent advice for you. True, you are a lousy Tarock player, but I like you anyway. Just promise you'll do what I'm going to tell you! You'll be sorry if you don't. Promise me."

I thought I'd like to know more about the nature of his advice.

"You are not in love right now," he continued. "so this is the right time. Later, when you fall in love, it'll be too late."

"Too late for what?"

"Have yourself castrated! That way you'll save yourself "soooo" much pain because you won't care if she says 'no' because you can't anyway."

The following week Mr. A. confessed that he was glad to be still in full possession of his manhood because his lady had finally said "yes."

I met a few other young men, all sons of my father's friends and rather well to do, most of them students at the local university. Since all of us were Jewish, we decided to start a private club, the "Intellectual Zionists," meaning, I guess, that we would talk about Zionism without having any intention of ever emigrating to Palestine. Having now at least somebody to talk to you after working hours, even if not friends, I should not have been so unhappy.

But I could not escape the fact that our factory was going from bad to worse; it was sometimes hard to meet the payroll and to meet our obligations. What hurt us very much was that many of our customers paid very slowly, some even went broke. I started to work less in the office and more in our factory. Perhaps, I thought, I could save some money by introducing better methods. But I was not at all prepared for Mr. S., the man in charge of production, giving us three months' notice!

"I enjoyed working here," he said, "but I found a better job. You will understand that I have to think of my family. Anyway, young Mr. Weinmann should be able to take over."

My father agreed. "This is your chance!" He said to me, "You can do it! The workers like you, they'll cooperate. Just be sure you get all paint formulas from Mr. S. before he leaves and learn as much as possible during these last three months!" This was January of 1935. I was just 20 years old. What if I make big mistakes, I thought? What if I ruin my father's business? How will we eat? This was not an intellectual exercise now. This was not studying Roman law. No time to be brilliant. This was real life.

My father reassured me. "In a way, I'm glad Mr. S. is leaving. He is by far the highest paid employee. I am also glad that I could give more money to you now with your greater responsibilities."

At about the same time, my father's partner of 35 years, Dr. Winter, informed my father that he wanted out. The Viennese factory was doing poorly, and he could not see any future for himself and his family in the business. So, my father bought him out, using his last reserves! Luckily my brother had just finished his studies with a PhD in chemistry and was taking over in Vienna. Truly, my father's capital *was* his two sons.

VIII

I DANCED WITH THREE GIRLS

Shortly before Mardi Gras, there was, and probably still is, a big dance in Vienna called the "Gschnas-fest," pronounced "Ge-Shanas" in Viennese German. The word does not mean anything. Neither should one look for any meaning in the elaborate decorations of the huge hall where this dance takes place, except that they are crazy, sexually-suggestive and expensive. So expensive are the decorations that in order to make money, the dance is held three times: First, for the rich people; the entrance fee is huge, but if you are somebody, you must be seen there and written about in the Sunday papers. Second, for the "artists," much cheaper but still covered by the press. Finally, at greatly reduced prices, was the Gschnas for the students. The dress code: come masked or without a mask; wear a tuxedo or a swimming suit. Anything goes. During the pre-Lenten time, called "Fasching," strictly Catholic Austria will be looking the other way, for this night only!

One does not go to this event with a boyfriend or girlfriend. As a matter of fact, it is best not to have one at all; why have the pangs of conscience later for any misdeeds committed at the "Students Gschnas"?

I lived in Bratislava, Czechoslovakia in February 1935, but that was only 35 miles from Vienna. And I was certainly in the right position, unattached but looking. Much too lazy to even think of a costume, I simply dressed in short pants and a T-shirt. It's hot there, I was told.

Almost everybody was of my own age, around twenty. I soon discovered that most of the girls wore masks, if not much else. There was already some dancing when I got there at 10 o'clock in the evening.

But at least for a while it seemed to be more fun just walking through the crowd, looking every girl in the eye, but certainly not only in the eyes, keeping free to choose a partner for a dance or two.

"Please dance with me, Frank," said a pleasant voice. "Don't you recognize me?" I looked at the girl, but could not see her face, which was covered with a blue mask that went well with her dark blonde hair. She had good legs, and a typical "Viennese figure," which means a little plump. I liked her.

"No, I'm afraid not," I admitted. "I usually remember voices. Yours sounds familiar, of course (a little lying is OK, I thought). "But how do you know my name?"

"I'm not going to tell you, not just now. Shame on you for not remembering me! As a punishment, you must dance with me."

We danced rather close. I feel sorry for the young people nowadays who think they are dancing, while really doing acrobatics by themselves without the nice feeling of being close to a soft body. After a while, I lifted her mask and saw a nice face, it could have been a beautiful face had it not been for a rather long nose in the middle. I guess she didn't take the chance of me still not recognizing her.

"I am Trude. We met at your cousin's birthday party a month ago, remember?"

"But of course," I lied. Actually, I did remember the party; we played some boring games. But I didn't remember her.

"You don't sound very convincing," she prattled on. "Anyway, my mother and your aunt are best friends. My mother made me go, that's how I got to that party. You were the only interesting boy there. I asked your cousin for your name. I remembered it, not like a certain young man who is dancing with me now but not holding me quite as close as before, I wonder why?"

She was right. I was not so sure I wanted to have anything to do with a girl whose mother was my aunt's best friend. And she looked so young. But, what the hell, this was the Gschnas, and we were supposed to have a good time.

"Trude, I'll remember you for ever and ever from now on, I promise. And I love you because you are sweet and beautiful and smart."

"Frank, you can bullshit as well as anybody. Why don't you quit while you're ahead? I'll tell you what: if you promise on your Boy Scouts honor to come to my birthday party a week from next Saturday, I'll let you go now. Just to make sure, I'll send you an invitation with my address."

The music had stopped. We looked at each other for a while. I gave her a quick kiss on the forehead. She was much shorter than me.

"Thanks for asking me," I said. "I really like you, Trude."

When Trudy said that she'd let me go, she only did what was required at the Gschnas. One does not stay with the same partner too long. I went my way, very pleased with myself, looking for more adventures, remembering my father's saying: "Our mothers have beautiful daughters too."

The evening was still young, not even midnight, and walking through the crowd I saw Hansi, my second cousin. She did not wear a mask and her dress was the typical Austrian "dirndl," a kind of stylized peasant's costume.

"I'm surprised to see you here," I said. "You, a second-year medical student, aren't you too proud for such nonsense as the Gschnas?"

"Thanks for insulting me. I think I'll become a dentist just for the pleasure of drilling your teeth."

"Hansi, the pleasure will be all mine! I'd love to be hurt by such beautiful hands."

"Frank, you B.S.-er. You are such a bastard. Why didn't you ever pay the slightest attention to me at our family gatherings?"

She was right. I considered family gatherings a bore and furthermore Hansi was not my type, though her face was pretty enough. She had an ever-so-slight mustache and always looked sloppy. Our fathers were first cousins but not at all close. While my father was a self-made industrialist and certainly an intellectual, hers was a well-to-do farmer some 20 miles from Vienna. I was surprised that he let his daughter study medicine. Hansi was a quiet girl, really somewhat misplaced at the Gschnas, I thought.

The music had started to play and I asked her to dance.

"I'm not living with my parents anymore; it was too far to commute to the University. I found a 'residence for girls,' very proper, of course." She blinked as if to indicate that this place was not all that proper, and she pressed her body very close to mine while we danced.

I reacted carefully. "I'm so glad you are in Vienna now. Don't you think we should see a little more of each other?"

"Yes, of course. Just come to my residence. We have a special room where gentlemen callers are admitted. I will give you my address. But right now, I'd like you to dance a little longer so when we get tired, we will rest, together, of course."

The dance floor had become very crowded, this was as good an excuse as any for us to dance very, very close. Or maybe we didn't dance at all. I have no difficulty guessing just what Hansi had in mind by saying we should "rest together," because I had seen a heavily carpeted room (called the "Egyptian Room") separated from the one where the dancing took place. It was much darker there, the wall decorations muted; there were a few tables and chairs on which nobody was sitting. Rather, it was the floor, which was being used for "resting" by couples who went about as far as one could go in a public place. I took Hansi there. We had a good time. There comes a time when nature calls, and boys and girls must separate. Afterwards, I returned to the dance floor, looking for more adventures but did not find anybody I especially liked. It was long after midnight now.

Getting hungry, I went to the buffet. While I ate, I saw Fred, who I knew well from our Sunday hiking group and his sister, Anny, who joined us once in a while.

"I must keep an eye on my little sister," Fred explained. "She is only nineteen."

"Very interesting. Our mother asked me to see that Fred did not get in trouble. You boys are terrible, everybody knows that," Anny said.

"Not me," I protested. "I am the quiet, serious, rather dull type."

"Is that so?" Anny wondered. "Let me find out on the dance floor." She smiled, took my arm, and we were off.

"Be good, you two!" Fred called after us.

"Anny, I must admit that I didn't notice before what a pretty girl you are," I said to her as we started to dance. "Definitely my type. Dark brown hair. I don't like blondes, you know, and eyes to match it. Not too skinny."

"I am NOT fat, I'm athletic!"

"Of course, perfect figure, also just the right height for me. And you are wearing such an interesting dress!"

"Well, it's about time you noticed! I made it myself, it took me hours."

Anny stopped dancing, and took me to a spot where there was room for her to step back. She looked at me with a serious smile. She was so beautiful!

"Tell me, Frank, what is my dress all about?"

I was put to task. I felt more apprehensive than I ever had before and examination at the University. I must guess right! Well, the dress was essentially of a thin, light gray material, sleeveless, with many strange designs sewn on. On the upper left side there was an orange circle on a blue background, rather small, with two diagonal thin red lines over it. To cancel it out? Across the chest I saw a few large, dark gray, irregular patches with a zigzag bright yellow line vertically sewn over them.

The lower portion of the dress was covered with a tree, as a child would paint it, but strongly bent to one side, with vertical, thin gray lines sewn over it. Obviously, there was a theme. A thunderstorm, perhaps? Then I remembered the hit song of the year, which had just reached us from America and called out loud:

"Stormy Weather."

Anny fell around my neck and kissed me. "Frank, I love you! Nobody guessed it but you! Fred said nobody would! Thanks!" Anny was really happy.

As I looked at her and she looked at me, I had a strange feeling. Whatever it was, I was 20 years old and had never had it before. A longing, so very pleasant, although it hurt a little. She had said to me, "I love you," but just as a figure of speech, I thought. But I really loved her! And after all the bragging and posturing I had done at the "Gschnas-fest" I could not tell her! After all, it was just the atmosphere of the place that had made me so bold.

In reality, I was still a timid boy. I danced a little more with Anny, but we were rather quiet now. Then we decided that it was getting late and we were both tired; since she had come with her brother, I did not even take her home.

I went to Trude's birthday party the next week. (My parents approved. "After all, your aunt's best friend's daughter must be a nice girl.") Quite a few young people were there, somewhat younger than I, who seemed to know each other well but were all strangers to me except for Trudy. When we sat down to eat, I found the place cards prepared on the table. I was sitting at Trude's left, the place of honor, I guessed, and she made a point of addressing me all the time. I couldn't possibly meet anybody else. And it surprised me to learn that she was only 17, too young for the Gschnas, I thought.

"Tomorrow, Sunday, our group will go for an outing to the Vienna Woods. Could you join us?"

Trude asked me just before I left her party. "We meet at 9 o'clock at the end of trolley number 38." I could not think of a good excuse and promised to be there.

Next morning, when I got out of the trolley at five minutes before nine, I saw Trudy already waiting. "Frank, I'm so glad you came," Trudy said, "Unfortunately, none of the others could make it today."

"Couldn't you just tell me yesterday?"

"Frank, I was afraid you wouldn't come just with me alone."

How could I tell her that she was probably right? As we slowly walked up one of the hills of the Vienna Woods, which I knew so well from my Boy Scout time, the crowd of hikers always present on a Sunday gradually thinned out. It was already quite warm when we got to a small meadow.

"How about resting here for a while?" Trude suggested.

We sat down near the path we had come up but after a while moved away to a more secluded spot where we had a good view of the city below. It was an unusually nice day for March, the grass was getting green.

"Let's lie down here," Trude suggested. "But come a little closer to me. Pretend you like me."

Soon, Trude kissed me as I had never been kissed before. I tried my best to answer in kind, but though I was more than three years older, I knew that I could learn much from Trude. I was a willing student.

In the following weeks, I really joined Trudy's crowd, all nice girls and boys. We went for Sunday outings, but only after spending Saturdays alone.

Soon we fell into a routine: Every Saturday, after coming to Vienna from Bratislava, I would call Trude. We would meet at a movie or a coffeehouse, and I'd take her home. Her mother usually had a snack prepared for us and we visited for a while, then her mother left, indicating she'd be back by 10 or so. As soon as we were alone, we sat down on a couch, always the same, and the kissing started and lasted for quite a while. Once, when I came home to Vienna after having worked at our factory in Bratislava all week, my mother told me:

"Your cousin Hansi asked for you. I heard she is very sick."

"Of course, I'll visit her," I said quickly. "I didn't know."

"Well, her mother called me. Hansi is at the General Hospital."

I had an appointment with Trude, as usual, but told her I'd leave her at a coffee house near the hospital and pick her up later. She understood.

When I came to Hansi's hospital room, I saw immediately that she must be indeed a very sick girl. Her parents, her sister as well as more relatives were there, some in tears. A cousin who, like Hansi, was a medical student, took me aside.

"Hansi has an inflammation of the cardiac sac. Fatal, I'm afraid."

"Does she know that?" I asked.

"Of course, she knows. She's a smart girl and knows medicine."

When I entered Hansi's room, she saw me immediately and asked to be left alone with me.

Actually, she didn't look bad at all, just red in the face.

"I'm glad you came, Frank. Please forgive my mother for calling you, but I really wanted to see you."

I had seen Hansi a few times since the Gschnas; we went for walks or to the movies. I had come no closer to her than holding her hand.

"Frank, I'm afraid we have no time for small talk, my parents want to be with me, for obvious reasons. I want you to hold me very tight, very tight."

I could not talk, but embraced her as well as I could. "No, tighter, much tighter. Put your hand on my breast, as you did at the Gschnas. I want you to hurt me, really hurt me."

I tried to make small talk about us seeing much more of each other after she got well.

"Whatever you say, Frank. Now kiss me goodbye." I could not help telling Trude all about my visit with Hansi when I met her at the coffeehouse where I had left her. I just could not hold back.

Trude cried a little. "Why do the girls like you so much, Frank? You really don't deserve it."

The next day I learned that Hansi had died a few hours after I had seen her. And Trude, I'm afraid, was right about me. I certainly did not deserve Trude's love because I betrayed her. Not once, but twice.

Early in the summer of the same year, I saw Anny, the "stormy weather" girl, again, more or less by chance, at one of the bathing beaches on the Danube, near Vienna. Annie was no great beauty (I never went for that) but more than just a good-looking girl with an excellent figure. Her mature, intelligent way of looking at things without the pretense I so often detected in Trude, attracted me. She was going to England for a few months, she told me, in order to improve her knowledge of the language, because she wanted to become an English teacher. We agreed to correspond. When she returned in the fall and I saw her again, I knew that I loved her. This time I managed to tell her! I also told her that I saw another girl regularly but would break up with her because I really did not love her. Anny understood.

When I saw Trude, I gave her the usual song and dance. "I like you, dear, but I am almost four years older than you; I'm afraid I am monopolizing you. Don't you think you should be more with friends of your own age?" Trudy saw through me immediately. "Don't tell me what you think. You found another girl and want to get rid of me."

I tried a different approach. "Trude, I am 21 years old, male, healthy. I have no intention of marrying for quite a while, but I want to have sex."

"How do you know I'd refuse you? You never asked me!"

We both realized that there was no point in arguing. I wished her luck.

Anny and I were in love. We drank wine together at the full moon, looking at each other. Though I never smoked in my life, I lit a cigarette for her and even put the darn thing between my lips because it came from her lips. During Christmas vacation, we went skiing with another couple. Officially the two boys would have one room and the girls another, but of course it wasn't so. With Anny, I learned the joys of sex.

I still spent the week in Bratislava, working in my father's factory and came to Vienna and to Anny only over the weekend. Anny had told me that she was working now too, giving English lessons and also cooperating with "somebody" singing records with English nursery rhymes.

"Frank, dear," she said one Sunday, would you mind very much if we couldn't see each other next weekend? You see, my friend with whom I am working has no time during the week..."

I looked at Anny. She looked away, I understood. It was over. It was then that I did something I'm ashamed of to this day. I called Trude, asking her to see me again, and she agreed. For the next two months Trude and I were "together again" as if there had never been an Anny.

But there was an Anny in my life, very much so. She called me, explaining that the recording business hadn't worked out. Would I mind...

Well, I didn't mind. Again: goodbye Trude; again, hello Anny. But this time we parted after only a few weeks. I think I bored her.

This was the end of my weekends in Vienna; from now on my friends, and love, would be in Bratislava. But I often think of the three girls I danced with at the "Gschnas-Fest." Hansi, who died so courageously, and Anny, my first real love. (I have no idea what became of her except that she escaped to England shortly after Hitler came to Vienna.) And as for Trude, the girl who taught me how to kiss? I saw her again, some 20 years ago, when I was on a business trip to New York. She had had her nose operated on and, in her late 40's, looked positively glamorous. Furthermore, she was holding down a big job with a leading New York publisher. My daughter and son-in-law, working for a television company, had just transferred to New York, and Trude helped them find an apartment.

"What do you think of my daughter?" I, the proud father, asked Trude.

"She is such a beautiful, sweet little thing," Trude answered, "and so intelligent! Too bad she is too decent ever to take a lover. You see, she married a man just like her father: nice, but a little dull."

"What do you think of Trude?" I asked my daughter.

"What a ball buster!" was her only comment.

Not having an excellent education like my daughter at Northwestern University, these words were not part of my vocabulary. But I figured it out.

IX

GOODBYE, VIENNA!

This time I mean it, I said to myself. I am not going to run to Vienna every weekend. I can't even hold a girl that way. I had loved Anny, and she had loved me for a while, but a girl probably needs a fellow during the week too! I'll be an obedient son and do what my father had asked me so often: try to feel at home in Bratislava, work hard during the week, but also see friends whom I can meet again on weekends!

First, I did what I thought then was only symbolic but proved of great importance later: I had the Austrian consulate in Bratislava change my official residence from Vienna to Bratislava. I was still an Austrian citizen, but one residing in Czechoslovakia. Next, I started to read the local Slovakian newspaper. When I found ad by a "young woman, transferred to the capital (Bratislava) and looking for company," I answered it. But when we met, we didn't click. (I wrote a story about encounter in a coffeehouse that is essentially true.)

I joined a "Rowing Club." Rowing on the river Danube was an important sport in Bratislava. There were three rowing clubs: Slovakian, Hungarian and German.

I investigated the Slovakian club first, but they were not my kind of people: mostly civil servants, very Catholic. I could feel they didn't want me. Since I could not speak Hungarian, it had to be the German club, which I found to be a catchall for all those who did not fit the other two. The members, all male of course, were mostly young professionals, industrialists, many Jews.

The membership fee was rather stiff, but that did not bother me at all. The club bought a lot of paints in order to keep the boats in good shape. I offered to sell them these products from our factory at a good retail price, but still lower than what they were used to paying. I think I was the only member who got money out of the club.

I soon found out that rowing on the Danube was nothing like paddling around in a little lake! The current is swift; it's not easy to hold onto the oars.

"Don't be afraid of the water, it won't swim away!" a veteran rower, who was acting as my teacher, explained. "And when you pull the oar, you must bend "way back, practically lay down, like a whore!"

The language in the "very exclusive" club was not very delicate. Neither were other habits, for instance, drinking beer. After all the boats were in, we would assemble in the clubhouse for a huge glass of beer. The problem was that the glass was shaped like a boot. Drinking was easy until only the beer in the foot portion was left. All of it would then rush out over the face of the drinker. The novice did not know that and thus got a baptism with beer. Oh, what fun!

When I was permitted out of the stationary rowing box, I was assigned to a boat with eight seats, four on each side. First we would invariably row upstream, and I soon found out why. In case of an accident, usually caused by the wrongdoing of an inexperienced rower, the delicate boat would turn over, and we had to swim home. But swimming against the current in the Danube is impossible. Soon I was taking long outings on the river. We would row to a village several miles upstream and dock there at an inn famous for its wine, but not just ordinary grape wine! This noble drink was made from currants grown locally and tasted like strawberry juice, sweet and smooth. I noticed that all eyes were looking at me.

"Have another glass," said one of the fellows with an innocent smile. "It's good for you, full of vitamins!"

After I finished the second glass, I fell off my chair, dead drunk. Somehow we got home without my input; downstream is easy.

I had become friends with a fellow my own age who told me one day: "Why don't you join us next Saturday afternoon? We are a group of three girls and only two boys; you see, one of the girls broke up with him.

"Thanks, but I have no intention of getting involved just now, "I said

"Don't get me wrong! These are three very respectable Jewish girls, a little too respectable perhaps! Would you believe they asked me to find out all about you before inviting you?"

Well, I had nothing to lose. After all, I had promised myself to try to make new friends. And friends we became, indeed, nothing more. The girls were all around 20 years old, from well-to-do families. I don't think I ever considered the obvious possibility that I, the son of a factory owner of excellent reputation but rather limited means, could "marry money." This was done all the time. There was nothing dishonorable about getting a dowry and investing it in the family's business. We saw a lot of each other for a few years until the Nazis made an end to the world as we knew it.

"Female company" without love is not enough to keep a young man happy. Neither were the rowdy activities at the rowing club. My work was strenuous. I was by no means sure I did a good job, although my father was always reassuring. One day he said to me:

"I know how happy you were in Vienna when you had the intellectual stimulation of the 'Kette' (the young Freemason's organization). Why don't you start a club here? Some of my lodge brothers and I would help."

I liked the idea. There was a similar organization in Prague, the capital of Czechoslovakia, called "Amicitia," (friendship). It was amazing how fast the word spread within the secret organization of the Masons. It took less than a month until a dozen youngsters, all sons and daughters of Freemasons of Bratislava, met and organized ourselves. We would call ourselves "Amicitia" like our sister organization in Prague. The Latin name took care of a possible language problem. But being in a smaller town, we would admit not only children of Masons, as was done in Vienna or Prague, but also friends of members. However, in order to protect our fathers, these friends would have to be "voted in" by our group. Every member had the right to suggest anybody he or she liked, but the actual admission could only take place after balloting. Only two votes against a prospect were permissible.

We would meet formally once a week, in the lodge building, but informally as often as we liked for outings and parties. For a few weeks, our father's lodges would provide speakers, afterwards we would be on our own. Being in the provincial capital, which was also a university town, quite a few children of Freemasons from small lodges in the provinces studied or worked in Bratislava; they soon learned about us and, having recommendations from their fathers, joined us.

The first problem we had to solve was which language to speak. The official language of the land was Slovakian. But quite a few preferred German or Hungarian. As a matter of fact, the mother tongue of only a small minority was Slovakian. The great majority of my contemporaries in Bratislava, whether well-educated or barely literate, spoke three languages fluently. Those twenty or thirty years older spoke only two: German and Hungarian.

Here is the explanation: the original language spoken, at least until the latter part of the 19th century, was German, although the city of Pressburg (the German name of Bratislava) belonged to Hungary, and even was its capital for a while. But in 1867, under the influence of nationalism which swept all of Europe, Hungary asserted its influence politically; the Hapsburg Empire changed from Austria to Austria-Hungary.

Since the new Hungarian rulers still under the Hapsburg Emperor were quite liberal and did a fairly good job, many citizens, especially the Jews, embraced Hungarian culture eagerly, to the point that quite a few changed their names in order to make themselves sound more "Hungarian." Thus, those born during this time actually spoke Hungarian better than German, although this language never died out.

After the First World War, Bratislava found itself in the new country of Czechoslovakia. The Czechs of the Austrian half of the old monarchy and the Slovaks of the Hungarian half formed the new nation.

Almost nobody in Bratislava spoke Slovakian except for the peasants who lived just north of the city. When some of the town's citizens found it expedient to have at least their children learn the new language, they hired Slovakian maids, the daughters of the farmers. Many of my friends learned the country's official language from their parents' household help. But a new problem arose when schools, especially a high school, had to be selected. Hungarian was politically unwise. Some chose Slovakian, but the children had to struggle too hard. The obvious compromise was German. At least it was a world language, which Hungarian or Slovakian was obviously not. But when it came to attending a university, the only one around was Slovakian! The result of such an education was rather crazy. My friends switched from one language to another and did not even notice it!

"How are you? It's cold today." Such words would be said in Hungarian because this was the first language my friends had learned from their mothers.

"I liked the play I saw yesterday though it had a very bad write-up." The speaker would now use German, since these are high school ideas.

"But the play is all wrong! Common Law does not apply in this case!" Slovakian would be spoken now. Common Law was discussed in law school.

It didn't take us very long to come to an excellent compromise about the language to speak at our meetings of the "Amicitia." Any language, as long as it was Slovakian, Czech (these two languages are so similar that the speakers easily understand each other), German, or Hungarian! As a matter of fact, I cannot remember a single incident when belonging to a different nationality or different religion disturbed our friendship. We merrily conversed in several languages. Luckily, for me, some of our members were from the Czech part of the country and did not understand Hungarian; for that reason, long speeches in that language were discouraged, short ones translated.

Never before or since have I had so many good friends. We met not only in the venerable building of the Freemasons Lodge, but more often it was in "our" coffeehouse!

"The usual?" The waiter would ask. He remembered everybody's order from one time to the next.

"Sure," the answer would be, "and of course, all the newspapers." A wave of the waiter's hand brought the paper boy, carrying not only local but also many European newspapers. Every coffeehouse would carry them. Many of us had at least a reading knowledge of English or French. The latter language was especially useful for me in reading the "Parisienne" (Paris Life), which was probably the most popular periodical. It contained so many saucy pictures.

The coffeehouse culture is actually the only thing I miss in America. Nothing we have here can take its place. Just to sit in a comfortable chair, sipping coffee (one cup would last all evening) while talking to friends or reading newspapers. *(Editor's note: this was written before the advent of Starbucks, where some of these same features can be found.)* One always knew whom to find in a certain coffeehouse and on what day! My father and his group of friends patronized a different coffee house, but would not be at all surprised when I showed up there.

Soon our "Amicitia" changed its complexion somewhat. It was all for the best, but the reason for the change was strange.

"I'd like to bring Ruth into the Amicitia, Carla, one of the founders of our group might say, many of us know her and…"

"No, I don't think Ruth would fit in with us at all," Steffi, another old member, objected.

"I've known her all my life, not that anything is wrong with her in general, but she is a little stupid, and too loud."

"All right, if you don't like her I won't invite her, of course," Carla conceded. There were many similar conversations. Many others knew the friends of the "old-timers." As in any small town, there may have been a few little feuds or controversies years earlier. But when one of the newer members, usually a Slovakian student or young professional from out of town, suggested a prospect, it was quite different.

"I have this old friend Janosh. He is from my home town," Milosh, a brilliant young Slovakian lawyer might say. "I think he'd make an excellent member of the Amicitia."

Well, nobody had ever heard of Janosh, therefore nobody could object. If Milosh said so, Janosh must be all right. And he was!

Besides the founders of our organization, mostly from old native German stock or else Hungarian or German Jews, and the Slovakians, there was a third group: children of Freemasons from out of town who heard of our organization from their fathers. They were automatically admitted. Since they usually would not know anyone and have a little harder time integrating, everybody saw to it that they, too, made friends.

During the question periods, which usually followed the presentations or lectures, I had noticed a tall girl who didn't seem to know anybody. She spoke up once in a while, in Slovakian, and always made sense. Just to be friendly, I talked to her, and found out that she was the daughter of a Freemason from Kosice, a town in eastern Slovakia. She was not a student at our university, but rather she was in Bratislava to perfect herself in her trade. She wanted to become a dressmaker. The most important reason for her coming to Bratislava, she admitted, was to get out of her little provincial town. I don't believe that she made a great impression on me; I didn't even know her name.

One evening, in "our" coffeehouse, I arrived late from work. I hadn't had time to eat and therefore ordered a light snack, the only one available: buttered bread, two soft boiled eggs, and a glass of water. As I ate the eggs and sipped water, I heard a voice behind me:

"Frank, you shouldn't drink water while eating eggs, it's unhealthy!"

I turned around and saw the girl who wanted to be a dressmaker.

"I never heard of such a thing. I do it all the time, and I'm still well," I said.

"Nevertheless, my father always says so," she replied.

"Your father is a doctor?"

"No, but he's usually right. Really, eat the eggs and the bread first, Frank. When you are finished, you may drink water."

I can't remember if I followed her advice or not, but I had a good look at this girl with the firm opinion who knew my name. I still didn't know hers. Her best features were her excellent complexion and her lovely smile. She wore glasses, and was a little overdressed. No great beauty, but nice.

"Frank, I know your name because our friends always address you, but you probably don't know mine: I am Teri Vidor."

This is how I met my future wife, the mother of my children, who died in 1975.

It was not "love at first sight." I only thought that Teri would be nice to have as a friend in order to practice my Slovakian. Our conversation had been in that language and I had not heard her using any other. But soon I got to like her more and more.

She was as tall as I was, and had an excellent figure. Actually, she was a little on the slim side, not the chubby "Viennese figure."

"Teri, when you'll be 40 years old and have filled out a little," I said to her (always the perfect diplomat) "you'll be very good-looking."

The language we spoke soon changed to German. Teri was quite fluent in that language, though with a Hungarian accent. Her command of languages was fantastic: her mother tongue was Hungarian; the language her family spoke at home. She was quite perfect in both Slovakian and Czech—a very difficult achievement. It might be comparable to an American who can speak with both a Texas and a Maine accent. Terry had learned Slovakian and Czech in high school. I never found out where she learned German, perhaps in a Jewish grammar school.

Besides, she had a fair command of French. After we had been in America for a few years, she spoke English with hardly any foreign accent.

Soon our friends of the Amicitia considered us a couple. The year was 1937 and business conditions had improved somewhat. Life had become a little easier. We were happy, and our friendship turned to love. But when the subject of sex came up, Teri was quite firm.

"It's not a question of me wanting it or not," she explained, "but I could never look my parents in the eyes if I broke my promise. When I left home, they made me promise I would never do anything they'd be ashamed of."

I knew her well enough already. There was no point arguing when Teri had made up her mind.

"That's it, my dear!" she would say.

Certainly, the year of 1937 and the first months of 1938 were some of the happiest times of my life. Not only was I in love and had good friends, but I felt a little more comfortable in my job. I slowly felt I knew what I was doing. In the meantime, my brother had finished his chemical studies and was now in charge of our factory in Vienna. My father's partner had left the business. From the beginning, my brother did a lot for our Viennese enterprise and soon it turned profitable.

At that time my father was involved in an incident I will never forget. He did a lot of traveling and was without doubt his own best salesman. We had a good customer somewhere in Bohemia, a building contractor who used a lot of our paint. Suddenly he stopped paying his bills. He owed a lot.

"I must find out what happened," my father said. "It isn't like John Gruber never even to answer our letters, but they did not come back." So, on his next trip to that part of the country, my father looked up this delinquent customer. This was before the time of credit cards; my father took cash along on his trips. But a few days after he left he called me long-distance, asking me to wire him more money.

"Will Mr. Gruber pay his bills?" I asked my father after he returned.

"Well, not yet," he answered. "Mr. Gruber is sick."

A few weeks later I saw a letter from Mrs. Gruber thanking my father for his generous gift, but that unfortunately her husband had just died.

My father explained: "Gruber was very sick when I got there, his business in shambles. Mrs. Gruber is destitute. I left her all the money I had in my pocket, she needed it."

In February 1938, we had a big celebration. My father was 60 years old. My mother invited all of our friends. Our family was happy.

A few days later, March 12th, Hitler's Nazis invaded Austria.

X

"DON'T LOOK BACK"

The year started so peacefully. My friends from the "Kette," the young Freemason organization of Vienna, visited our sister organization in Bratislava. The speaker for the occasion was my brother. I can't remember what he spoke about, only that he was a huge success. I basked in his glory. The Viennese invited us back for early April, but by that time the Masons of Austria had ceased to exist. I believe Hitler hated them almost as much as the Jews. Why did every dictator of the right or the left suppress the Freemasons? Probably because they stood for brotherhood.

It's more than half a century since I left Austria; certainly, time enough to forget the bad memories I have about the inhabitants of that country, the bitterness. And yet, I find it difficult not to become emotional even, to be fair, when thinking back to March 12, 1938. Actually, Austria had been a semi-fascist country long before that date. There were no political parties. Both the Socialists on the left and the Nazis on the right officially didn't exist. After bloody battles with the government, they were forbidden. No election had taken place for many years, but the government functioned, was fairly popular, and tolerant to those minorities who had no political opinions. Austria's friend was fascist Italy; Hitler's Germany was officially an enemy.

When Hitler threatened to annex Austria, the Chancellor, Kurt Schuschnigg, felt strong enough to ask for a plebiscite on March 12, 1938. He was sure that the Socialists, though officially forbidden as a party, would vote for the government. But Hitler took no chances. On the morning of March 12th, his forces marched into Austria and experienced no resistance because the military, as well as the police, was riddled with Nazis. On March 10th, the good Austrians had loudly professed their hatred for Hitler. On March 12th, they loved him so much.

The persecution of Jews started immediately, and with the cooperation of most of the Austrians.

Since practically everybody wore a swastika (just where did these emblems, strictly forbidden until yesterday, come from?), it was easy to recognize the Jews. Citizens of foreign countries wore little national flags in their lapels; only Jews wore nothing! Jews were caught in the streets or in their homes, often with the cooperation of the janitors, and on their hands and knees were forced to scrub the pavement, often with a toothbrush. Elderly Jews who had gray beards were especially preferred to perform for cheering crowds of Viennese.

Am I quite fair in my memories? Probably not. Let's assume that out of two million Viennese only five percent, or 100,000, we're directly involved in mistreatment of Jews. Well, 100,000 yelling people is a big crowd and can do lots of things! Did anybody resist? Of course not. Unlike in France or even Germany, nobody in Austria resisted the Nazis. That might have been unhealthy.

I learned two lessons in March of 1938. I'll never forget them:

1. Mistrust yelling crowds, regardless what they are screaming for or against. Most of the shouters are only there to have fun.

2. Educated liberals, even if they have strong opinions, are totally ineffective when it comes to any showdown. They quietly evaporate.

My brother, always a realist on the pessimistic side, decided immediately to leave Austria; my father was not sure.

"Oh, it will blow over; now that Hitler has all he wants, he'll be satisfied and leave us alone. Wait a while!"

But my mother advised differently. "Call your grandfather. His brother emigrated to Chicago in 1885; he died long ago, but his wife and children are there. Grandfather will write them and ask for help!"

(Half a year later, my brother was on his way to Chicago after making a last effort to convince himself whether staying in Austria might be possible for him. He asked for the opinion of the president of one of our German suppliers, who knew him well from trade conventions. An unsigned, hand-written letter on neutral stationary came back: "Dr. W. Leave, fast!")

The Viennese factory was "sold" to an "Aryan" employee for one mark. He soon ran the business into the ground. All we got after the war were a few hundred dollars for the real estate.

"Good riddance!" both my brother and I said.

Almost immediately, Jews who were Austrian citizens and had their residence in Austria, could no longer enter a neighboring country without a visa. But I had the good luck to have my official residence changed to Bratislava, Czechoslovakia a few years earlier. My passport stated this fact; therefore, I could travel freely, the only member of my family who could do so.

I'd like to refute a myth one often hears in America to this day. A rich American benefactor would claim, "I got XYZ out of Germany." Not so.

Until the end of 1941, it was not difficult for most Jews to leave Germany (not Poland) after leaving all of their possessions there, which most were glad to do. The problem was not how to get OUT of Germany, but rather how to get INTO another country, for instance the U.S.A. Not only were the American consuls not at all helpful, but even within the U.S. quota system, established in 1924, much was done to make it difficult for Jews to obtain a visa. What the above-mentioned benefactor may have done was to help with American, not German procedures.

I don't remember how my father got to Czechoslovakia (probably the Czechs let him into their country because he provided work for some of their citizens), and once there, he knew better than to return to Vienna.

My mother was left to dissolve our Viennese household and joined us in Bratislava half a year later. I guess my mother may have mourned for what she had to leave behind: the beautiful apartment with all the expensive furniture, the grand piano, paintings. But if she did, I never heard her say so. Actually, the Nazis permitted the Jews to have containers with household goods sent to an overseas country, but my mother only "emigrated" to neighboring Czechoslovakia.

"Never mind," my father said to us. "We still have our factory in Czechoslovakia. We'll become Czech citizens; we'll work hard."

As a matter of fact, my father even tried to convince my brother Charles, who was allowed to visit us once he had his American visa, to stay with us. There'd always been a "special relationship" between my father and Charles, his firstborn son who looked like him.

"There's room for all of us," he would say. But my brother's mind was made up.

"No, I'm not going to stay anywhere in Europe. Hitler will start a war sooner or later. All of you will have to leave. No country will be safe. As a matter of fact, as soon as I get to Chicago, I'll start working for your immigration." He looked at me. "And that includes your girlfriend Teri, whom I like very much!"

Charles arrived in the US in October 1938, on Columbus Day. (As a matter fact, Terry and I also arrived on Columbus Day, but in 1941, and my mother on Columbus Day, 1942!) He managed to get a job immediately at the American Decalcomania Company. He was hired to check the paint the company bought, a large budget item.

"I have a suspicion these s.o.b.'s are screwing us with the price," the boss told Charles. "I don't trust my purchasing agent very much. You say you are a paint chemist? Make sure that at least the quality is good!"

Two weeks later Charles reported back. "The quality is fairly good, at least adequate. I analyzed the paints carefully, and I have a suggestion: we can make these same paints right here in your plant for less than half the price! I have already investigated where to buy the raw materials and the equipment for manufacturing. Here is my written proposal."

A few months later, American Decalcomania started to manufacture paints. The savings, due to eliminating the considerable profits of our suppliers, were enormous and made it possible to underbid all competitors, as well as actually raising the quality of the merchandise. The difference in price between raw materials of lesser or higher-quality became meaningless in the finished product.

Not only did my brother's position in the company quickly become very secure (in the Depression year of 1938 an important consideration for a penniless immigrant whose command of English was none too good), but he also felt confident enough to do what he had planned all along.

"My parents, my brother are still in Germany," he told his boss, George Eisenberg, during one of their long walks on Saturday afternoons. "I can and will issue affidavits for their support. But, other than my salary..."

"How about your relatives who brought you over?" Mr. Eisenberg asked.

"I'm afraid there is a little problem. They seem to feel they've done enough signing affidavits for me, my uncle and aunt."

"Doc." This was how my brother was called by Mr. Eisenberg (I guess he was proud to have a Ph.D. on his payroll). "I'll be only too happy to give them the affidavits they need. And more: as soon as your brother is here I'll give him a job. You can write him that. Just be sure to tell your relatives not to bother anymore. I am taking charge of your family!"

Mr. Eisenberg was as good as his word. Just why was he so nice to my brother?

There are, of course, the obvious reasons: the time, which was early 1939. Although the war in Europe had not yet started, it was a well-known fact that the Jews had to get out of Germany. This was a few months after the infamous "Kristallnacht."

(Editor's Note: Kristallnacht, known as the "Night of Broken Glass," was a series of coordinated attacks against Jews throughout Germany and Austria on November 9 and 10, 1938. The name comes from the shards of broken glass that littered the streets after Jewish-owned stores, buildings and synagogues had their windows smashed by the Nazis and others.)

Furthermore, no doubt Mr. Eisenberg wanted to insure the loyalty of my brother. But there was more to it, I believe, and in the interest of truth, I must state it.

Our family members were Austrian, German-speaking Jews. Our relatives in Chicago may have been born in the U.S.A., but as far as Mr. Eisenberg was concerned they were still "German" Jews. But though also born in Chicago, he was like the great majority of

American Jews, a "Russian" Jew. Now, close to the end of the 20th century, the old animosity has ceased to exist. But in 1939 it was still alive. The Russian Jews (most of them came to the U.S. in the two decades before the First World War) had not forgotten that the "German" Jews, who had arrived in the U.S. earlier, hadn't exactly greeted them with open arms. As a matter fact, they wanted to have nothing to do with the "uncivilized" Russian Jews. They only extended "charity" to them, as Jewish law commanded. Mr. Eisenberg had asked my brother to tell his relatives that he, the Russian Jew, was taking over. "Charity" went the other way now.

Back in the summer of 1938 there was talk of war. Hitler, not satisfied with having annexed Austria, now wanted to have the German-speaking part of Czechoslovakia as well. However, that country was not only a strong democracy, but also had a good army.

Furthermore, it had a mutual assistance treaty with France. We know what happened eventually: the sellout in Munich by the British and French governments. "PEACE IN OUR TIME." *(Editor's note: The Munich Agreement was a settlement permitting Nazi Germany's annexation of portions of Czechoslovakia along the country's borders mainly inhabited by German speakers, for which a new territorial designation "Sudetenland" was coined.)*

But a few months earlier we were living in a fool's paradise, trusting the noble Western powers. Actually, during the summer of that fateful year of 1938, I had a great time. Why not? I was in love!

Earlier that year I had met Teri's family, who I visited while I was in Kosice, a town in Eastern Slovakia, where she was brought up. I was on a business trip, trying to sell paints to some of our industrial customers.

"Have you also tried to sell to the two leading paint stores in our town?" Terry's father, a very tall, good-looking man, asked me.

"I'm afraid our company was never successful."

"Well, try again. Both owners of the stores are my brothers. They are Freemasons, and so is your father. I'll talk to them."

The next morning, I got a lesson in "networking." Rudolph Vidor, my future father-in-law, had indeed talked to his brothers, the Masons. In both stores, large orders were waiting for me; the owners showed me invoices of their present suppliers. I had no difficulty in underbidding ever so slightly the prices they paid.

While Rudolf Vidor was a very successful representative of leading textile mills, his wife was a quiet woman who managed to make me give her all the worthwhile information about my family and me without ever seeming to be nosy. My future father-in-law had all the good ideas. Matilda, my future mother-in-law, all the common sense. It took me not long to realize that Teri was the apple of their eyes. Her younger sister, Magda, a beautiful girl (she, Rudolf and Matilda all perished in Auschwitz a few years later) also tried to be very friendly, but we had language problems. She knew no German and her Slovakian was poor. I, of course, did not know Hungarian. On the other hand, both my future father and mother-in-law were perfect in all three languages.

Teri first met my mother in Vienna, in June of 1938. My mother was about to join us in Bratislava. She knew she had to leave our apartment but would have liked to get some of her jewelry out. This would have been, of course, against German law, and my mother was not about to risk her life smuggling. But Teri, who could freely travel with her Czech passport, volunteered to visit Vienna, put on my mother's jewelry and brought it to Bratislava. (The two ladies liked each other instantly. This would become important later because my father, once he realized that we all had to emigrate, tried to insist that I travel to the U.S. "unattached" as my brother had done. There were bad arguments but my mother always managed to be the peacemaker. Finally, my father also got to love Teri. Much later, in Chicago, the two ladies were to spend many years together.

It was also in the summer of 1938 that Teri and I, as well as my best friend and his girlfriend (my friend was killed by the Nazis; I don't know what became of his girlfriend, a sweet girl, but statistically speaking the chance of her surviving the war was close to nil) spent two weeks in the high mountains of eastern Slovakia, a region not unlike the high Sierras in the U.S. There were strictly separate rooms for the girls and boys, not at all unlike the winter vacation I had spent with Anny, my first real girlfriend. But to this day, I remember this trip as one of the most beautiful in my life. The lakes were so blue, the forests so green, the snow-covered mountain peaks so white, the rushing streams so pure. No, we certainly had no idea that our peace was just about over.

As late as September 1938, our newspapers and our radio assured us that Hitler would never dare to invade Czechoslovakia.

"We'll stand firm against aggression! We ae not Austrians! The whole international community is with us: France, Great Britain and the Soviet Union. All will help us to defend our country!"

Well, that was not to be. Treaties are made to be broken.

"Czechoslovakia is a far-away country about which we know little, said Neville Chamberlain, the Prime

Minister of Great Britain. Edouard Daladier, France's Premier, concurred. "One can live with Hitler."

Well, in October, 1938 we learned about "PEACE IN OUR TIME." *(Editor's note: this was the phrase spoken on September 30, 1938 by Chamberlain in a speech praising the Munich agreement.)* Hitler was to get the German-speaking part of Czechoslovakia; the southern counties of Slovakia would be given to Hungary; even Poland (this is little known even now) was rewarded for keeping quiet about the rape of her brother Slavs (Czechs and Slovaks) by being given a few towns in northeastern Czechoslovakia. Our factory in Bratislava seemed to be safe. It was in Petrzalka, an industrial suburb of the city, definitely a Slovakian town.

One day in late September we woke up to the blaring of public loud speakers mounted on trucks, which slowly cruised through the streets.

"The village of Engerau (nobody had used the German name of Petrzalka for years) will be incorporated in the German Reich within 48 hours."

We could not believe it. We were a part of Bratislava and most of the industry was located here!

Soon we found out the truth. We were south of the Danube; the Germans had decided that the river was to be the border! Some of our workers, those of old German stock, were elated.

"Long live the DEUTSCHE PARTIE," screamed an old, well-trusted man who had been with my father for thirty years. He knew that we were Jewish, but he didn't realize he would lose his job and that our plant would close.

My parents took the news calmly. "I'm only glad Charles is in America. You'll see, he'll get us out!" my father said to my mother and me. "We'll survive!" (He was almost right. He would die in Cuba in March, 1942. My mother would join us later.)

We sent my mother to a friend of my father's, a brother Mason in Bratislava. My father and I tried to save whatever we could.

"DON'T LOOK BACK!" my father said to me as we slowly walked to the trolley, which was to take us across the bridge to temporary safety. I never did.

Frank's Mother Marianne

Frank (left) 2 Years Old, and Charles, 5 Years Old, 1916

Frank as a Young Boy

Frank (right) and Charles with Mother Marianne

Frank (right) and Charles with Father Heinrich

Frank's Parents Marianne and Heinrich Weinmann

Teri's Parents Rudolf and Mathilde Vidor

Teri Vidor (Weinman) as a Child

Teri's Sister Magda Vidor Bettelheim

Teri's sister Magda Vidor and her
husband Dr. Martin Bettelheim

153

Teri & Frank in Bratislava, 1938

Teri in Kassa (Kosice), Hungary

Wedding Day October 25, 1939, Prague

Frank and Teri in Chicago, 1942

Frank with Francie (right) and Linda (left), 1950

Frank's Cousin Dolfe Bruner & Wife Tamara in Israel

Teri & Frank at Home in Skokie, Illinois, early 1960s

(left to right) Frank, Linda, Francie & Teri in Skokie, 1971

Teri & Frank at Frank's 60th Birthday Party, 1974

Teri Weinman, Teaneck, N.J, 1974

Frank with Grandchildren Dana (right) and
David Schwartz, Teaneck, N.J., 1974

Wedding of Frank and Frances (Alt)
Weinman, Skokie, January 23, 1977

Frank & Frances Weinman

Frank and Frances with Granddaughter
Jennine Lichterman, 1988

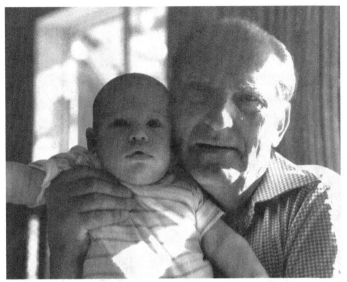

Frank with Grandson Ricky Gelber, 1985

Frank with (left to right) Frances, Daughter-
in-Law Maureen Alt, Granddaughter Jennine
Lichterman, Son-in-Law Maynard Lichterman

Family Photo. Back Row (left to right) Frances Weinman,
Nephew John Weinman, Rodica Weinman, Son-in-Law Stuart
Schwartz, Daughter Judy Lichterman with Granddaughter
Jennine, Daughter Dr. Linda Wolf with Grandson Jonathan
Gelber, Son-in-Law Dr. Alex Gelber, Frank, Granddaughter
Dana Schwartz, Sister-in-Law Marilee Weinman, Brother
Charles Weinman. Front Row (left to right): Grandson
David Schwartz, Daughter Francie Schwartz, Grand Niece
Samantha Weinman, Grandson Ricky Gelber. 1988.

Family Photo. Back Row (left to right): Daughter-in-law
Maureen Alt, Son George Alt, Granddaughter Yvette Alt,
Son-in-Law Dr. Alex Gelber, Frank, Son-in-Law Stuart
Schwartz, Granddaughter Dana Schwartz, Grandson David
Schwartz, Grandson Jonathan Alt, Son-in-Law Maynard
Lichterman. Front Row (left to right): Daughter Dr. Linda
Wolf, Grandson Ricky Gelber, Grandson Jonathan Gelber
Frances Weinman, daughter Francie Schwartz, Granddaughter
Jennine Lichterman, Daughter Judy Lichterman, 1994.

Frank's 90th Birthday Cruise. Back Row (left to right) Grandson Jonathan Alt, Son-in-Law Dr. Alex Gelber, Son George Alt, Grandson David Schwartz, Son-in-Law Stuart Schwartz, Alex's Mother Anda Gelber, Frank, Dr. Jeremy Miller (Yvette's Husband), Grandson Jonathan Alt, Jeremy Bash (Dana's Husband), Son-in-Law Maynard Lichterman, Maynard's Brother Mark Lichterman, Grandson Ricky Gelber. Front Row (left to right): Daughter Judy Lichterman, Granddaughter Jennine Lichterman, Daughter Francie Schwartz, Jami Lieberman with Great Grandson Jacob Miller, Deborah Alt (Jonathan's Wife) with Great Granddaughter Jordyn Alt, Granddaughter Yvette Alt with Great Granddaughter Simone Miller, Granddaughter Dana Bash, Daughter-In-Law Maureen Alt, Daughter Dr. Linda Wolf. (2004)

Sentimental Journey to Europe, Vienna, 1996

Frank & Francie in Courtyard of Frank's
Childhood Home in Vienna, 1996

Frank and Cousin Otto Weinmann, Vienna 1996

Brothers Charles & Frank Weinman

(Left to Right) Grandson Dr. Jonathan Gelber, Son-in-Law Dr. Alex Gelber, Grandson Ricky Gelber, Daughter Dr. Linda Wolf

Frank's 95th Birthday with (left to right) Daughters Francie Schwartz, Judy Lichterman, Dr. Linda Wolf

Frank's 95th Birthday with (back, left to right) Grandchildren
Jonathan Gelber, David Schwartz, Ricky Gelber, (Front
left to right) Jennine Lichterman, Dana Bash

Frank Weinman 1998

Frank Weinman

XI

MOTHER, FATHER AND FIANCÉE

During the years preceding 1938, my mother must have hated Saturday afternoons, when her husband and her two sons paid no attention to her! At two o'clock I would come "home" to Vienna after spending a week in Bratislava. There was a quick lunch, then the three men in her life retired to comfortable chairs and discussed business: how was the week in the Austrian and the Czechoslovakian factories? Which important orders came in? What technical problems arose? But my mother, the lady of the house who had waited all week for me, her younger son, was entirely left out. She did not participate in our meetings, which we three men obviously enjoyed! And she knew that as soon as we were through talking, I would call some girlfriend and be off.

Unfortunately for all four of us, she would often get an asthma attack around three o'clock in the afternoon: a violent attack that would make her suffer terribly. All we could do was watch her suffer, pity her, and wait until she felt better. Then the three men would continue their discussions. After all, we knew that her asthma had plagued her for many, many years, but to make matters worse for her, she must have sensed our annoyance. Did she really have to get her attack every Saturday?

In early 1938 my mother was 48 years old and had been married for 27 years. She had dutifully given birth to her older son eleven months after her wedding, and three years later to me, the younger one. Although the marriage had been, more or less, arranged by mutual friends, there was always love; real love between my parents. There was nothing they wouldn't have done for each other! My mother had had a fairly decent education for her time, but there was not much for her to do, and my father, older by eleven years, may not always have been very easy to get along with.

Her mother, my maternal grandmother, was a domineering woman, married to a nice but weak little man, my grandfather. She had three daughters and one son, my uncle. Even I, as a mere boy, could see that my grandmother did not think much of her daughters; only her son seemed to be important. The three girls were brought up to wait on their brother. Luckily, he was a decent fellow who, though sickly in his youth, lived to be 100 years old.

My father, with all his love for his wife and sons, was also a very strong person. From the point of view of my mother and me, my mother did not, and could not do very much, especially after she broke her hip at age 35. She walked with a strong limp for the rest of her life. She was to be loved, to be pampered, and to love us.

Then came March 1938, when life as we knew it came to an end. My father and I left as soon as we could for Czechoslovakia. Men were in great danger, and my brother could do no better than to work on his emigration to America. That left my mother (without a maid by that time) to dissolve the household, and to fend for herself as well as she could. Sometime during the summer of 1938 Teri, my girlfriend and later my wife, visited her. Teri, as a citizen of Czechoslovakia, could travel freely, although one could never know if the Nazis would really respect the foreign citizenship of a Jewess. In any event, the two women liked each other instantly. (Whoever invented the myth that there must be discord between mother and daughter-in-law?)

They decided that Teri would put on all my mother's jewelry and get it out to safety, to Czechoslovakia, where our family hoped to spend the rest of our lives. My mother even spoke the Czech language since her childhood. Only my brother would go to America.

Well, soon after, my mother came to live with my father and me. We had a nice little apartment in our factory waiting for her. But soon we lost the factory! We moved in with a bachelor friend of my father's.

Now we were refugees.

I frequently saw Teri, who lived in Bratislava.

"Frank, you love your Teri and she loves you," my mother said to me one day. "Why don't you give her a ring?"

"But mother, how could I afford that now?"

"No problem. I'll give you a diamond from one of my rings; you can get a simple gold band for very little money."

One evening I slipped this ring on Teri's finger, shortly before she moved to join her father's family.

She wore the ring until the day she died.

Late in 1938 my father, my mother and I moved to Prague, the capital of the country, to wait for our emigration. We had a tiny apartment: one small bedroom, a bathroom and a kitchen where I slept on a cot. My father's nerves, and probably mine as well, were badly frayed. There were really bad words between us. More often than not, the reason for our quarrels was that I would not promise to emigrate without Teri (who had not come to Prague with us). I insisted I would never leave without her.

"Look," my mother would say to my father. "These two young people found each other, they are in love."

"How selfish can they be?" my father screamed. "Why should all the burden to care for us be on our older son? How can Frank be so selfish?"

Mother would be between us two hotheaded men in this tiny place, trying to spend as little money as possible since our resources were obviously limited. She tried and succeeded very well to cook for us, to wash and clean and sew for us. There was no more maid, and I'm afraid neither my father nor I were much help when it came to housework.

On the other hand, my mother was free of asthma attacks while living in Prague, maybe because she felt so needed. When it came to preparing all of us for emigration, her advice and decisions prevailed.

To this day, I often wonder just how much my mother influenced me. True, during the first years of my life, I may have been closer to our nanny then to her. Later, when school or even the Boy Scouts were the most important things in my life, I probably did not see as much of my mother as I could have.

But from the first memories of my life until the time she died, when I was almost 40 years old, I always knew how much she loved me! As a matter of fact, I felt sure that I, not my brother, was her favorite child. When my father went on business trips (sometimes he was gone for the better part of the week) there was no doubt my brother was "the man of the house." But I was the one who was allowed to sleep in my father's bed next to her (king or queen size beds were unknown, there were only twin beds). I was given that privilege.

In 1925, after my mother had the complicated fracture of her thigh and had to stay in bed for several months, I wondered what I could do to cheer her up. I was 10 years old and could not bear to see my mother suffer so much!

"I know that you always wanted a daughter," I said to her. "Well, you'll have your wish this evening; just look."

With the help of our maid, I had dressed up as a Czech country girl (two pillows in front under my shirt). I sang a song in a fake Czech accent and I danced for her. My mother laughed until tears came; she forgot her pain for a moment. I was so happy.

My father had witnessed my performance. "I cannot thank you enough!" he said to me later. "I'll never forget what you did for her."

In the summer of 1938, not long after we lost our Viennese factory and Hitler was screaming about Czechoslovakia, my father made a decision.

"You know that I'm an optimist," he said to me. "I predict that Hitler will never get anywhere with his ambition to destroy Czechoslovakia. But just to be sure, we should have some ready cash."

"How can we do that?"

"We'll stop paying our bills. I've been in business since 1910 and never thought of such a thing. But on the other hand, all incoming money will be taken in cash."

"Won't our creditors sue us?"

"Not for a while, I'm sure," he said. "We can always explain later." And that's how it happened that there was enough cash for my parents to live.

When we moved to Prague, later in 1938, we thought we'd be on our way to America within a few months. But emigration wasn't to come for three years.

"I feel like a defrauder," my father said to me on the train from Bratislava to Prague. "Money in my pocket, leaving debts behind."

I tried to rationalize. "You have been a good customer to our suppliers for decades. They will understand."

Then, bad news from my brother in Chicago.

"Unfortunately, I have not been able, so far, to get affidavits of support from our relatives in Chicago," he wrote. "They are very, very nice to me, but they say that they've done enough for the family already as far as taking on obligations. But I am still trying. Also, I'm looking for other sponsors."

This was the worst possible news because we couldn't register for emigration until we had affidavits.

My father's most important time of the day was when the mail came.

"Anything from Charles?" he would ask if, by chance, my mother or I were at the mailbox before he could get to it.

"Let me open it!" "Let me open it!" he demanded. He absolutely had the privilege of seeing his older son's letters from Chicago first. Luckily my brother wrote at least twice a week: about the enormity of the city, the elevated train, the museums, but most of all about work and how well he got along with his boss.

"You'll see. I'm going to get a job too. I'm only 61 years old!" my father said to me. "And the three of us will work together, just like before."

"Yes, I agreed. "Of course, Teri will be with us too and also working, and mother will keep house for all of us."

"Oh, no. You cannot, absolutely cannot be burdened with a wife. Just like Charles, you have to come to America unattached," my father said.

Now an argument started, getting hotter as it went on, until my mother managed to get between us. Then, sometime in February 1939, the mailman brought a big package from Chicago. My brother, together with his boss, sent us not one but TWO affidavits: one for Mr. and Mrs. Henry Weinmann, my parents. The other one for Mr. and Mrs. Frank Weinmann. That was for Teri and me.

Sometime in late 1937, Teri had needed a job. She didn't want to become a dressmaker, but that was the profession her parents had selected for her.

"A good dressmaker always finds work," her father would say.

"Furthermore," he said, "THE NEEDLE IS INTERNATIONAL." (Actually, he was right. When we came to Chicago, Teri found a job immediately, and she also managed to make good money on weekends, doing alterations.) Back in 1937, Teri hated this kind of work. However, she needed an excuse to stay with me in Bratislava so she wouldn't have to return to her parent's town.

Fortunately for us, a friend of mine named Heidi had just started a small business of knitting and hand weaving. She needed a helper and I suggested Teri. Luckily, Heidi had just found a new boyfriend--she married him later-- thus, no competition between the girls. The two women worked quite well together.

Once, when Teri went home to her parents for a few days, she took one of the frames used for hand weaving with her.

"You've got a good thing going," her father, an expert in weaving, said to her.

"I'll make a drawing of the frame; it's easy to duplicate and could not possibly be patented because it's too elementary. Of course, you won't compete with your friend now, but one never knows what might happen!"

A year went by. When I moved to Prague, Teri did not care to stay in Bratislava.

But before following me to Prague, she wanted to make some money of her own. (Her hometown, Kosice, having been in southern Slovakia, was now a part of Hitler's friend Hungary.) Teri certainly did not want to ask her father to support her. Always resourceful, she found a temporary job in a small town. She would teach all the Jewish ladies there how to hand weave. Of course, she would also sell them the necessary yarn, at a good price. It all worked out splendidly. Teri's father supplied the frames, and I was charged with the task of purchasing yarn in Prague and mailing it to her. (Of course, Teri's father told me where to go, what to look for).

On the last day of 1938 Teri visited me in Prague. We wanted to spend New Year's Eve together. The next day she would return to the small town where she was working. She only brought a small handbag. But we had no place to go! No decent hotel wanted to rent us a room.

"Show me your wedding certificate!" he hotel receptionists said. Finally, we sat down in a coffeehouse and felt sorry for ourselves.

We had not seen each other for weeks, but there seemed to be nothing we could say to each other. Everything seemed to be so hopeless.

Suddenly we heard a voice behind us. "I've been looking at you young people. What's the matter with you? Why do you look so sad?"

Turning around, we saw an old man with an encouraging smile. "Sit down with us, we'll tell you," Teri said to him.

So, we poured our hearts out to this stranger. We loved each other but had no place to go, not tonight nor ever.

Though speaking perfect Czech, Teri was a Hungarian now, and I was a German refugee. There was no future.

"Don't say such stupid things!" The old man interrupted. "Shame on you! I'll make a prediction: since you are probably Jews, you'll want to get out of this stinking Europe; to Palestine or to America, perhaps; just don't give up! Not ever! But look at me. I'm an old Czech, a university professor. I helped build my beautiful country, now I see it falling apart. This madman Hitler will get it. Then there will be war, and nothing good for us will come afterwards. Someday, my country will be resurrected, but I won't live to see that. But you, your life is still ahead of you!"

The old man kissed Teri on the forehead, patted me on the back and sat down at his lonely table.

Teri would often speak of this old Czech when our future looked hopeless. And every one of his predictions was to come true.

Teri checked in at a hotel, alone, and traveled back to her job the next morning. We did not see each other again for more than two months. Finally, in early March, Teri wrote the letter I had been waiting for:

"I'm through with my work here, I will come early in the morning on the 15th of this month. I even have a place to stay. A lady whom I've known from home, who is in Prague now, will be renting me a room. And do you know our friend Heidi is also in Prague and will be married the same evening?"

Later, Teri and I often talked about the 15th, the "Ides" of March, 1939.

"I was so looking forward to this day," Teri would say. "We'd see each other again, attend our friend's wedding. I'd meet your parents again and make sure that they both like me; we'd start planning our emigration."

Early in the morning, long before Teri's train was to arrive, I was sitting in a park, watching the buds of trees and bushes. None had opened yet, but I could feel spring was coming. This time I had done my homework and found a hotel where we could stay together for the first time.

What really happened on March 15, 1939 made it one of the worst days of our lives, for the country we were in, as well as for all of Europe.

When I came to the station, I was advised that the train would be late, it might possibly not arrive at all, but nobody would tell me why. I went to Saint Vaclav Square, the center of Prague, not far from the railroad station. There I heard one policeman say to another:

"HITLER IS COMING. THE GERMANS ARE TAKING OUR COUNTRY."

The "rumor" spread quickly. Soon huge crowds formed, but the police kept the streets open. Shortly before noon, Hitler's gang goose-stepped down Saint Vaclav

Square, tanks rolled in, German flags with Swastikas were flying. The Czechs stood on the sidewalks, bowed their heads, and cried. Hitler had broken his solemn promise to the British, the French and the Italians half a year earlier: that he would respect what was left of Czechoslovakia after "Munich" and never, never take a single Czech.

I went back to the railroad station and was told that Teri's train had just arrived. There had only been a delay until the "political situation" between the new state of Slovakia and Germany was clarified. Teri had no idea what happened. When I told her, she cried. Like all the Jews of Czechoslovakia, she had loved the country.

Heidi's wedding did take place, as scheduled, but there was no joy at all. The couple decided immediately to emigrate to Romania, the groom's birthplace. (I hope they survived and are now somewhere in Israel. Statistically chances are fairly good; a little more than half of the Romanian Jews survived the Holocaust and eventually moved to Israel. Both Heidi and her husband were healthy, smart and resourceful.)

"Tonight, we'll sleep together." Teri said to me after we checked in at the rather shabby hotel. ("Miramare" was the hotel's fancy name. "Look at the Sea." A prophetic name. Prague is many hundreds of miles away from the nearest ocean.)

The "time" was right, Teri said. We had read about the "rhythm" theory; all we knew about prevention of pregnancy came from books. We promised each other, again, that we'd always stay together from now on, come what might. Soon we'd be in America.

The next morning, I brought Teri to the room she had rented. We hoped she'd stay there until our emigration, and I went to my parent's apartment in order to prepare them for Teri's arrival. They knew she was already in Prague and could, of course, guess where we had spent the night. I was apprehensive. How would my father react? My brother's two affidavits and come a few days earlier, one for my parents, the other one for Teri and me. Well, I could have saved my worries! As soon as Teri walked into the door, with her quiet smile that conquered everybody, my father loved her. Furthermore, Charles had sent the affidavit for "Mr. and Mrs." Frank Weinmann, and my father always respected his older son's judgment.

"Let's celebrate together!" He said to us after a while. "No use mourning for Czechoslovakia. We must think of ourselves: To America!"

He brought out a bottle of wine with four glasses. "Let's drink to our future. The four of us should soon be with Charles who, I hope, will soon have a wife as lovely as Teri!"

Within a week or two, Teri started a class of hand weaving on her "special frames." We had lots of family in Prague (after all, my mother was born in Bohemia) and soon a relative of mine, Trude Bruck, a young beautiful woman, got some students for Teri. Money was not to be Teri's problem.

A few days later the American consulate advised us that we wouldn't get our visas for two or three years; our registration numbers were too high (a lie as we found out long after the war). The consulates were advised by the American state department to stall on immigration of Jews. The "quota" was never filled. The consulate said we should try to emigrate somewhere else.

"I don't feel very well," Teri said to me a couple of weeks later, "not actually sick, but nauseated."

"Oh God," I screamed. "Did you have your period?"

No, she had not. It seems that March 15th had not been the "safe day" we had figured on. Teri confided in her landlady who advised her to jump from a chair many times. That would help. But when it did not, the good lady asked her to look for another room.

Teri and I had been unhappy before and, during the coming years, would be unhappy many times again. But nothing hit us like Teri's pregnancy! How could we emigrate anywhere with a baby?

We turned to Trude Bruck, my beautiful cousin, for help. After all, she might know of a doctor who…

Well, she did. (Of all my Czech relatives, she was the only one who survived the Holocaust in a concentration camp, probably in a brothel for German officers. She hinted as much in a letter we got from her after the war.)

Trude recommended someone we could trust. Abortions were illegal; it had to be in the doctor's office.

Teri had found a new place to live; when I took her home after the operation, the only time we ever took a taxi, the driver looked at her:

"Don't worry, Mrs. I'll drive extra carefully," he said.

I told my parents, who by that time were used to Teri's daily visits, that she had a bad cold and could not leave her place for a few days. The next day, while I was at Teri's apartment, the bell rang. It was my mother.

"I just wanted to know how you are," she said to Teri, and had a long, good look at her. Then she touched her forehead. "Thank God, you don't have any fever. Be sure, Teri, to call a doctor immediately if your temperature should go up. And don't get up too soon."

I'm sure she did not believe in Teri's "cold" for one moment, but guessed what had really happened.

My mother never mentioned the "cold" again but made it a point to drop in on Teri for the next few days.

I kept myself busy in Prague studying various things I thought might be helpful for the emigration.

All a waste of time, as it turned out. I even made money by contacting some of our previous customers and offered to get them the paint they used to buy from us, advising them that I had taken all the formulas with me. Then I had a former competitor manufacture the merchandise from our formula and pay me a commission. But I felt threatened in Prague; I was a young, able-bodied young Jew doing nothing useful. I had to find something the Nazis might respect and, at the same time, prepare for Teri and myself an alternate destination if we could not get to America.

I felt I could do no better than to join and do volunteer work for Hechalutz (Hebrew for "the Pioneer"), an organization which prepared young Jews for illegal (from the point of view of Great Britain) emigration to Palestine. It was at that office that I met my best friend again.

XII

MY FRIEND ANTI-HACHSHARAH

I had met Anti (short for Antonin. Last name: Feuer) at the German Rowing Club "Danube" in Bratislava. Speaking with a strong Hungarian accent he seemed misplaced.

"Don't you feel a little strange here?" I asked him. "You hardly speak German at all."

"That's true," he answered in Czech. He knew already that I didn't speak Hungarian.

"But where else should I go if I want to row? The Hungarians don't want any Jews, I understand. The Slovakians wouldn't want me either."

He explained to me that he came from Podcarpatsko, then the eastern-most province of Czechoslovakia, now part of Ukraine.

"My grandparents spoke Yiddish, my parents Hungarian. I was educated in Czech schools because my father, a prominent lawyer in the town of Munkach, wanted me to speak the language of Prague, the country's capital."

"How come you are here now, in Slovakia?" I asked.

"After I finished law school, a job was offered to me in Bratislava. Don't you know that we Jews are the only perfect Czechoslovakians? The Czechs and the Slovaks really don't like each other, but we love the whole country, as it is, because it's a democracy."

Anti loved whatever he was involved in at the moment, and he did it well: sports, his job, music. But most of all he loved girls, and they loved him. I could never figure out why he was so successful with them. He was short, not a great talker. I never heard him pay a compliment to a girl. And while he may have been good-looking, there was nothing striking about him: black, straight hair, a high forehead; only his big, searching eyes were special; they seemed to look at you and know all about you.

When Hitler invaded Poland on September 1, 1939 and what was to become World War II began, I was working at the Zionist organization of Prague, Hechalutz.

My job consisted of interviewing and registering young Jews. I did not get paid; the organization was funded by contributions from abroad. Every penny had to be used for helping our members emigrate to Palestine. I felt what I was doing was useful. After all, war or no war, Hitler wanted to get us Jews out of Europe. Neither the Conference of Evian, France (in the summer of 1938), which was supposed to open opportunities for emigration for German Jews, nor the "Kristallnacht" a few months later, induced any country to open its doors to Jews. The only possibility for mass emigration, at least for young and able-bodied Jews, was Palestine. True, the British, who were in control of the country, had recently in their "White Paper" forbidden practically all immigration of Jews to Palestine.

But the Hechalutz still organized transports by small ships. Once these ships landed in Palestine, after evading the British shore patrols, the Palestinian Jews helped to hide the immigrants. If the ships were caught by the British Navy, the Jews were sent to internment camps; first to Mauritius, a tiny island near Africa, then to Cyprus. They were only fully liberated in 1948, after Israel, as an independent state, welcomed them home.

One day, a short time before Hitler started the war, Anti showed up at the office of Hechalutz carrying a big suitcase. I had last seen him in Bratislava almost a year earlier.

"I could not see any future for myself in Slovakia," he explained, "and I wanted to make my way to the west. I almost made it. I was already out of Germany. But the French caught me and sent me back. My Czech passport didn't impress them; they didn't want any more Jews."

"How about your girlfriend Adry?" I asked.

"Oh, I left her with her parents. She's better off without me and I without her in these times. I don't want to stay in Europe, only get to Palestine. Life there would be too rough for her."

"So now you want to join Hechalutz?" I asked.

"Sure. When does the next transport for Palestine leave?"

"Well, Anti, first you'll have to go on Hachsharah."

"Hachsharah? What's that?"

"You know what 'Kosher' means?"

"Sure. Kosher food. That's religious Jewish food."

"Yes. But Kosher really means 'fit.' Kosher food is food 'fit' to eat. 'Hachsharah' comes from the same root. It means 'to make fit.' Well, before being admitted to a transport, we have to make ourselves fit."

"Do we have to take some kind of a bath?" he asked.

"No. You see, Anti, all this was explained to me when I first joined Hechalutz a month ago; that's why I'm so smart. Anyway, going on Hachsharah means spending a few months on a farm, doing hard work there. Afterwards, we'll just have to wait for a transport until our turn comes."

"But I'm a lawyer. I never did any physical work."

"Neither did I. But in Palestine, we'll have to join agricultural settlements, be farmers!"

"How come you are not on Hachsharah?"

"I'm waiting. There not enough farmers who want to accept us for training. Also, I can live with my parents, at least for the moment. But you have no place to stay. You'll be given preference. Within a few days you'll get an assignment. In the meantime, you'll stay at 'Bet Chalutzim,' the House of the Pioneers. You see, Anti, we are highly organized. Of course, tonight you'll have dinner with my parents. Believe it or not, you'll see Teri again."

For the next week, Anti spent most of every evening with us: my parents liked him immediately.

As a matter of fact, after I left Prague in the spring of 1940, they looked on Anti as a substitute son. (Later, in Chicago, my mother would often tell me how she watched Anti, whom she would see every few weeks when he was between assignments, change from a soft, fat Jewish boy into a lean, athletic man.)

But Teri, when she saw Anti again, could at first not forgive him for abandoning his girlfriend Adry in Bratislava.

"How could you leave this girl who loved you so much? Do you think only of yourself?"

"Teri, I promise you, the next time, when I meet a girl who is really for me, and I for her, we'll stay together as long as we live. And what's more, if Frank and I should ever be together without you, I will make sure he does not fall for any other girl because you two are made for each other!" Somehow Anti always found the right words.

After the war broke out, it became much easier for the Zionist organization to find farmers who would be willing to "train" young Jews. As I was soon to find out, they used us more or less as slave labor. There was an acute manpower shortage, especially because the Slovakian migrant workers would no longer come to the Czech lands. While the Nazis never trusted the Czechs, they make sure that the Slovaks, who now had their own state, we're drafted into a Slovakian army that would later be used as cannon fodder when Germany attacked the Soviet Union. Anti was quickly sent to a farm, and I didn't see him for a month or two because I, too, was given an assignment soon afterwards at a different place.

Teri never became a member of Hechalutz, not that she wouldn't want to go with me to Palestine, but she was simply not strong enough for a Hachsharah. And as a Hungarian citizen, she was in no danger. She could always join her family.

I was sent to a sugar beet farm in Hribsko, a tiny village about 30 miles from Prague. It was reached by first taking a train to the nearest railroad station, then walking for an hour on a dusty or, after the rains came, muddy country road. There were 30 or 40 of us working in the camp, almost as many girls as boys. Being 25 years old, I was one of the oldest. Most of the others were still in their teens. As I soon found out, the majority came from a Zionist youth group called "Blue-White" (the Jewish national colors to this day). They had known each other for many years, and hoped very soon to be sent on a transport to Palestine. The leader of our camp was barely 18 years old; a nice enough fellow but immature. He was a pampered Jewish middle-class boy for whom the Zionist movement had been a kind of glorified Boy Scout experience. I doubt that he, before Hitler, had any intention of leaving Prague, his hometown. But in the fall of 1939, the older leaders of the Zionist Youth movement had already emigrated. Whoever was left was simply promoted. Luckily, the organization had been set up well; even less able leaders could carry on for a while.

And as I said, the farm was assigned to grow sugar beets. It was our task to get them out of the ground, and with a sharp knife, cut off the green top. Essentially we worked behind a tractor pulling a plow loosening the dirt around the beets. We had to pull the beets out and throw them on the ground. Unfortunately for us, that could only be done by bending down. Thus, for many hours we were not permitted to straighten up! The tractor was driven fairly fast; we had a hard time keeping up.

"You Jews call yourselves intelligent people!" the farmer, riding the tractor, would scream. "The uneducated Slovaks work faster than you!"

I soon noticed a strange phenomenon: those of us who, like me, were older and much less physically fit than the teenagers, complained less and took hardships better. It was not a question of muscles but of willpower!

The same story with the girls. They were in charge of picking up the beets, putting them into baskets and carrying a back to a truck, also hard work. And the older ones performed better, not the teenagers from the youth movement who may have been much better skiers or ballplayers.

Our accommodations consisted of bags of straw, placed on wooden racks. About ten boys or girls slept in one room; there was no facility for heating; presumably all work would be finished before the onset of winter. There was also a kitchen. Two or three girls were in charge of cooking, or rather of preparing meals from whatever foodstuffs they were given. Since we stayed in the fields all day, there were only two hot meals: breakfast, consisting of hot soup and bread with marmalade. And for lunch, we each took our piece of bread along. Dinner was again mainly bread and soup. but often the "kitchen girls" were able to find some cabbage overlooked when it should have been harvested, or even apples not picked up after they had fallen from the trees. The farmer gave us enough flour to bake bread with, and also enough potatoes for soup. But our diet was almost entirely fat-free and also quite low in vitamins. Soon our hands started to bleed.

Strangely enough, those of us who were at least 18 years old were also given two cigarettes every day! Since I was the only boy who did not smoke, I gave my cigarettes to some of the girls who did, but not for any "favors" in return. We were all much too tired for any frivolities. But still, during the long evenings when we sat around the petroleum lamps that were much too dim for reading, I guess there was some good conversation.

"When we get to Palestine" (strangely enough nobody said "if" we get to Palestine), how will we live? Will we be dirt farmers with not enough to eat for the rest of our lives? Sure, we'll help build "Eretz Yisrael" (the Land of Israel) but what will our standard of living be?"

"Oh, maybe as good as the farmer's; the one who rides the tractor."

"Will we have any intellectual stimulation? Can we ever get to Jerusalem or Tel Aviv? Can we continue with our studies?"

"Well, maybe so. But we should never forget that only agriculture, only our tilling of the soil of Eretz Yisrael, will redeem the land! We don't need lawyers or stockbrokers or even industrialists, only farmers." In many ways, we were living in a never-never land, trying to forget the present, waiting for the moment when we would board

195

the small ships which would carry us down at the river Danube, into the Black Sea, then to the Mediterranean and finally to the coast of Palestine.

Still, many friendships formed, often between boys and girls, though I doubt that there was any sex. We were always tired (not that weariness could necessarily influence a bunch of healthy youngsters). Even the fact that it was impossible ever to be alone, somehow a couple finds ways. Most important, I believe, was our somewhat monkish attitude. We all had one-track minds. Think only of Eretz Yisrael. Once I sat next to a girl to whom I had given my cigarettes. We obviously liked each other, we talked and accidentally our hands touched.

"Next Sunday Teri, my fiancée, will visit here," I said quickly.

The girl moved away, a little regret in her eyes. "I'm so happy for you that you found somebody already. You are a decent fellow."

Teri really did visit me the following Sunday at 2 o'clock in the afternoon. That's because we worked until one. It took half an hour to return from the field and half an hour to wash up. The rest of the week, Monday through Saturday, we had to be at our station at sunrise and didn't come home until after dark. There was little time for such luxuries as a good wash.

Teri arrived before I was ready. The walk, from the railroad station, had tired her out. She was carrying a sandwich for lunch. There wasn't even a place for her to sit down while she waited for me. We kissed and decided to go for a walk just to be alone with each other. We talked very little. Teri told me about my parents and that she was getting along just fine with her class of hand-weaving students. I described my work on the farm, making it appear a little less hard than it was. Then we were silent, just walking and looking at each other.

"Why don't you eat your sandwich?" I said finally.

She unpacked it and tasted it. "It's so good; your mother made it. Have a bite!" She broke off a piece of the sandwich and put it into my mouth. Then another piece, and another. Suddenly, she laughed:

"There's nothing left. You ate it all!"

"I'm so sorry; you must be hungry after the walk from the station."

"Never mind. I'm glad you enjoyed the sandwich. I'll eat tonight!" We laughed together, happy to know how much we loved each other.

I had been at the farm for several weeks when good news reached us: for more than half of our group the "Hachsharah" was over. They would join a transport down the Danube. (As I learned later, the transport was successful. Only six weeks after they left, the miserable

boat that carried my friends reached Palestine. The
weather on the Mediterranean had been favorable: fog
prevented the boat from being spotted by British ships.)

A new group joined us at our camp, and among them
was my friend Anti. Since the old leadership, consisting
mostly of members of the youth movement "Blue-White,"
had left with the transport, there was room for new people
to fill the vacuum. Anti soon emerged as the one who
could best talk to the farmer. After all, he had been a
lawyer, and also immediately commanded respect from
those who had been in our camp before.

"We won't have to work such long hours anymore,"
Anti reported to us after he had had a conference with
the farmer. "We Jews actually stepped into a Slovakian
farm workers contract; their hours will be ours. On the
other hand, we are going to furnish a man to run the
tractor; I told him that we have a very qualified fellow.
The farmer liked that because it will free him to do other
chores. Furthermore, one of our women will act as his
secretary. She'll write letters for him and do a lot of other
paperwork. One of her duties will also be to allocate the
food for us. Anyway," Anti continued his report to us,
"from now on we will eat a little better. My friend Emma,
who will be the farmer's secretary for the next week, will
see to that. And my friend George, when he sits on the
tractor, might just make it run a little less fast."

Quite possibly, Anti favored those who came with him from the Hachshara where he had been previously. Both running the tractor (the task fell to George who was really qualified) and playing the farmer's secretary, were easy jobs. But everybody benefitted. After one week, Anti saw to it that one of the girls who had been in our camp before he got there was given the soft job of sitting in the farmer's office. Anti was a born leader; soon he had everybody's loyalty.

There were other changes. Some of the young women and men new to our group were Orthodox Jews. They prayed every morning and evening and they had to get up even earlier and go to bed later than the rest of us.

"How come you work on Shabbat?" I asked Shmuel, a big fellow with ear locks, the best worker in our camp, who never seemed to be tired.

"There is a war on," he explained. "Hitler is making war on us. He's trying to kill us. We are trying to defend ourselves by working. To save a life, somebody else's or our own, we may break the Sabbath."

Suzy had been one of the "old" girls on our farm who usually worked in the kitchen. Since Anti had only met her when he joined us, I had known her before he did. She was a quiet, big girl; not exactly beautiful but extremely pleasant. I don't know how Anti and Suzy first got together, but soon they were a couple. Everybody knew and respected that.

I couldn't forget how in a different world, long ago, Anti had dropped "his" girls after a few weeks.

"You remember Adry?" I asked him. "Will it be the same with Suzy?"

"Frank, believe me: Suzy and I, we'll be together as long as we live. We really love each other! But there is more to it. Suzy is a Czech, Jewish girl. She grew up on a farm and knows how to work. She is intelligent, you know." Adry was "sweet," but a lot of brains she didn't have.

When I found an opportunity to work in the kitchen, I said to Suzy:

"I'm sure you know that Anti is a good friend of mine. But…"

"You are afraid he'll 'use' me?" Suzy laughed. "He's mine! Never fear! I know how to handle him! We'll make it to Palestine together, somehow.

Unfortunately, this was not to be. I left the farm in October 1939 because my time was up. If there was to be another transport, I had the right to be on it. But I kept in touch with Suzy and Anti. The last time I saw them was on a bitter, cold day in February 1940. Anti was in charge of a farm that was essentially nothing more than a barracks to keep the snow out; there was no heat of any kind. Suzy, the only girl, was cooking on an open stove. About two dozen boys, the roughest looking Jews I would ever see, were felling trees and chopping wood, which they loaded onto trucks.

"I'll miss you!" were Anti's last words to me when we said goodbye.

In 1946, in Chicago, I got a letter from Suzy (I had given her my brother's address). It was written in Czech, the only language she knew.

"Anti is gone. He was too decent a fellow to live. Our baby is gone too. I'll try to start a new life."

Much later I learned that the Nazis, when they knew they had lost the war, killed all young male Jews in the Czech work farms. According to the Wannsee Protocol of 1942:

"There had to be no strong survivors to propagate the Jewish race."

XIII

WEDDING IN PRAGUE-
HAPPINESS IN BRATISLAVA

In October 1939, in Prague, Teri and I had to take stock of our chances of ever getting out of Europe. We could wait for a transport to Palestine. I was eligible now. As a matter of fact, I received the exit visa from Germany (Prague was now a German city) as well as an entry visa to Slovakia, since all transports left from Bratislava, the capital of the country. But how good were our chances? Not good, we had to admit to ourselves. While the last transport had succeeded in reaching Palestine, the next one might never get organized, or so we were informed. (There was one more attempt to leave Bratislava on a miserable ship sailing down the river Danube; it ended in disaster. In Romania, bandits killed all aboard.)

The other chance we had to leave Europe was for the U.S. After all, we were registered for emigration at the American consulate in Prague. But it would take two years before "our number" would come up.

"My Hungarian passport will expire on the first of December," Teri told me. "Without a valid passport, I can't travel anywhere."

"But as a Hungarian citizen, you can't get an American visa. The quota for Hungarians is filled for twenty years to come! Only as my wife are you eligible to get on the German quota!"

"But I can't stay here without a valid passport and really want to see my family."

We arrived at the obvious solution to our dilemma: we would marry now in order to make Teri eligible for an American visa, but the next morning she would take a train to go "home" to Hungary just before her passport expired! Before the Hungarian authorities knew about her marriage to a German, she would renew her passport and meet me in Bratislava.

Our wedding in Prague, late in October 1939, was not something we would later joyfully remember. In the City Hall, about thirty couples were lined up. A Czech judge asked us to say, in unison:

"I, bridegroom or bride—here you must state your name—am herewith marrying you, my bride or bridegroom. Now you must give the other name."

That was our wedding, except that the judge now admonished us to stay true to each other in spite of the short ceremony. My parents and a distant relative of Teri's (he perished a year later) were the witnesses. My father wanted to take a room in a hotel for us.

"Even a slave is entitled to a wedding night!" he said.

But we didn't want that. "We'll wait for happier times." The next morning, Teri left. (Thirty-five years later, in our Temple in Skokie, Illinois, we repeated our "wedding vows" in a solemn ceremony. It was as if we had a premonition of Teri's death a year later.)

I would stay in Prague for six more months, living with my parents and working for Hechalutz. Soon it was clear, even to the greatest optimists among us, that all emigration to Palestine was over for the duration of the war. Our office became only a distribution center for Jewish workers on Czech farms. We hoped that the Nazis would respect the usefulness of our groups for agriculture (there was a severe labor shortage) and leave us alone. They did, until just before the end of the war when they knew all was lost. Then they proceeded to kill all young male Jews.

Sometime in late 1939, there was an ad in all newspapers: "All male German citizens between ages 18 and 45 years of age residing in Prague must register for service in the German armed forces." While I knew that Jews were not taken into the German army, the ad stated that ALL German citizens had to register, and that included me.

On the designated day, I showed up at the place of registration, taking care to have documents showing that I was Jewish. Sure enough, I received an impressive-looking official document, with my picture, signed by a German officer, stating: "UNTAUGLICH DA JUDE." Meaning, not fit because Jewish. This document would come in handy later with a Slovakian border guard. But at the time of registration, those who saw it, all good Germans, envied me. "You Jews have it made, as always. You don't have to go to war."

In January 1940, I came down with a severe case of appendicitis. And appendectomy was performed in the only hospital open to me: The Jewish Hospital of Prague. The Jewish community of Prague maintained it. I was treated as a "charity" patient since I was a "refugee."

(Isn't it strange: those who paid for me were dead a few years later and I survived them.)

After the operation, I stayed in a room with five or six other patients. One of them was a violin virtuoso who had been refused admission to the U.S. by the American Consulate because he had a mild hernia. Though advised by his doctor against an operation (the man was in his 60s and had a weak heart), he decided to have the hernia fixed in order to be able to emigrate to the U.S. We watched him die; the operation had been too much for his heart. The anti-Jewish attitude of many American consulates was well known. They did their best to keep Jews out.

In June 1940, with a heavy heart, I left my parents. It was clear to me that I had no chance for emigration as long as I stayed in Prague. Most likely I had no chance anywhere. At least in Bratislava, the capital of the new independent state of Slovakia, I would be with my wife. Perhaps we could get our American visas in Hungary, Slovakia's neighbor to the south. My parents encouraged me to go. I wouldn't see my father again.

"Be good, always." These were his last words to me. I traveled lightly: one small suitcase containing a suit, a pair of shoes, six shirts, some underwear, a few photos and very little money. I shared my third-class compartment with a bunch of German soldiers.

"The war is seventy-five percent won already!" they kept telling one another. "From now on, we won't even have to fight anymore."

They couldn't be blamed for being so confident. Belgium and the Netherlands had fallen. France was as good as lost. Denmark and Norway were occupied. The British would probably have given up, since they couldn't fight alone.

On a beautiful June morning Teri and I met in Bratislava. We hadn't seen each other since our wedding the previous October. She had come from her father's house in Hungary (though his city had been a part of "pre-Munich" Czechoslovakia until 1938, it belonged to Hungary in 1940), while I had left Prague, now part of Germany. We both knew Bratislava well; we had met there in 1936, in happier times, when I worked in my father's paint factory. After the Munich agreement, the Germans had occupied that factory, being south of the river Danube.

Meeting again in June 1940, we first had to look for a room. Nominally, Slovakia was an independent country then, but a creation of Nazi Germany. A ghetto had just been established. Jews could only live in a certain part of the city, and all Christians who lived there had to move out. The Jews who were left were charged with "inviting" their fellow religionists into their apartments. For practical purposes, this meant that Jewish apartment owners were in a hurry to sublet empty rooms to childless couples, fearing otherwise that they'd get large families.

A Mrs. Deutelbaum advertised a room. Teri had brought a little money from Hungary, and so we rented it. We did not know, of course, that the landlady was a witch, or so it seemed to us soon enough.

I'm not sure if there are Jewish witches; but if so, "The Widow Deutelbaum," who always referred to herself by that name, would qualify. She was actually not bad-looking. About 60 years old, fat, with pitch-black eyes smiling at us until we paid for the first month with most of the money we had. Then she screamed:

"I know your kind, you Godless Jews who made Hitler because you don't observe the Jewish laws."

"You," she turned to my wife, "don't you ever dare to set foot in my kosher kitchen!"

When we had finally closed the door to "our" room, from the inside, we laughed and kissed. And that started one of the happiest years in our lives.

But how could we be happy, living in surroundings where we were despised; in a town that relegated us to a ghetto; in a country openly stating it wished us dead; that would never acknowledge us as even second-class citizens; in the middle of a war; in a world where nobody wanted us? It seems to me that short of great physical pain or hunger or death of a close relative, happiness is not greatly influenced by what goes on around us.

In spite of our strictly illegal status, we both found work quickly. Terry gave classes in knitting and hand-weaving, she was an expert in both and took advantage of the fact that many women (not only Jews) wanted to learn something new. Advertising was unnecessary; the news about our return to the city quickly spread among our friends. I contacted one of our former salesmen who had worked for my father's factory for many years.

After the usual greetings, I came right to the point.

"Mr. Kuerti, I need work, any kind; I have to make money to feed my wife and myself."

Not much explanation was necessary for Mr. Kuerti. A tall, strong man in his fifties, he was certainly a man of the world. He was not greatly bothered by legal restrictions the Slovakian government had set up against Jews working; he knew how to get around them. A proud, Orthodox Jew himself, he knew better than to offer me money. Rather, he did the traditional thing:

"Mr. Weinmann, (we never got to calling each other by our first names), don't worry. I'll set you up in business. We'll both make money."

"But how? I have no permission to work here, certainly no capital."

"Never mind. As a chemist, you know how to make things; I can sell."

This was the way a partnership began which lasted for almost a year, until I ran away to Hungary in order to get my American visa.

Mr. Kuerti knew of a shed that did not seem to belong to anybody. It was approximately six by ten feet in size, had two walls and also a roof of corrugated tin. Most important, there was a stove inside, fit for cooking. Also, a sturdy table. The shed was in an open field.

"You can make paints here, also adhesives I can sell," he said. "Some of the raw materials I'll procure; others you can perhaps get from former suppliers of your father's factory. Of course, I'll lay out the money."

How much Mr. Kuerti told me with these few words! First, that he had confidence in my ability to "manufacture." Second, that he would be available to help. Third, and most important, that I should not be too proud to use my connections as the son of my well-known father.

It really worked out, and we made money almost from the beginning! Mr. Kuerti hired a gypsy who went to the city dump and found paint cans there. I emptied them carefully; cleaned them by boiling them in lye and then, using the traces of paint I had preserved from the cans, I made them "look like new." Since I had no paint mill, I decided to make floor polish, which Mr. Kuerti sold to restaurants. What little raw materials I needed I got for very little money, from local suppliers who knew me from "before."

But Mr. Kuerti was more ambitious!

"They use a lot of adhesive for walls, to put up announcements or proclamations. It's not only for paper to stick to paper. Do you think you could make that? I could sell many barrels of it."

I had no idea how to produce such an adhesive, but that was not hard to learn by spending an afternoon in the city library. The question was how to get raw materials, and in fairly large quantities. In a war economy such as we had in Bratislava in 1940, it was very difficult to get raw materials.

I am surprised now at the courage, the chutzpah, I had when I was 26 years old. I went to a competitor of my father's former factory, a much larger enterprise than ours ever was. It was actually a subsidiary of a German firm. I had met the manager only once or twice when my father had sent me to manufacturers' meetings he found too boring. I knew the manager's name, not much more, other than that he was German. Probably a Nazi. I also learned that he had the reputation of being a decent fellow. I still had a few of the calling cards left that I used when working for my father. I sent one to the manager, who received me immediately, inquired about the well-being of my father, and finally asked me what he could do for me. I could not help looking at a huge portrait of Adolf Hitler on his desk, but thought it best to come right to the point.

"As you know, we lost our factory. I spent some time in Prague but had to leave that city. While I am waiting for my American visa, I'm doing some, well, a little manufacturing, if you can call it that, but I'm finding it difficult to get raw materials. I thought perhaps you could help me out."

He looked straight into my eyes, waited a moment, then rang for his secretary.

"This is Mr. Weinmann, he owned a paint factory until recently. Please find out what he needs and give it to him. Also, establish the price we paid for the material and charge him the same amount."

He turned to me and stretched out his hand. "I trust this will be satisfactory. I hope you make it to America. The best of luck to you!"

What this man had done was more than fair; he had practically given me a gift. I found that frequently during the Hitler years, Germans tried to be decent on a one-to-one basis. Anyway, I was in business now, making lots of adhesive at a good price, but wondered who used it.

"Why, the city of course," Mr. Kuerti told me. "Nobody else could use that much. I have my connections, you know. You see the posters they are putting up all over the city; they are using our adhesive."

I felt myself blush. The posters Mr. Kuerti, the Orthodox Jew, was referring to read, in part:

"DO NOT BUY FROM JEWS! ANY SLOVAK WHO BUYS FROM A JEW IS A TRAITOR."

Our lives consisted of much more than work in Bratislava during 1940. We had good friends there and saw a lot of them. On Saturdays and Sundays, we left the city for the hills nearby. In winter, I even went skiing, for the last time in my life, in an outfit borrowed from friends. We had only Jewish friends; any social contact with Slovaks, Germans or Hungarians (all three nationalities existed in Bratislava) would have endangered not only us but also them. One day as Teri and I were going for a walk, we saw Fritz, a German fellow who had been one of our best friends before 1939. He was in a Slovakian soldier's uniform. He was obviously surprised to see us, stretched out his hand, then thought better of it and gave us a smart salute as if we had been officers. But I saw a tear in his eye when he looked at us.

My wife refused to study English. "We'll never make it to America, anyhow," she would say. I could understand her and did not argue. There was a certain superstition, perhaps, because we did learn Spanish together, from a book called "A Thousand Words of Spanish." Who knows? "A Thousand Words of Silence," this was the theme of our New Year's Eve celebration of 1940. Conditions had become very bad for Jews, there was no hope left. A dozen friends had gotten together for what we thought to be the end of our last year on this earth. There were gruesome decorations on the walls (one of us was a painter) and yet we managed many laughs. Young people are that way, I guess. None of our friends who participated in this party survived the war.

In January 1941, we came to a decision: we would do everything possible to stay alive, even if it meant leaving friends, or environments we knew well. We would take desperate chances. Our lives might not be immediately threatened, but it would not take long until all Jewish life in Slovakia would come to an end.

Unfortunately, we were right. Therefore, Teri, who still had a valid Hungarian passport under her maiden name, returned to her father's house in order to wait for me until I could join her there, illegally of course. Maybe, just maybe, we'd still make our way to America.

It feels strange to be the only survivor since Teri, my wife of 36 years, died in 1975. My father-in-law, his wife, and his younger daughter all were killed, as was Mr. Kuerti and his family. Fritz, our German friend, did not survive the war either.

XIV

DIFFERENT ACCENTS

In May, 1941, I had to get to Hungary because my American visa was waiting for me there. But I was in Slovakia and the Hungarian government would not let me in. On the other hand, I was not allowed to stay in Slovakia either. There was only one way out of this dilemma. I had to illegally cross the border between the two countries, both allied to Hitler's Germany.

Trying to learn as much as possible about the best place to get across without getting caught, I was advised that the mountains of eastern Slovakia were not heavily patrolled. This was several weeks before the Germans invaded the Soviet Union. Eastern Europe seemed to be peaceful. The Jews in Slovakia were persecuted because that's what Germany wanted. However, the Slovakians were not very good at it, they did not care one way or the other. I was told that a Jewish family named Hirsch lived close to the point where I wanted to cross the border; they would help me. Their house was high up in the mountains, eight day's walk from the nearest railroad station.

Not wanting to make myself conspicuous by asking questions, I had studied the local map beforehand. I took a night train, arrived early in the morning and started my hike towards the Hirsch's house, carrying all my possessions in a backpack. As I walked on a narrow dirt road I was alone, slowly climbing through a forest for several hours. In the early afternoon, I left the trees behind me and found myself on a ridge where I could see my way ahead for several miles. The road climbed only slightly now. On my right was the forest I had just left; on my left I saw a deep valley, actually a narrow, steep ravine leading upwards towards my road. There was a little waterfall where the valley ended. Right above it my road crossed a brook, and then followed the other side of the ravine. A short bridge across would have saved me half an hour's walk.

As I looked at the road on the opposite side of the ravine I saw a soldier walking towards the waterfall; in fifteen minutes or so we would meet. This was what I had good reason to dread: a border patrol. He must have seen me as I had seen him. If he arrested me, I would be sent back to Germany, no doubt to a concentration camp. This would be the end of me. I considered running back into the forest but there was no way for me to escape. I had been told that these border patrols were usually made up of mean, trigger-happy soldiers. If he would shoot at me across the ravine he could not miss. Then I thought of simply walking until we met and trying to push him down into the ravine. I was quite strong at that time; a surprise attack might work. But this was not my style; I have never been a man of violence. I decided to keep on walking and somehow try to talk the soldier out of arresting me.

We met on the little bridge above the waterfall. He was quite young, probably still in his teens. Though he carried a big rifle, he did not look like a soldier, his uniform seemed too big for him.

"Na straz!" he shouted. Well, these words, the Slovakian equivalent of "Heil Hitler," were used for patriotic greetings in the new State of Slovakia. But literally translated, "Na straz" means something like "watch out!" I did not think it a good idea to greet him with the same words and just bid him a good morning.

"What are you doing here?" He asked me. He spoke with and East Slovakian accent, the local dialect which sounds different from West Slovakia, the official language of the country, which is what I spoke well at that time.

"I am a tourist," I answered, "I have my backpack, as you see, and I love this beautiful country."

"Beautiful country, my ass. Don't you know that you are near the border? You have no business walking around here. I should arrest you."

I've got to stay cool, I told myself. "But I have business here. I am visiting my friend, Mr. Hirsch."

"Don't bullshit me. You don't even know the Hirsch Jews."

I did not know what to say. The soldier's pink face got red with excitement. Whatever I said might be wrong. Better to wait for him to ask me something.

"Show me your passport!" He commanded, after hesitating for a while. He must have remembered "Standard Procedure for Border Patrolling."

"Sure. I'll get it right away." I slowly opened my backpack to find my passport and tried to think of a good answer for his obvious next question, but could not find one. I handed the document over to him.

"You have a German passport?" The soldier obviously recognized the swastika on the cover, the emblem of Slovakia's big neighbor and protector.

"Yes," I said.

As he inspected my picture on the inside of the document, a sheet of paper fell out. He picked it up and studied it for a long time. It also had my photo pasted to it.

"This is from the German army, sir?" He asked, politely. This soldier was smarter than I thought.

Obviously, he had recognized and translated the words "Deutsche Wehrmacht." Of course, in May 1941, this expression could be found in his Slovakian newspapers all the time, in its original German.

"Yes, it is." I answered as briefly as possible. No use getting involved in any details, I thought.

"What does it say, sir?" he inquired.

The moment of truth had arrived. I decided to play it straight.

"It says UNTAUGLICH DA JUDE." I read to him in German.

"What does this mean in Slovakian? You see, sir, I do not know German.

"It means that I am not fit to serve in the Army because I am a Jew."

This Slovakian soldier, this peasant boy stuck into a uniform, had an enormous sense of humor. He laughed and laughed, then he put his rifle on the ground and slapped his thighs with both hands, and laughed some more.

"You are a Jew? Funny, funny! That's why you wanted to visit the Hirsch Jews. I thought you were a spy, with your stupid city accent that only my school teacher has. Nobody speaks that way around here. I thought maybe you were a Russian. You know, of course, we are at peace with the Ruskies. But I don't trust them, and their country is only a few kilometers from here right now. You are not a spy; you are only a Jew! Funny! But what the hell are you really doing here?" The soldier was still laughing.

I thought I might as well try to take advantage of his good humor and tell him the truth.

"I want to go to America, but I have to pick up my visa in Hungary."

"Sure," he interrupted. "You are a smart man. You know, my mother keeps on telling me I should go to America. 'Janosh,' she says, 'don't trust the Germans, don't trust the Russians, don't trust the shitty Hungarians in the next valley. Don't trust anybody.'"

"But you have your own country now," I said. I did not know what to make of this soldier's confidential talk; better be careful and flatter him.

"You are the masters of your own beautiful state of Slovakia."

"Bullshit. We farmers will get screwed one way or another. The guys in the capital who are running our country now do not even talk like I do; they talk funny, like my teacher did. Of course, if I go to America, I'd have to learn the American language. My uncle Milosh writes it is quite difficult, it does not sound at all like Slovakian or Hungarian."

It may have been nice chatting with this soldier, but I wanted to go on. As a matter of fact, I could not even be sure that he would really let me go. Again, I thought the direct approach might work best.

"Is it still far to the Hungarian border?" I asked.

"No, a couple of hours. But if you really want to visit the Hirsch Jews first…" He started to laugh again.

"You and the Hirsch Jews! Old man Hirsch has a beard all the way down to his belt and he always wears a hat. You don't look at all like him! How come you are a Jew too? Anyway, I went to school with his younger son, a smart fellow, and strong! He beat me in arm wrestling every time. But, let me tell you, I can shoot better than he can. Nobody can shoot like me. I can hit any bird flying high up in the sky!"

I am so glad I did not try to run away, I thought.

"Well," he prattled on, "if you really want to see the Hirsch's, you cannot miss. Just go straight ahead on this road for about an hour and you'll see their house. Tell them Janosh sends greetings.

By the way, let me tell you: be careful the Hungarian border guards don't catch you. These bastards are mean! They beat you with their rifles! I get along with them, of course, I speak their shitty language but they don't know one word of Slovakian; they are stupid. They cannot even catch the gypsies who cross the border all night right under their noses, smuggling coffee and tea. When I catch them, I beat them up but good. They should work like I do. By the way, I hope you don't have anything like that in your backpack."

I assured him that I had only personal belongings; but just to make sure I ask him to see for himself and open my backpack. He looked in a side pocket and the first thing he found was the picture of my fiancé.

"She sure is pretty," he said, "is she already in America?"

"No, she's waiting for me in Hungary."

"Oh, well, then don't keep her waiting any longer. You know, my uncle got a girl into trouble here and had to run away to America or the police would have caught him. He is a miner in Pennsylvania now; stinking rich; he sent us a picture: he wears a tie and a hat. I should really go to him. Maybe we will meet sometimes in America!" He looked down, onto the waterfall.

"But much water will flow until then!" he said softly. "I hope I will not be in the war." He stretched out his hand and looked into my eyes.

"You better go now. Be careful and good luck," he said, and finally gave me the traditional Slovakian farewell.

"S Bohom (God Be with You)." I took his hand and shook it.

"S Bohom," I answered. There is no difference between the eastern and western Slovakian dialects in this traditional greeting.

XV

JEWS, GYPSIES AND HUNGARIANS

I decided to visit the Hirsch family after all, although the Slovakian soldier had advised me that "I couldn't miss" finding my way to Hungary. Furthermore, my father-in-law was expecting me at a certain time at a Hungarian railroad station early the next morning. I had no trouble finding the Hirsch's place. An elderly man was sitting in front of the house, skull cap on his head, busy with his afternoon prayers. He paid no attention to me.

A young man came out of the house. "You must be the man who wants to cross the border tonight," he said. "They wrote me about you, from Bratislava. You're lucky the border patrol didn't catch you!"

"He did. Janosh sends you greetings!" I told him of my adventures.

"So, you and Janosh had a little fun!" The young man, who didn't look all that different from Janosh the soldier, laughed. "Have a bite to eat, rest a while, will go in an hour, after the sun sets."

The old man had finished his prayers. "Sholem Aleychem" (peace be with you) was all he ever said to me as he went into the house.

"They pay me a little, the Jewish community in Bratislava, for every man I get across the border, but very little!" The son said to me. "You have a nice wristwatch. Maybe you won't need it anymore?"

I could take a hint. The watch had been a present from my mother., But I was sure she would have wanted me to part with it if my safety was involved. I gave him the watch.

"By all means, have it!" was all I said. I was not sure I liked this man very much. After a while he brought me a plate with a few hot potatoes; I ate them gladly; after all, I had not eaten all day. We left at dusk, first going up across a pass between two hills, then down. I saw a few huts.

"Are we already in Hungary?" I asked.

"Oh no, we are still in Slovakia. But all you have to do now is go down to this gypsy camp; they know you're coming; they will take you to Hungary!"

"But I thought you are my guide!"

"No. Just go fast! I have to leave." He disappeared without another word.

What was I to do? I felt betrayed by young Hirsch. After all, he had said himself that he got paid for leading me across the border. But I had come this far. I had to take my chances with the gypsies.

I saw about a dozen men as I entered the only hut that was lit. They seemed to have known that I was coming because they greeted me with loud voices, probably more than a little drunk. But they spoke Hungarian! I understood next to nothing.

"Do you speak Slovakian? I asked in that language. "German?" They just laughed at me.

"Magyarul (Hungarian)!"

But after a while, one of them said in more or less broken English, "I was America. Work hard. Bad country." I was happy to have found somebody I could talk to, I thought, only to discover that this man had just about exhausted his English vocabulary. After much screaming and laughing, another man pointed at himself, then at me, and said:

"Magyarorszag (Hungary)!"

Obviously, he was to be my guide. But when I tried to take my backpack, he motioned to me that it was too heavy; I was to go without it. Well, I thought, this is it. I am in no position to argue.

We left. He gave me a small bag to carry, but he had a big, obviously heavy bag on his back; no doubt he was a smuggler. What if the Hungarians or Slovakians catch us, I thought? Not only are we crossing the border illegally, but also we are smuggling.

Suddenly my guide pulled me down. "Katonag" he whispered. I did not understand but soon realized that he had seen soldiers. After a while—it must have been an hour—he motioned me to go on.

But not long afterwards, he pushed me to the ground again, hard. He must have seen soldiers again.

I had seen nothing in the pitch-black night but I had to trust his judgment. This went on for several hours. Go on, down, go again. I was getting very tired. But finally, we were on a highway just as it was getting light.

"Magyarorszag!" he said, took the bag he had given me to carry, shook hands, pointed at the highway for me to follow and disappeared.

I followed the road for only a few minutes when I saw a railroad station and my father-in-law standing in front of it with a big shawl in his hands. He motioned for me to be quiet, hugged me, and put the shawl around my head and chin.

"You have a bad cold, you are hoarse, you cannot talk at all," he whispered into my ear in German.

Only his smiling eyes welcomed me; he didn't say another word to me as long as other people were around, knowing that I knew no Hungarian, but not wishing me to speak another language. He was well-prepared. With two railroad tickets in his hand, he motioned for me to board the train that soon arrived. Even on the train I watched him discussing me with a Hungarian soldier who asked everybody lots of questions; my father-in-law spoke for me since I was obviously sick; I pretended to try to talk but was too hoarse. Finally, the train pulled into the station, we got out and walked a few minutes until we got to my in-laws' apartment; Teri was there as were her mother and sister; we all laughed and cried.

A few days later a buggy pulled up before the gate of the house. I recognized the gypsy who knew a few words of English. Without saying anything, he threw my backpack, the same one I had to leave behind, on the sidewalk and disappeared.

No one had told me that gypsies could be so honest.

The city where the Vidor family (my in-laws) lived was named Kosice during the Czechoslovakian period, 1918 to 1938, and is so named again since 1945. However, under Hungarian rule, roughly coinciding with World War II, this city changed not only its name, to Kassa, but also its language! Suddenly very little Slovakian was heard; almost everybody pretended to have been a Hungarian all the time. (Sometimes I wonder what would happen in many California cities if suddenly Mexicans were to rule. Would English disappear?)

Not speaking Hungarian, I had to be silent when not at home. There was one exception: The Vidor's had a dry goods store, and during market days, twice a week, I was asked to act as cashier. The store was always full of customers, all Slovakian farm women from the surrounding hills. They spoke only Slovakian; they liked me and had a lot of fun with me.

"So, you are the new young man; be sure to marry one of the Vidor girls!" one of the women customers might say. "Don't live in sin!" Or another might say, "I'd gladly give my money to such a nice young fellow." Another would say, "Look. I did NOT steal this cloth; not this time, anyway!"

Business was very good and the Vidors made a lot of money. Unfortunately!

There was no incentive for Jews to emigrate! Hungry seemed to be a nice, free country. When the Nazis took over in 1943, they did it through a local party organization, the Hungarian National Socialists, similar but not exactly the same as their German brethren. The Hungarians used the "arrow cross" as their symbol, while the German Nazis, of course, used the swastika. If anything, these "Hungarian Nazis" were even more cruel than the Germans.

Jews like the Vidors had no idea what was in store for them. Eventually, all over the country except in Budapest, the capital, Jews were collected and shipped to Auschwitz. Anybody over 45 went directly into the gas ovens.

But when I was there, in 1941, life was good, in spite of the war against the Soviet Union a few hundred miles to the east. Teri and I frequently went to the local swimming pool or had nice walks, and loved each other very much.

In July, we got our American visas. Unfortunately, we did not see the slightest possibility of getting out of Europe. We were surrounded either by Germany or by war.

XVI

BRUNHILDE

Had it been a month earlier, it might have been possible to reach America via the Soviet Union, through Siberia. But now Hungary, as well as all of her neighbors, was directly involved in the war with Russia.

We were trapped. The American visas, which we had been anxiously waiting for since 1938, seemed to be useless. Then, suddenly, we heard a rumor at the Jewish community center in Budapest: the most unlikely way to travel might be open for us, right through Germany, occupied France and Spain. This sounded crazy.

I had been glad to be out of Germany but now I should go back? Furthermore, why should the Germans let us pass through their country?

But still, it was certainly our duty to pursue even the most unlikely of possibilities.

Furthermore, we had nothing to lose. I was in Hungary illegally and could be picked up by the police at any moment.

All we could learn at the Jewish Community Center was that we might contact the HAPAG, a German office which, before the war, had been in charge of shipping goods from Hamburg, Germany to New York. However, since the outbreak of the war in 1939 no more German passenger ships were sailing the ocean, nor did any American (nominally neutral) ships stop in Germany. The HAPAG branch in Budapest still existed.

So, one morning in July 1941 Teri and I went to that office. We had our story well-rehearsed: she would do the talking if Hungarian was spoken (since I knew only a few words of that language), but if the employees should prefer to speak German, I would be in charge.

We found the office closed, with a sign on the window: "Business Hours from 2 to 4:30 PM."

When we returned a little after 2 o'clock, we entered and saw a young man behind the counter who spoke to a customer in Hungarian. But there was also a woman, probably in her early 60s, sitting in a private office in the back. She seemed to be in charge.

She was also busy, negotiating in German with two important-looking gentlemen. We just stood there, waiting to be noticed. After ten minutes or so the woman waved us to approach her with a contemptuous expression and motion. We had a good look at her now: she was a stout, tall woman with a lot of unkempt gray hair falling over her shoulders. She reminded me of the composer Richard Wagner's "Brunhilde," after she had gotten old and seedy.

"What do you want?" she barked at us in German. Certainly, Hungarian, the language of the land, would have been more appropriate; we had not spoken as yet. I told her that we had heard of the HAPAG procuring transportation for Jews trying to emigrate from Europe. She did not let me finish.

"You goddamned Jews," she interrupted with a screaming, screechy voice. "What makes you think I would waste my time on you? I am talking to more important people now! Maybe I might see you at 6 o'clock but now out with you before I kick you in the behind!"

As we left the office we saw the sign again: business hours from 2 to 4:30 PM. We looked at each other, more bewildered than hurt. Why did that terrible woman act that way? It just did not add up. She let us wait; she might well have guessed what we wanted. Why had she screamed and cursed when addressing us? Finally, when she threw us out, she had, in a way, asked us to come back after office hours. Perhaps she would ask us for a bribe when she was alone with us. But if that were her intention, why be so rough and mean?

Having nothing to lose, we returned at 6 o'clock and peeked through the window. The young man had left. "Brunhilde" was sitting at her desk, working on a stack of papers. Trembling, we entered the door. The woman got up, stretched out both arms and said:

"Welcome! I am so glad you came back; I was afraid you would not make it. Please excuse my behavior this afternoon, I must do that for appearance sake; a show I put up for these people!" Hinting with a gesture who "these people" were, she let us know what she thought of them.

"Sit down," she said with a mellow voice, really reminding us of an opera singer. "Tell me all about you, I can probably help."

She was no prettier than before, but now she looked more like a friendly grandmother who could not take care of herself because she was too busy with her grandchildren. I was too surprised and moved to speak; Teri got a hold of herself first and explained that we finally got our American visas but could not find any way out of Europe. The woman turned to me:

"Earlier today, you spoke German perfectly well but your wife has a Hungarian accent. What is your nationality?" She inquired.

I told her that I was born and raised in Vienna and that I had first an Austrian, then a German passport. Now we had a "stateless" document and were in Budapest only for the purpose of obtaining our American visas.

"Don't tell me how you got to Hungary, I do not want to know," she said. "They are treating you dreadfully but, believe me, it will get much, much worse. You should get out as fast as you can; all Jews should. Right now, there is a good chance."

She explained to us that she was collecting the names of all Jews now in Hungary who had an overseas visa and, once a week, sent a list to Berlin with a request to provide transportation to Spain. She continued to tell us that she assured "Berlin" that she personally interviewed us and that we were not wanted by the German police, and owed no German taxes. Therefore, it was in the interest of Germany to get us out in order to have fewer Jews in Europe.

"The charge from Budapest to Madrid will be 500 Reichsmark per person, to be paid when you receive your tickets; this includes the commission to this office (so, no bribe is solicited, I thought). You will travel from here to Munich by train, then fly from Munich to Madrid."

"You see," she continued, "the wind is blowing from the right direction in Berlin, as far as you are concerned, but it will only be for a very short time. I implore you, hurry! It will not be long before terrible things will happen to all European Jews. It is already very bad in Poland but it will get much worse."

We worked in the HAPAG office, with "Brunhilde" (we never learned her real name) for more than an hour. An enormous number of questionnaires had to be filled out; the Germans are fond of these. The slightest error or omission would mean that "Berlin" would not act on our case. We thanked her and asked how long it might take before she heard from "Berlin" on our behalf.

"You will be on the sixth list; I already received the first three lists back from Germany. You should get good news in about four weeks. God willing." She really used the German words "so Gott will."

"Brunhilde" had not said anything that could be construed as asking for a bribe; there was not even a request for a down payment. We thanked the old lady as we left the office and heard her mumble something like "this is the least I can do as a German woman."

We felt on top of the world. In four weeks we could be on our way! Even if it took a little longer, this was only early August, our American visas were good until October!

"Now you might as well start learning English," I said to Teri on the train as we traveled back to Kassa. "It looks like you might need it!" She agreed.

But why had "Brunhilde" made the prediction of terrible things to come? What did she know? How high was she in the German hierarchy? Why should all Jews be in a hurry to get out of Hungary where, until now, the summer of 1941, they had hardly been bothered? There did not seem to be any imminent danger for native, Hungarian-born Jews as far as anybody could tell. It was not until much later, after the war, that we learned of the infamous decision of early 1942 (the infamous "final solution") to let no more Jews out of Europe.

ALL JEWS WERE TO BE KILLED, WITHOUT EXCEPTION.

Starting from the west (France, the Netherlands) and progressing to the east, all Jews were to be shipped to Poland and killed there. The Nazis did just that. Only the arrival of the Russians saved the Jews of Bulgaria, a good part of those from Romania, and about half the Jews from Budapest. My wife's parents and sister were not among those saved.

Obviously, the rumors we had heard at the Jewish Community Center were true.

"Brunhilde" could indeed help us. Her promises seemed too good to be true. Furthermore, 500 Reichsmark per person was not very much money for the transportation provided; and most important, it would have been impossible for most Germans to book an airplane flight from Munich to Madrid in 1941; only diplomats or business people of high priority had the right to fly.

XVII

SURVIVAL

"Joregelt kivanok!" These sounds woke me up from a sound sleep on a couch in my father-in-law's apartment in northern Hungary. I knew about 100 words of the Hungarian language in August 1941; it seemed safe to repeat the greeting that means, "I wish you a good morning."

But as I opened my eyes I saw a policeman staring at me. What I had feared for several months had finally come to pass. I was to be arrested for being in the country as an illegal alien.

"I'm afraid you have to get dressed quickly." My father-in-law was talking to me now, in German.

"Mother already woke up Teri."

I looked at my watch: it was 5 o'clock in the morning.

"But Teri does not have to go; she is a Hungarian citizen!" I mumbled.

"The police do not think so," my father-in-law said, and I saw tears in his eyes. Teri was his oldest daughter, the apple of his eye.

"Because she is married to you she is a German now, like you."

Oh my God, I thought. I had imagined my Teri—his Teri—to be safe in her father's house. Jews had hardly been bothered so far in Hungary as long as they were Hungarian citizens. We had been married in faraway Prague two years earlier because this was the only way Teri could register with the authorities for immigration to America. As a matter of fact, we had finally received our American visas just a few weeks before our arrest, and were preparing for our departure. Somehow, the American consulate must have contacted the local police, for whatever reason. Except for my in-laws, there was nobody in all of Hungary who knew that we were married. As I got dressed, I saw that Teri, as usual, was calm.

"They'll let us go as soon as they see our American visas," she said.

My mother-in-law joined us, crying. "Why couldn't you stay in Budapest just one day longer; they wouldn't have found you there."

This was true, of course. We had just returned from Budapest, Hungary's capital, where we had made preparations for our departure. I learned later that quite a few people had been saved from being arrested that day by pretending not to be at home: The Hungarians were not very thorough at investigating.

The policeman spoke up again; somebody translated for my benefit.

"I'm sorry to do this, I have nothing against German Jews, but my orders are to get you to the local high school. And I must tell you that you should take warm clothes along, you will be transported to Siberia."

In spite of our misery, I had to laugh. The Germans had invaded Russia just two months earlier. They and their Hungarian allies could hardly be as far as Siberia yet.

An hour later we joined a group of 10 or 15 people in one of the classrooms of the high school. A few more kept coming, all carrying large suitcases. We talked and commiserated. The police had picked all up the same morning. After a while, an important-looking policeman joined us and gave us a short speech in Hungarian. I was almost the only one who did not understand him! What kind of foolishness is this, I thought? There is a score of people here whose only crime, besides being Jewish, is that they are not Hungarian. But almost all understand and speak that language; most of them were born here though their grandparents came from somewhere else.

Teri translated for me: the police officer explained that "many important people" were working for our release. We should be patient. As a matter of fact, nobody seemed to be very excited. Just the opposite: there was much laughter. A little old Jew was even giving advice to Hitler:

"He made a mistake, he should have asked me, instead of invading Russia he should have tried Italy, it's warmer there and the wine is better!"

"No," said a burly young chap, "he should have sent a few more bombers to England. When the English give up, he could use me as an interpreter. You see, I speak English. I was born in America."

He said a few words in English with an impossible Hungarian accent. Probably for my sake, much of the conversation was conducted in German.

Suddenly an old lady started to scream: "You fools, don't you realize we are all going to die in Siberia? I will never see my grandchildren again!"

Around noon sandwiches and coffee were brought in. A policeman explained that our relatives had sent them. Anyway, he said, we should not be afraid. All would be well with us. He told us we could use the washrooms of the school but only one at a time, always with a policeman waiting at the door.

During all this time, Teri kept calm, participating in neither the frenzied jokes nor in the hysterical screaming around us. At 4 o'clock in the afternoon she whispered to me:

"I only hope we can stay together. My father will do everything to get us out, but I'm afraid."

She was interrupted as the important-looking policeman who had advised patience in the morning came in. He said something. I did not have to wait for a translation because everybody got up, very quietly, and took his or her suitcase. We marched out of the school – half the town seemed to be watching us – and were loaded on a bus leaving in a northeasterly direction, towards Poland.

Teri and I were separated as soon as the bus stopped half an hour later. We didn't even have a chance to say goodbye. All men were loaded on a train and traveled another two hours.

We were not taken to Poland but rather to makeshift camps near a small Hungarian town (now Ukrainian) surrounded by beautiful wooded hills.

A Hungarian concentration camp could in no way be compared to a camp run by Germans or Austrians. There were no watchtowers, no barbed wire, and only wooden fences. We could have wandered off into the forest because only one bored policeman watched us. Actually, the men's camp I was in consisted only of a few half-finished wooden huts with straw inside. Except for fleas and bed bugs, we slept peacefully. There was a kitchen somewhere, not staffed by inmates but by old soldiers who prepared food for us, which was quite edible and enough to keep us from starving. We were not asked to work, not even to finish the buildings in the camp; being afraid of fall and winter, we'd gladly have done so.

I asked to see the commander of the camp who showed up once every few days.

He saw me, was polite (he spoke broken German with me) but showed no interest in my passport with an American visa in it.

"I have no orders about you other than to keep you here," he said. "No idea how long you'll stay here. A lot of places not many kilometers away are worse than this camp. I hope you get to America. If you do, tell the Americans that we Hungarians are good people, not like others."

We tried to organize ourselves. I was in charge of giving English lessons to beginners, but at a different time of day I took lessons from a man who knew more English than I did. We played chess on homemade boards. There was even a man who told us Bible stories and interpreted them.

Of course, we figured that we would be shipped to Poland; this had already happened to many Jews in Czechoslovakia. More important, I had not heard a word from the women's camp where my wife was interned. We were so much in love. Had she never met me, I thought, she would be safely in her father's house.

Three weeks went by. Then, on a hot day in the middle of August, I was called to see the commander of the camp. He asked me to sit down.

"I have orders to let you go," he said to me in his broken German. "Since you have an American visa, we won't hold you here any longer. Your wife is being dismissed, too. I'll even give you papers which will prevent you from being arrested again. But hurry, there is one more train out of here today, it's only 6 km to the station."

I tried to thank him but he interrupted: "Be sure to tell the Americans that we Hungarians are decent people," he said once again.

I said goodbye to my fellow inmates, packed my suitcase and ran to the railroad station. In the hot August sun, I managed to run four miles carrying that heavy suitcase! And I was lucky. Just 10 minutes later the train came and in the evening I was back in Kassa. I walked to my father-in-law's apartment and found Teri already there! She had been dismissed from the women's camp one day earlier.

(A little later we learned that all Jews who had been picked up together with us were sent home in September. There was a rumor, probably true, that Hitler had asked Miklos Horthy, the Regent of Hungary, to send all non-Hungarian Jews to Poland. Horthy, who was no doubt an anti-Semite but still a human being, informed Hitler that he'd rather have these Jews interned in Hungary. They might be needed as workers because Hitler had asked him to send all able-bodied young men, as soldiers, to the

Russian front. Later, the whole thing was forgotten and the Jews sent home.)

I was so exhausted that I could hardly kiss Teri. I fell asleep on the carpet in the living room, unable to stand or sit or to undress. But, as in a dream, I heard Teri say:

"The sixth list has arrived from Germany; we can go to America."

XVIII

A DIFFICULT DEPARTURE

It seemed so easy. In August 1941, my wife and I had our American visas, good for entry until October 1. Equally important for us, the German authorities in Berlin had sent us transit visas for travel through Germany. Being in Hungary, then completely surrounded by the fighting of World War II, this was the only possible way to the west. Together with the transit visas, we were given the complete routing and tickets, all for comparatively little money. Our route was to take us by train from Budapest to Vienna and to Munich, then by airplane across France to Madrid. Spain was neutral during the war, thus all we had to do was get transportation across the Atlantic Ocean.

We'll never know why the Nazis were so nice to us: they gave two Jews extremely scarce airplane accommodations. Now, half a century later, this seems almost unbelievable. After all, this was the second half of 1941. Just a while later, in January 1942, the infamous Wannsee Conference decided that all Jews then under the domination of the Nazis were to be killed, without exception. *(Editor's note: The Wannsee Conference was a meeting of senior officials of Nazi Germany, held in the Berlin suburb of Wannsee on January 20, 1942. The purpose of the conference was to ensure the cooperation of administrative leaders of various departments in the implementation of the final solution to the Jewish question.)*

One possible explanation for why the Nazis were helping us might have been that Germany was not yet at war with the U.S. The German foreign office might possibly have been urging their government to show the Americans that the third Reich was still a civilized country. They may have been hoping to prevent the U.S. from joining the war on the side of Great Britain.

My wife and I were in a happy mood when we presented ourselves at the Spanish consulate in Budapest to apply for transit visas. This was a minor formality, we thought. After all, being already on our way to America, we should certainly try to get there as quickly as possible. Generalissimo Franco's Spain of 1941, right after it's murderous Civil War, was hardly a place in which to linger!

A lady at the Spanish Consulate carefully looked at our family passport with the American visa.

She seemed very pleased.

"Good, you are going to America," she said in Hungarian. "And how are you planning to get to Madrid?"

My wife showed her the German documents. "I believe you will find these all perfectly in order," she said. "Aren't we lucky?"

"You certainly are! I only wish you could take me along."

A lengthy conversation in Hungarian followed. It was the kind only two ladies who like each other at first sight could carry on. My wife translated the essential portions into German for me.

"You have your ship tickets, of course?" The clerk turned to me, speaking broken German.

"Well, practically," I explained. "As soon as we get to Madrid we'll wire my brother who is in Chicago; he will then send us the tickets."

I showed her my brother's letter explaining the situation: "Since trans-Atlantic accommodations are scarce, the actual tickets will only be issued to persons already in Spain; otherwise the shipping line won't know that the prospective users will actually get there."

The lady's features, so pleasant until now, turned stern.

"I am sorry. We cannot give you a Spanish transit visa. As you know, Mr. Franco is very kind to Jews, but too many Jews are already in Spain and cannot get out. His Excellency, the Consul, has received instructions directly from the "Caudillo" (she used Mr. Franco's official title, meaning leader) not to issue any visa to Jews unless they already have ship tickets. Come back when you have them."

Nowadays we call such situations a "Catch 22." We could not get ship tickets until we reached Spain, but neither could we receive a Spanish transit visa until we had ship tickets.

I could not see any way out of our dilemma. Just to be sure, I wired my brother: "Cannot get Spanish transit visa without ship tickets." His answer came the next day: "Sorry, but you must get to Spain first."

It was my father-in-law, a man experienced in extraordinary ways to do business in Central Europe, who found a solution to our problem. He did two things:

First, he sent a wire to a travel bureau in Budapest whose owner he knew. He asked that he send a wire back to him: "Have transatlantic tickets for Mr. and Mrs. Weinmann from Spanish harbor to New York. Stop. American Express." We would later pick up the wire as proof that we had steamer tickets.

Second, he sent a letter to the lady at the Spanish consulate who had talked to us.

He sent it to her home address, which he somehow had found out. In this letter, written in especially flowery Hungarian (as my wife translated to me), he thanked her for the excellent reception and special courtesies she had extended to his children. He stressed that his children (my wife was 24 years old at the time, I was 27) were still rather inexperienced and therefore the information she had so generously given us was all the more appreciated.

In order to show his appreciation, he was taking the extraordinary liberty, for which he begged forgiveness, of sending her a bolt of the best English fabric, suitable for a fine suit. He mentioned in his letter that he had been the representative of a large English textile mill and therefore still had some material in stock. If the fabric might find favor in her eyes, he would be more than happy to send her another bolt of fabric that any good tailor could make into an overcoat, which would protect her from the harsh Hungarian winter.

My father-in-law guessed that the nice lady at the Spanish consulate might have considerable influence, in which case a little bribe, as well as the promise of more to come, might be helpful.

We allowed a few days to pass in order to make sure that the bolt of fabric had time to arrive; then we presented ourselves at the Spanish consulate once again. We decided to let my wife do the talking. I felt she'd do a much better job than I would. Furthermore, the lady was obviously more comfortable speaking Hungarian rather than German. As soon as we saw her, we could guess from the special look she gave us, that my father-in-law's fabric had indeed found favor in her eyes.

My wife handed her the fake telegram, which we had picked up at the travel agency. She also made a speech I did not understand. In no language I know of can one express oneself as politely as in Hungarian. The lady looked at the wire, turned it over, put it on her desk, looked at me, looked at my wife, then said to her in a low voice:

"Az semi."

I knew just enough Hungarian to understand what this meant: "This is nothing."

The three of us just stood there. I looked at my wife; my heart skipped a beat. After a long, long time, in reality probably only 10 seconds, the lady turned to me. She was breathing hard.

"I'll take this "telegram" (the tone of her voice made quite clear what she thought of it) to the consul anyway. I think His Excellency is having a good day today. Maybe, just maybe. Give me your passport."

She disappeared through a door leading into another office. We sat down on a bench, holding hands. Oh God, I thought, what will happen now?

She came back in no time, holding our passport over her head, smiling at us:

"His Excellency signed your visa! He was doing something important; I said to him: 'just sign here' and he did! Congratulations."

Teri thanked her in Hungarian as I did in German. Then I added for good luck:

"Muchas gracias." Yes, the lady got the second bolt of fabric.

It was early September 1941 now, and our American visas were good until the end of that month. Certainly, we had no time to waste! First, a wire to my brother giving him the good news and asking him to get in touch with us at American Express in Madrid. Then a trip to HAPAG, the German office that had procured the transportation to Madrid, asking them to fill in the actual day of our flight from Munich to Madrid. We wanted it to be as soon as possible, of course. This, I believed, would be the last possibility for trouble, at least until we reached Spain. But everything went smoothly: our departure date was set for September 15: an early morning train to Vienna, then to Munich overnight, leaving that city for the "flight to the west" on the afternoon of September 16.

It was in Budapest, right after I had picked up the train and flight tickets, that I had a strange adventure. I was alone. My wife had more than enough to do to get our suitcases packed. My immediate task was to cross a fairly busy street in order to get to the railroad station for our trip back to Kassa where my in-laws were living. But I could not muster the courage to leave the safety of the sidewalk in order to cross the street! I was sure some vehicle would hit me. I told myself how crazy this fear was; even violently bit my lip just to make sure I was not dreaming. But it was no use. No, I was not dreaming. Yes, I was afraid to cross.

There must be a way out, I thought, and finally I hit on the solution to wait for an old lady, as frail-looking as possible. Then, when she would cross, I would attach myself to her. If she made it to the other side of the street, so would I.

As luck would have it, within a few minutes a lady showed up carrying a cane, barely able to walk. I pretended to help her and once safely on the other side I thanked her, feeling both silly and relieved. To the best of my knowledge, this is the first time I have ever told anybody about this incident.

I had good news from my parents, who were still living in Prague: there was a good possibility of them getting to Cuba. The dictator of that island nation may have been guilty of many misdeeds, but for $5,000 per person, a Cuban visa could be had. My brother's financial abilities seemed to be endless, though I knew that he could not possibly have a penny to his name. He had come to the United States only three years earlier! Only much later did I learn that his (and later also my) boss gave him practically unlimited credit. For this he got my brother's loyalty, which transcended any employer – employee relationship. He also got my brother's knowledge as well as his ability to work endless hours.

Just a few days were left for my wife to be together with her parents and younger sister; I tried to give them as much time as possible alone. But we took the meals together, of course, and one evening I said to no one in particular:

"Wouldn't it be wonderful if all of us could start a new life in the United States?" I was not prepared for what followed. My father-in-law, always the mild-mannered, accommodating man who loved me like the son he never had, and who had always helped me, turned on me, screaming:

"How dare you say such a thing! Not enough that you take my older daughter away to a strange, foreign country; now you want me to leave my homeland too! Everybody knows me here; I am an honorable man! Do you want me and my family to be beggars somewhere in America?"

This proud, good-looking man, well over six feet tall, started crying. It is easy to psychoanalyze him now, with hindsight. Not only would he never see his elder daughter again, but also this highly intelligent man knew in his heart how precarious his own situation was. Not to be able to provide for or protect his family was intolerable for him.

All I could do at that moment, with the whole family sitting down at dinner while the maid was serving us, was to go to my father-in-law and embrace him.

"Please forgive me, I am so sorry I hurt your feelings; you know best what to do."

Of course, we made up immediately. But after that outburst, I was very, very careful about how I spoke to my father-in-law. I have often blamed myself for that. Perhaps it still would have been possible for him to save his family; they all had Hungarian passports, they might have been able to fly to Italy. Later, when we definitely learned that Teri's family had perished, my wife told me not to blame myself.

"No, my father would never have agreed to be a fugitive, a refugee. Not for the loss of money: he had enough self-confidence to think he could always make money. It was his pride. Do you know," she asked me, "what hurt my parents more than anything else? That they could not give me a dowry to help us start our new life in America."

Of course, it was impossible to take money out of Europe. At the last moment, we were advised by the Jewish community center in Budapest that we were indeed allowed to take with us something like the equivalent of $20 (figured at the purchasing power of the 1900s, not 1941) in Hungarian currency. That might get us a room in a cheap hotel in Madrid for one night. Furthermore, we were allowed to buy $10 in actual American currency! We could hardly believe it. Five, two dollar bills, looking as if the ancestors of the Hungarians had brought them along under the saddle of their horses when they came riding from Asia. Two dollar bills were as uncommon in 1941 as they are now. When my American relatives saw two of them (three precious bills had been changed in Madrid) they wondered how come we'd already had time to go to the races!

Other than precious metal, jewelry, works of art or other valuables, there were no restrictions on personal belongings that we could take with us, as long as we only had one suitcase per person.

"We have to be able to carry our suitcases ourselves," my wife explained to her mother, who wanted to give her too much.

"But all the beautiful towels," my mother-in-law complained, "the pillowcases I had made for you! How can you show to your new relatives in Chicago what kind of house you come from?"

Finally, we decided to take one towel and one pillowcase along. They haven't been used since, and I cannot convince my daughters to take them.

The day of our departure soon came. My father-in-law insisted on accompanying us to Budapest. He even boarded the express train to Vienna with us, staying until the first stop. Other than to send our love to Teri's mother and sister, we did not speak, not one word, until he was ready to get off the train. We all felt sure that we would not see each other again.

We had taken sandwiches and cookies along, which kept us going for almost a week. Arriving in Vienna in the late afternoon, we left our suitcases at the station and went for a long walk. The last time I had seen this city had been more than three years earlier when huge banners were greeting "The Fuehrer." Then, everybody who was not Jewish had been wearing a swastika. Nobody did now. Vienna looked a little shabby; one could see few young or even middle-aged men. We slowly returned to the station. I felt no attachment to the city I had once loved and believed to be the only place on earth where one could live.

We arrived in Munich early in the morning. A city bus, fare included in the airplane tickets, was to take us to the airport in mid-afternoon. So, why shouldn't we look at the famous Hofbrau House?

It still amazes me how carefree we were, but it's just impossible to keep two young people down. Neither of us had ever been to Munich before; we enjoyed ourselves looking at all the beer drinkers.

At the airport, our suitcases were supposed to be checked for any valuables we might take out of Hitler's Reich. It had been suggested to us that we sew gold coins into our overcoats, or put diamonds into the heels of our shoes, but we decided against it. Once in America, we had no doubt that we'd make a living, so why take chances?

I have often been asked whether we did not mind leaving "everything" behind? No, not at all, unless "everything" included the people I loved. As it happened, we could have packed the crown jewels of Hungary in our suitcases; nobody paid any attention to us. A policeman waved us through and wished us a happy journey.

It was a strange feeling, sitting in the small airplane, surrounded by German high officers and important-looking businessman. We were the only Jews onboard, of course. Teri was the only female passenger. Until the last moment I was afraid we might be ordered off the plane, but everything went smoothly. A few hours later, as the sun was already sinking, we saw Barcelona and the blue Mediterranean below us. Never in our lives had we seen anything so beautiful. We were in the "West."

It was already dark when we arrived in Madrid. For one of our two-dollar bills, a friendly cab driver agreed to take us to a hotel downtown which was "muy barato" (very cheap). We stayed there for seven days because the next morning, at American Express, there was a letter from my brother containing five $20 bills. We were rich. Otherwise, the news was mixed. We should present ourselves at an agency of a Spanish steamship line; they would "do their best" to get us transatlantic passages.

The "agency" turned out to be a one-room office; a friendly Dutchman who spoke perfect English took care of us.

"Welcome, welcome. I have many wires from your brother; he really worries about you. I only wish I had somebody like that in America. Anyway, we'll take care of you."

"Yes, soon," I replied. "Our American visas expire in a couple of weeks and the consul in Budapest told us there is no renewal."

"Please, don't worry. First, it does not matter when your visa expires as long as you are on a ship before it does. And I am almost sure I will get you on a ship; your brother guaranteed all financial arrangements. Believe me, we are the best brokers in Spain."

He sent us home and promised to call us at our hotel as soon as he had good news. He told us that in the meantime we should look at the Prado, the famous museum. "Of course, as soon as I call you, you must leave immediately." We did not feel very good about this agency; obviously, they were scalpers who bought unused ship tickets and sold them at high prices. As far as the Dutchman was concerned, the "guaranteed financial arrangements" were the main thing. In other words, my brother had asked him to get us on the ship at any cost.

There was really nothing we could do except try to enjoy ourselves in Madrid.

After all, we wouldn't come back very soon! We visited the Prado, certainly one of the most beautiful museums in the world. Otherwise, Madrid looked terrible. We saw many bullet holes dating from the civil war that Spain had suffered a few years earlier. Unfortunately, the sandwiches we had brought from Hungary were soon eaten up; food was rationed in Madrid and we, being foreigners, had no food stamps. When we asked the lady who ran our hotel for advice, she had a good suggestion: "Shrimp. You can buy them at the street vendors. Very nourishing."

For almost a week we lived on shrimp. To this day, I cannot look at shrimp, but they kept us alive then.

An adventure I had in Madrid again proved to me that "the female is the stronger of the human species." One day when I was rather hot we were going for a walk. I carried my jacket over my arm. Suddenly it became too heavy for me to carry and the sun too bright for me to see anything. I'd have fallen down if my wife had not caught me. The strain of waiting for the ship tickets had become too much for me, but she carried on.

Then, on September 21, 1941, on my wife's 25th birthday, we received "the call."

"I have your tickets, but you must hurry. I booked a first-class compartment on the night train to Bilbao for you. The ship *Magallanes,* with you on board, will sail tomorrow morning at 9 o'clock."

When I picked up the tickets at the agency, I asked for the price.

"One thousand dollars each, including the train. I know that's a lot of money, but ship tickets to America are scarce nowadays."

I blushed. My brother was well paid; he proudly informed us of all the raises he got: he made $60 per week, a lot of money for 1941. But $2,000 was much more than half of his yearly income, and furthermore he'd have to pay for our parents. (My parents did indeed get to Cuba just a few weeks before Pearl Harbor, after which all transatlantic passenger travel stopped. We could still talk to our father on the telephone before he died, of a stroke, in March 1942. Our mother joined us in Chicago a few months later.)

I never repaid my brother, nor did I offer to do so. That would have been an insult, I believe. To have brought his family to America by himself, in 1941, away from certain death in Europe, should forever be to his credit.

The ship tickets were in our pockets. For the first time, we had good reason to believe that we'd really get to America, away from the war. We'd leave the uncertainty that being unprotected by any law brings with it. Soon, we'd be able to walk on the street, sleep in a bed, eat, breathe, without the strong possibility that somebody – more likely than not connected with the government – might arrest us, even kill us.

After all, the Spain of Generalissimo Franco was as much a police state as was Germany. All one had to do was to look at the ruined buildings, the lack of food, the listless people to know it!

The train ride from Madrid to Bilbao proved to us again that there was danger all around us. At midnight scores of policemen boarded the train, and many passengers were forcibly taken off, but not from our car which had only first-class compartments. Our travel agent who had booked us in the first-class section had obviously done the right thing.

Getting off the train in Bilbao, we had two new observations.

"The names of the stores are in a strange language, not in Spanish," said Teri. "Now we really can't…"

"Of course, this is Basque country. Look: Banca Guepuckao," I read. "But I'll bet they'll give us a few pesetas for American dollars anyway." Even stranger than the language: never had I seen so many beautiful women.

"I'm glad you're coming back to life; for a long time, you did not notice anything. But you are right," Teri admitted. "They are beautiful. Anyway, look all you want, in an hour we'll be gone."

(A few months later in Chicago, an FBI agent tried to interrogate me about the harbor of Bilbao: how large, how many ships, easy or difficult to get in or out? I would like to have helped, but all I could remember was a strange language and beautiful women.)

One last moment of fear before we boarded the ship: would the Spanish policeman who looked at our passport notice that our American visas were due to expire before we got to New York? He certainly did, but his reaction was interesting:

"Be sure you don't get off the ship when she docks in Cuba, not even for one minute. If you do, the Cubans will send you back here to Spain! We really don't want you right now! I wish you a very good journey."

We had not been aware that our good ship *Magallanes* would stop in Cuba. As it happened, one month later, my parents would be on the same ship, on its next and last trip, on their way to Cuba also.

The ship looked big to us. We had never been on an ocean liner before. Only later did we learn that ships that cross the Atlantic don't come much smaller. The first thing we noticed were huge Spanish flags painted on both sides of the ship and also on the deck.

"The German submarines respect our flag; they should not take us for Englishmen," said a purser who gave us a list of the passengers.

There were four pages. The first two contained the names of all those traveling first class to Cuba and to New York. The third page, by far the longest list, contained the names of all those other than first class headed for Cuba. And the fourth page: the passengers to New York. But our names were not among them.

The steward conducted my wife to the ladies' section and me to the men's. There were eight bunks in the small cabin. I inquired and was shown the page of the first-class section. Sure enough, there we were: *Senor y Senora Francisco y Teresa Weinmann*. It seemed the second class had sixteen passengers to the cabin, the third several dozen. But when it came to eating, we first-class passengers were seated at separate tables and served decent food on porcelain plates, with silver cutlery on white tablecloths.

And my brother is paying for this, I thought!

We soon learned that our ship was not big at all, but small, old and slow. It would take two weeks to La Habana, Cuba, and then another week to New York. Our shipmates consisted of three distinct groups: Spanish businessman who all traveled first class but who had paid, as I later found out when I became friendly with one of them, a small fraction of the horrendous price charged my brother. Then there were a number of Jews with many children who came from Belgium or Holland. How they got to Spain I never found out. They spoke Dutch or Yiddish and obviously did not want to have anything to do with us. I'm pretty sure they took us for German spies. As a matter of fact, we were the only German-speaking passengers. Finally, by far the largest group consisted of Basques emigrating from Spain. They were all women. My Spanish was not good enough for long conversations, but luckily, we found out that many of them spoke French. My wife and I befriended a 19-year-old girl, beautiful, as were all the Basques.

"How come we don't see any of your men?" we asked her. "You must have brothers, husbands, fathers…"

"Hush," she interrupted and looked around to make sure that none of the ship's crew could hear us. "Our men are not allowed to emigrate. But many of them are waiting for us in Cuba; from there we will travel together to Venezuela, Ecuador, or Colombia."

"But how did they get out?"

Again, she looked around before she answered. "Sometimes they went fishing and forgot to come back home. You know, we Basques are not afraid of the sea. Once in England, they made it across."

As far as the Basques are concerned, the civil war in Spain, which lasted for many years during the 1930's and was certainly fought as bitterly as any war, was not yet over.

On the second day of our trip across the ocean, Teri remembered a silent promise she had made to herself without ever telling me.

"Now I want to learn English. Let's begin. I have no time to lose."

Was it a superstition, a fear to tempt fate that prevented Teri from studying English earlier? She was quite a linguist: perfect in Hungarian. She also had no foreign accent in Czech or in Slovakian, especially difficult for very similar languages (this is like an American being able to speak like somebody from Georgia or from Maine and be judged a native in both states).

Besides, she could speak and read German and French well enough. And now English! Her progress was unbelievably fast. (Within a few weeks, she was able to follow easy conversations; a few months later, she read newspapers. Her best language teacher was the actress Irene Dunne: she would see the movie *The Naked Truth* over and over again and tried, successfully, to imitate Dunne's way of speaking. Within a few years, she had less of a foreign accent than I did. And my daughters claim she had none.)

We had a smooth crossing of the Atlantic until the day before we were supposed to land in Cuba. Then came a message from the captain:

"There is a hurricane south of Florida; we will do our best to stay out of its way, but it may not be possible. I want you to have a second drill for the lifeboats immediately!"

We'd had our first drill the day we boarded the ship, but nobody took that one very seriously. Now, this was another matter! We still could not believe it; the weather was still sunny and warm. But the captain's weather report was unfortunately quite accurate. Soon, heavy clouds were racing across the sky and huge waves came from out of nowhere. But there was still no rain. I stood on deck, firmly leaning against the railing, watching our ship bounce up-and-down.

I did not believe a word about rumors we could be in real danger. Then suddenly I heard a scream. I turned around just in time to catch an old lady who came flying across the deck. I put my arms around her and held her firmly. She was hysterical until somebody took her off my hands. Had I not been standing where I happened to be and grabbed her, she would not have fallen into the sea, but would have bounced hard onto the railing. The next day the lady's daughter, one of the Basque girls, screamed all over the ship in Spanish and in French, pointing at me:

"He is a hero! He saved my mother!"

For years afterwards, Teri would kid me and call me the "Mother Savior." But at the time of the hurricane, when it really hit us, nobody felt like joking. It was raining hard now, even through the windows of the dining room. Nobody ate. We could see huge waves practically on top of us. Then our ship seemed to stand on a mountain of water, and we stared into nothing. Of course, we were afraid, everybody was, we'd never get into the lifeboats if the ship started to sink; so much for the drill!

"There are big sharks in these waters," a friendly man who sat at our table advised us. "No outside help could come in time."

Teri and I looked at each other with tears in our eyes. Was it possible that we had come this far, only to die now? But no, we agreed, God would not do this to us. Whether it was our trust in God or the skill of the captain that saved us, I'll never know.

Anyway, the next morning the weather was beautiful when we sailed into La Habana. Most of the passengers got off and that made it possible for Teri and I to move together into an empty cabin. As sorry as we were that we'd never see the beauty of Cuba except from aboard ship, we finally had the opportunity to be alone. That was more important for us then all the palm trees of La Habana.

On October 12, 1941, Columbus Day, we arrived in New York. The Statue of Liberty was there to greet us from far away. Being first-class passengers, we were never examined when we got off the ship. The clerk who looked at our expired visas just said:

"Welcome to this country. You made it just in time."

Indeed, we got a grand welcome. My aunt and my cousin from Vienna met us (they were American veterans who had been in this country for over two years). The New York salesman from the company my brother was working for also greeted us. He was an impressive looking man who obviously knew his way around; I guess my brother did not trust anybody but a "real American" to guide us.

Unfortunately, I had a little difficulty understanding him. Not only did he talk very fast, he had a strange accent I had never heard before. He was from Brooklyn.

My brother insisted that we should stay in New York for a few days to enjoy the beauties of that city before coming to Chicago to work. He even rented a room for us for a few days.

Obediently we spent all our energies sightseeing from early morning to late evening. To me, New York looked exactly like the picture postcards I had seen many times before, so why waste our time? Only when big brother insisted we see the "Rockettes" at Radio City Music Hall, did we doubt his wisdom just a little bit. We must look at a bunch of scantily dressed girls raising first one leg and then the other, always with a stupid grin on their faces?

Then came the long train ride to Chicago. We had been instructed to get off in Englewood, just one stop before Union Station. Being afraid to miss the stop, I turned to a friendly porter, a big black man:

"Would you please be kind enough to tell us before we get to Englewood? We are supposed to get off there."

He answered. But I did not understand one word except, "SHORE."

What kind of a shore did he mean? Lake Michigan, perhaps? And then a great fear overcame me: if everybody in Chicago talked like this man, how would it be with me at work, all my diligent studying of the English language for nothing!

I need not have worried. Before we got to Englewood the friendly man gave us another big speech. Obviously, he had understood me – laughed and took our suitcases.

Our train slowed down. I saw my brother running along the track, grinning like the full moon when he saw us. He had not changed much during the three years we had not seen each other. He only looked a little fatter to me.

XIX

WE WERE NEVER POOR

"This is your apartment!" my brother Charles said to us.

"Can we afford it?" Teri and I wondered, asking in unison.

"Yes, you can," my brother answered. "I paid the rent for the first month, of course. But by December 1st, you'll have your first paychecks. By the way, the rent is $40 per month including all utilities."

Teri and I looked at each other. We had been married since late October 1939 and this was November 1941. For the first time, we'd have our own place.

"I'll leave you now, unpack, make yourselves at home," Charles said. "If you need anything, ask the hotel manager. There is a telephone on the table."

Our apartment, in the west side Chicago neighborhood of Austin, consisted of a large room, about 15 by 15 feet. But one of the corners was occupied by a tiny kitchen containing a gas stove, a small refrigerator, a sink, and shelves with pots, pans, drinking glasses, plates and silverware. Two interior doors fenced off the opposite corner of the room. Inside were a shower stall, a sink, a toilet and a stool. In the middle of our place stood a table and two chairs. What made the room look so large to our European-trained eyes was the absence of a chest of drawers. But there were two closets, more than large enough to accommodate all of our belongings. We couldn't believe our eyes. Such luxury! A window on one side of the room allowed us to see the outside, actually the feet of passersby, because our room, as we soon learned, was called an "English Basement." One had to step down a few stairs from the main floor.

We unpacked. Suddenly Teri called out: "You'd better call the manager. They forgot to give us a bed! But wait, maybe it's hidden behind this large door we haven't opened yet!"

Sure enough, there was a bed indeed! Only it was in the vertical position. In order to open it, we had to reach up and bend it down to the floor. It all worked perfectly well. The bed was now close to the corner containing the bathroom.

"They have it all figured out, these clever Americans!" Teri said. Of course, we had to move the table and the chairs in order to make room for the bed. The room looked rather crowded now. But then, we needed the bed only at night. So, having five dollars in our pockets (a gift from Charles, "the last money you'll need from me" he had said when we tried to thank him), we felt very, very rich. This was on a Tuesday. The next Monday we'd both start working in our new jobs, we hoped.

Teri knew just what kind of job she would be looking for.

"I can sew. There must be people who need alterations. We'll try 'ladies clothing' in the department stores."

So, the next morning we started to look, but there was one slight hitch: our conversations, so far, had been in German. In German, a department store is called a "warenhaus." I translated: "a warenhaus must be a warehouse." After much asking around in the commercial center of Chicago, called the "Loop," we were directed to a street that indeed contained warehouses, not department stores. It was late afternoon when we detected our mistake, but we were dead tired and decided on a different approach: we'd look at the "help wanted" ads in the newspaper.

"They want power sewing machine operators not far from us, within walking distance, do you want to try?" Luckily, Charles had left us a map of Chicago.

Well, Teri was in luck. The factory where she applied for a job was situated in a Czech neighborhood. Teri was hired because she could easily communicate with the forelady who was Czech. She was to start the next day. Later, Teri discovered the most likely reason why she'd gotten the job: most of the machine operators were black; the forelady was glad to see a white face.

"All I can say is that they didn't fire me," Teri told me when she came home the next day. "They should have; I didn't know what I was doing. These sewing machines are not at all like the ones I had at home. They run awfully fast and make a lot of noise. I had to undo some of the work I had done. Luckily, the forelady was very patient. But tomorrow I'll do a better job!"

Indeed, she did, because Teri was "invited" to join the I.L.G.W.U., the International Ladies Garment Workers Union, which guaranteed her the minimum wage of 35 cents an hour, or $14 per week minus small deductions. She kept the job for half a year or so and always cherished her union card. (After she died in 1975, we found this card in a little box together with some of her favorite souvenirs.)

As for me, I was to be paid $25 per week, a good starting salary for a laboratory assistant, which I was soon to become at my brother's company.

After all, this was still before America entered World War II and the Depression wasn't really over yet.

Our total income was more than adequate. Almost $39 per week. Expenses, all calculated per week: rent $10; transportation to work (a streetcar ride cost seven cents), $2; food (a dollar a day) $7. Incidentals, including entertainment, etc., $3. Altogether only $22 against an income almost seventeen dollars higher!

In order to compare these 1941 figures with the value of money at the beginning of the 21st-century, one should use a factor of 20. The rent would thus correspond to $800 per month. Food for two would be $20 per day and so on. Of course, no provision for clothing or health at all. By the way, one of the figures mentioned above needs a little elaboration: "Incidentals, including entertainment, etc."

What does the "etc." stand for? Allow me to explain. Every evening we pulled down our "Murphy Bed" (that's what it was called). For the first time in our married life, we had our own bed! But we had to be so careful. In Prague, in 1939, we had been careless with disastrous consequences, resulting in an abortion. We didn't want that to happen again! But when I asked in a drugstore for a "rubber," nobody knew what I was talking about. Only after I asked my brother for help, (he, after all being a veteran of three years' life in America) did I get what I needed: condoms.

"Entertainment" consisted of going to the movies as often as possible, always beating the 6:30 deadline when the admission price changed from 17 cents. We saw every film playing in our neighborhood theaters, some more than once. One, *The Awful Truth*, starring Cary Grant and Irene Dunne, we may have seen five times.

"I want to talk like Irene Dunne," Teri said. "She speaks so clearly. I can understand every world she's saying!"

Well, paying 17 cents for an hour and a half of excellent language teachers—nobody could beat that!

"After all, I was sent to a Slovakian school when I was 10 years old," Teri continued. "I didn't know a word of the language and I managed. English is easier."

We also listened to a little radio my brother had given us: news, soap operas, everything. It took us less than a year after we landed in America to switch from speaking German together to speaking English. Since Teri knew so many languages (Hungarian, Slovakian, Czech, French, German) nobody could place her accent. Some called it French, some Swedish. Many of our friends couldn't hear any foreign accent at all.

My knowledge of the English language had been quite good for a greenhorn. I had studied with a British teacher when I was 16 and 17 years old and started to read English books and newspapers soon afterwards. In 1939 and 1940 I even made a little money giving English lessons! But Teri had refused to even look at an English grammar book while we were still in Europe. Superstition? Probably.

"If we ever get to America, I'll learn," she had told me repeatedly. She was right. We landed in America on the 12th of October (Columbus Day), 1941, and by November 1st, we "had it made," we felt. Teri already had a job; I started to work at the laboratory of the "American Decalcomania Company" on the first Monday of the month.

"What would I do, what can I do?" I asked my brother who would be my immediate boss.

"Don't worry," he said, "I have work prepared for you."

Indeed, he had, although I realized soon that what I was doing was "make work," not real work. In other words, what I was doing didn't need to be done. But who was I to argue? My task: measure the viscosity of paints, before and after adding various thinners, actually a good way of introducing me to the materials I'd have to work with later. I was given a white laboratory coat; everybody in the lab wore one. Besides my brother, my co-workers consisted of Burt (we would become good friends later), whose specialty was adhesives, and Maxi, a young man of somewhat limited intelligence, but of unlimited adoration for my brother. His function was to keep the lab clean, wash all the glassware. He told me: "I know when 'Doc' is through with an experiment: when every single beaker and flask and tube is dirty and he says: 'Maxi, start washing.'"

"Doc," of course, was my brother. Maxi tried to call me "Doc" too, but I explained to him that I had no Ph.D.

"Well, a Master's degree is pretty good too," Maxi said. I didn't know what to say, so I just smiled. My problem: I had no idea what a "Master's degree" was and certainly didn't have one, nor a Bachelor's degree. I did finish high school but couldn't even prove that! For many years to come, I would feel like a fraud, calling myself a chemist but having no diploma.

At noon on my first day of work, Charles (nobody called him by his first name, only "Doc") introduced me to the owner of the factory, Mr. Eisenberg. I was to thank him for everything he had done to "bring me over." I had a little speech well-rehearsed of course and the Big Boss shook my hand and said: "Frank, if you are anything like your brother, you'll pay me back with good work."

I promised to do my best. "Well, you're speaking good English," Mr. Eisenberg said. I wasn't sure if that was a compliment or not. As I had already noticed, many immigrants regarded my rather fluent English with suspicion. After all, their parents' English was usually poor.

There was a special relationship between my brother and Mr. Eisenberg, the sole owner of American Decalcomania Company. It had started soon after Charles got a job there as a chemist in late 1938. Both Mr. Eisenberg and Charles told me the same story:

"Doc, I think I'm getting a royal screwing from my suppliers," Mr. Eisenberg had said. "You say you're a paint chemist. I'm buying a lot of paints. Do I pay a fair price? Find out!"

A week later Charles reported back: "They don't overcharge you, there's too much competition. But we could save you at least half the cost."

"How?" Mr. Eisenberg asked.

"We" (Charles never said "I") can make the paints right here. After we get a paint mill and mixers, all you have to buy are the raw materials."

That's just what happened. Charles saved the company a huge amount of money.

A month or two later, Charles mustered all his courage and asked Mr. Eisenberg to co-sign the "Affidavit of Support" for his younger brother and his wife; after all, Charles was a penniless refugee himself. Mr. Eisenberg also gave Charles a huge loan to pay for our ship tickets as well as those for our parents, to be paid back in monthly installments. I never asked Charles whether I should pay him back or even how much money was involved. That would have been an insult!

Decals, also called "transfers," are essentially prints on special paper, a temporary surface, to be transferred to their final surface by our customers. The decal may be as small as a tax stamp for a wine bottle or as big as a decoration for a large truck. Well, we made our own paint at the time I was hired. Soon I was involved in color matching and writing of formulas. That was easy for me. After all, I had done that in our father's factory in Czechoslovakia.

XX

A GREENHORN'S THANKSGIVING

"Meet cousin Edith. Meet cousin Jack. Meet cousin Lilly. Meet cousin Dick. Meet cousin Marie."

The introductions continued for quite a while. There must have been two dozen cousins in the room and all seemed to be talking at the same time. My brother, a veteran of three years in America, had warned us.

"You'll think you are in a zoo, but on the wrong side of the bars. Somehow, you'll live through it. This is a command performance."

This was November, 1941 and our extended Chicago family was celebrating Thanksgiving as it had for many years. But for my wife and myself it was a new experience. We had come to this country only two months earlier and felt very rich, since we both had jobs already! And we knew a lot: when asked how we liked America, the correct answer was, "I do not like it. I love it!"

Then came the next question: how was it in Europe? They've had war there since 1939, for more than two years, so how did you get out? We had been cautioned not to go into any details. It was no use.

Nobody really wanted to know that our main problem was not getting out, but rather how to get in, into the U.S.A. or to any other place. Whoever asked us about the "Old Country" was sure to be too preoccupied to listen. If he was a Gentile, it was because he did not care very much: if a Jew, because he felt guilty for not having done enough to bring others to America. Actually, my wife had it easier than I about not talking too much. Her English was very poor. I spoke the language fairly well.

Our first feelings, when we had seen the Statue of Liberty as our ship sailed into New York Harbor, were actually mixed. Gratitude, of course: our odyssey of three years had come to an end. We were "here" now. This was the land we had been trying to reach and much more often than not it seemed to be impossible. But from now on, no more suffering; no more waiting in hiding. Real life was ahead and we were both young, in our twenties! We should have been very happy, and happy we were.

But...yes, there was a "but," a feeling of emptiness brought on by fulfillment. For three years we had so longed for this moment, never quite believing it could come, certainly not daring to think beyond it. What could one do if the vague vision that had kept one alive becomes a reality? After redemption, is there still hope?

How could we forget our loved ones who stayed behind? And how about the strong warning not to "spread rumors," not to report bad news. Maybe the Statue of Liberty was best viewed from the ocean, from the outside. Well, now here we were at Thanksgiving dinner.

Soon I found out that it was a good idea to talk mostly to elderly lady cousins. The cousins of our own generation seemed to be only interested in football. I did not understand this game; it took me a while to find out that football was not necessarily played with the foot and that the ball was not really a ball, as I had known it. I thought all balls were round. And the players do not like to play with this ball! Rather, they hang onto it, mostly selfishly, as long as the opposition will let them. After a while, the room we were in seemed to become too small for all the noise; I felt queasy and wished I were somewhere else.

"You cannot leave yet," said my brother, who must have read my thoughts. "The Thanksgiving meal will come now; we are here to eat, don't forget!"

I realized that the strong odor of food mixed with cigar smoke, had something to do with my queasy feeling.

"All into the dining room!" Cousin Marie commanded. My wife and I, preceded and followed by assorted relatives, squeezed into the dining room and looked at several long, narrow tables of various heights covered with a collection of white and near-white tablecloths and many large trays of food. Collapsible metal chairs were already set up, but so tightly that they almost touched each other. When we sat down behind our name plates, my wife whispered to me:

"Are we not lucky to still have our slim European war figures?"

The relatives sitting next to us on both sides were not so fortunate and spread out towards us.

Elbows sticking into our sides made eating difficult but, luckily, not impossible. The food was excellent: typically American, we were told; it had much to do with native Indian food. There was turkey and cranberries, which we had eaten before, but also sweet potatoes (delicious) and pumpkin pie (too spicy) which were new to us. And besides these goodies, a lot of other dishes were served. Probably thanks to the common heritage of our cousins and us, they tasted familiar: distinctly Central European, specifically Bohemian. The dumplings were good enough to be served in any restaurant in Prague or Vienna, or even by my mother!

Unfortunately, there was too much conversation during the dinner, we would have preferred to concentrate on eating. The shouting across the tables made us a little nervous. We had to answer all kinds of questions about our trip across the Atlantic (yes, we were seasick), about our three-day stay in New York City, about conditions in the "Old Country." Nobody really listened to the answers; there was too much noise in the dining room.

One of my elderly lady cousins shouted over to us from the next table that she would pick us up next Sunday in order to show us the city of Chicago. My wife smiled politely and consented, no doubt hoping that I would explain to her later what our good cousin had said. But I had a problem with the words "pick up." The context of the sentence clearly indicated that she would call for us in our one-room apartment.

But to "pick up," I thought, meant to stoop down, grasp an object or, better still, a person who needs help, and lift it up. In order to be picked up, one has to be down. But, I thought, my dearest rich cousin, whose excellent food we are eating, don't you understand? We are not down now. Where were you, cousins dear, when we were really down, way down, and desperately in need of help? A simple letter from you, called an "Affidavit of Support," a strictly formal letter, would indeed have helped us immensely. I had asked for such a letter, which could have made the difference between life and death to us. Why did we have to wait until my brother, himself a new immigrant, was financially able to send such a letter to us?

Perhaps you, all my dear rich cousins, were afraid that my wife and I might eat too much of your good food?

Coffee was served. Then cousin Dick, a wealthy doctor, rose up, banged his crystal wine glass with a silver dessert fork in order to get attention, and gave thanks to the Lord for the wonderful country He gave us to live in. A country so different from war-torn Europe, from which two newly-found cousins had just arrived. Everybody applauded. This called for a gracious reply, I thought, especially since all the cousins were looking at us. So, I rose up from my cramped position at the table and gave thanks: first, to the good Lord above and second, to my brother, who had worked so hard to get us to this wonderful country; an extremely difficult task for him since he had to do it all by himself.

All my cousins must have thought that I delivered a good speech; I got much applause. Soon, all of us got up from the table, or rather tables, and stretched. My wife whispered to me:

"Can we go home now, please? Tomorrow is a working day; I'll have to lift all these heavy coats at the factory."

Cousin Marie must have read her mind. She shouted: "There is much work to do now, cousins!"

What now, I wondered silently.

Again, cousin Marie took charge. "The first three girls and three boys to the kitchen, aprons and towels are prepared! Two more clear the table of the dishes! And you," she pointed at my wife and me, "might as well also go into the kitchen and watch; learn how to do it, become Americanized!"

Sure enough, three "girls," aged 32 to 68, donned aprons and started to wash dishes. Three "boys," including the doctor, took towels and dried. Marie put herself in charge of putting the dishes away.

Somehow it worked. There was not too much confusion. Fifteen minutes later a new crew took over, this time including my wife and myself. Afterwards, a third crew finished the job.

"Cousin Marie is certainly a good manager," I said to my wife as we were walking home. "She knows how to make us cousins work and get the job done. But could she not have hired help for the occasion?"

"Don't you see," my wife answered, "after two generations in America, they are still Bohemians. They will not spend a penny unless they must."

A few days later, during a business meeting on December 1, 1941 I was asked about the war in Europe. Before I could answer, a potential customer interrupted me:

"You realize of course, young man, that we Americans are already in this war. We are in it as deeply as can be."

I thought it prudent to get a bad attack of coughing. I did not want to tell this chap what war was really like.

XXI

NO WAR ON THE HOME FRONT

On the first of December, 1941, we received very good news: my parents were on the way to Cuba! For $500 each (courtesy of Mr. Eisenberg, of course) my mother and my father had received visas to Cuba. The Nazis granted exit visas to all Jews who could prove that they would leave the Third Reich forever to a destination not in Europe. (We'll never know what made the Nazis do that, but it is a fact that just a few weeks before the infamous "Wannsee Conference" in January 1942, when it was decided that all Jews in Europe were to be killed, emigration of Jews was still in favor.) My parents arrived in Havana just in time!

We all know what happened on December 7, 1941.

Some events are so important that we remember forever what we did, where we were, who was with us when they happened; certainly, the bombing of Pearl Harbor is one of them. Of course, we had read in the newspaper that Germany, and even more so Japan, could be enemies in a declared war. But even at the moment a high-ranking Japanese special ambassador was in Washington talking to our Secretary of State. Surely, the two gentlemen wouldn't waste their time if there were no hope for peace. On the other hand, Hitler was more likely to attack us, so we thought. A few German submarines in New York, Boston, Philadelphia or even on the Potomac River in Washington could do a lot of damage.

On that Sunday, Teri and I were sitting at our table in our Chicago apartment listening to a beautiful concert broadcast from New York when an announcer interrupted: Japanese airplanes were bombing Pearl Harbor. A hoax, we first thought, similar to the reports of an invasion from Mars reported earlier. But soon we learned that war had indeed come to the U.S.

We all expected to be drafted shortly, and Charles decided to marry his fiancée immediately; she should have a pension, after all, you never knew. Charles and Marilee Bernstein were married on December 19. It was a very happy marriage lasting until my brother's death in 1998.

All young men were asked to enlist. Foreign citizens who did so were promised almost instant citizenship. But when I presented myself to the local draft board, a kind, elderly gentleman interviewed me.

"Just wait, young man, until you are drafted. I know the company you're working for; you'll soon be involved in the war effort. You are a chemist with some experience in the paint field," he said. "I believe you should stay where you are and keep working. Work hard, young man, and do all you can for your new country."

I thought this man was crazy. I am no real scientist. Guys like me must be a dime a dozen. But a few days later, my boss told me about a manpower table he was filing with the government that would make several employees, including me, automatically draft exempt.

In simple words: no man working at that time in the laboratory or several other departments would ever be drafted. We all received little cards declaring that our military classification would be "2B." (Explanation: "1A" meant subject to immediate draft; "3A" was a family deferment – those men would be drafted later. "4F" was the classification for men who were not fit to serve for physical or mental reasons.) Thus, our category, "2B," implied that we were quite OK, but too important for the war effort to serve in the military forces.

"I'm afraid this country is crazy, and we're going to lose the war!" I said to my brother. "How can a country as dumb as this ever defeat Hitler?"

"Well," he said, "America is such a powerful country that we'll win in spite of our foolishness. Of course, it's silly to say that our work is really essential for the war effort."

Everybody was making speeches, from the precinct captain all the way up to the president, about how our mighty industry would get going soon. The president even promised that we would have 100,000 warplanes within a few months. Few believed him.

Frank Weinman

All of a sudden, so it seemed to me, there were changes: leaders of industry who had said only a few months earlier that they despised the "cripple in the White House," offered their services to the government for one dollar a year, and they were accepted. When the time frame the president had projected for those airplanes was over, we had almost twice as many.

As for me, I was immediately put to work on a new project: printing decals to be transferred to military vehicles. Numbers and insignias were needed which, while clearly visible from the ground, could not be photographed from the air. The specifications were clear: the color had to be different from the military olive drab; the markings must be "non-specular," a military word for having no gloss, dull. And finally, the decals should be easily applied to jeeps or tanks coming off an assembly line.

The color had to be a bluish-gray, which the black-and-white films (Verichrome), common at the time, could not distinguish from olive drab. It took me only a few tests in our camera room to establish the right shade. However, the second requirement, "non-specular," was difficult to meet. Obviously, all our competitors were furiously working on the same project, all with poor results. The problem: decals are printed on gummed, glossy paper which makes every decal look glossy after it is transferred, face-down.

Luck was on my side. Charles and Burt, the adhesive chemist, we're working on manufacturing our own decal paper (another of my brother's suggestions which would save the company lots of money). I had the idea of making such a paper with a rough surface that would give any paint a flat non-specular appearance after being transferred. The transferring was to be done with a mixture of water and organic solvents that would soften the paint sufficiently to make it adhere to the jeeps or tanks. To make a long story short, I was successful. Those of you who were riding in the jeep during World War II, please note: the numbers on that jeep were made with my formulas, in our factory.

I had known a bit about organic solvents from my previous experience, but not really enough. Realizing that, I enrolled in an organic chemistry class at the Illinois Institute of Technology and was lucky to have an excellent teacher. After Organic Chemistry 201 (Chemistry 101 was general chemistry; I didn't need that) came Org. Chem. 301 and 401. At the end of every semester, I would get a postcard with my name, the professor's name, the course, and also the letter "A."

"I don't know why they're sending me this postcard," I said to Teri. "I know that I attended the lectures."

Only much later would I learn that "A" stood for a grade, not attendance. Actually, I took the course only after completing a one-month course for laboratory assistants. One of the reasons I took this course was to familiarize myself with the English expressions for lab equipment. I didn't know the English words. One can easily carry on many a conversation without using words like "Erlenmeyer flask" or even "test tube!"

We were taught to set up distillations, viscosity measurements, conversions between the metric system (I was familiar with that, of course) to ounces, quarts, gallons, etc. Unlike my classmates, these expressions were new to me.

Since there was no time for me to go home between work and classes, I stopped for a nickel candy bar at the school cafeteria. I pointed at one of them, but the sales lady couldn't see what I wanted. Finally, she screamed at me: "For goodness sake, name it!"

But it was difficult for me to do that. How could I say: "Give me an 'Oh Henry'? It sounded stupid, but finally I learned it.

We worked hard, certainly long hours. Monday through Friday from seven in the morning until six in the evening, with half an hour for lunch, and Saturday from 7 AM until one in the afternoon. I frequently stayed even longer in order to finish a distillation. And no raises could be given as long as we did the same work we had done before. For practical purposes, in order to get more money, one had to be "promoted" to a different job. In my case, I was declared to be a "Senior Research Chemist." After all, I had done important research, which benefited the war effort.

I did indeed get a raise! After all, thanks to me, our company was the only one to come through with a solution to the difficult problem of marking military equipment. I couldn't help thinking: in the Italian army they probably just painted the damn numbers onto the vehicles, but in the U.S., we must have order, the numbers must all be of the same size. But who was I to quarrel with the Armed Forces of our great country! So, I was now making $35 per week.

This raise, which Mr. Eisenberg personally initiated, had several important consequences. The superintendent of our company started to think of me not just as "Doc's" brother, but also as somebody to be promoted later. Teri was overjoyed.

"We are on our way!" she said. "Furthermore, I think I can quit my job—the military coats we are now sewing are very heavy, I could use a rest. I'll still keep working, of course, but at home. I'll do alterations! I've become friendly with the manager of our apartment hotel; he'll see to it that some of the ladies in our building will send me work. Of course, I'll have to buy a sewing machine. It costs a lot of money, but we can afford it now!"

Our room was a little crowded after the sewing machine arrived, but Teri soon had more work than she could handle and made good money. Even more important for her was that she had free time now whenever she wanted! Charles introduced her to the wife of the superintendent of our plant; the two ladies became good friends. Teri's English improved quickly.

Jack, the superintendent, a man in his early forties, was a transplanted Californian.

He had owned his own decalcomania company near Los Angeles but had gone broke and was glad to find a job working for Mr. Eisenberg. Jack was an extremely able man; he knew all about our business; he could fix machines; he got along with everybody, so why couldn't he make it on his own?

"Too much competition in California," he said. I drew my own conclusion: one cannot work in California. After all, if Jack went broke there, nobody else could succeed. But, many years later, my brother gave me a different explanation: "As able as Jack was, he wasn't a good businessman. He fell in love with his own product rather than realizing that one must make a profit to stay in business. Somehow he could manage everything except money."

Jack and I also became good friends.

"I want you to work in every department," Jack said. "You already know paints. But you should know more about printing, about photography, even about machinery. The only way to learn is to do the actual work." Mr. Eisenberg approved.

So, I worked first in the photo department, then for a few weeks actually did screen printing, "pushing the squeegee" as it was called, a rather low-class job.

One day, after work, Charles took me aside for, as he said, a serious conversation.

He talked to me in German. He hadn't done that for many months.

"Frank," he said, "I must tell you a very sad fact. You are not well-liked in our company. As a matter of fact, many people actually hate you."

I was surprised, shocked; but I knew better than to doubt his words. He had too many connections. I was dumbfounded. "But why?" I wondered. "I haven't done anybody any harm, I'm always cooperative. I'm glad to talk to anybody who talks to me, during work, in the lunchroom..."

"That's just it. FRANK, YOU TALK TOO MUCH!"

Charles emphasized these words: "You're telling others too much about yourself, about the plans the company may have for you. First, that's nobody's business. Second, you create envy. Quite a few must wonder why you, with your foreign accent, a newcomer to our company, and to this country, should have opportunities they don't have. And third, probably most important, you are a Jew."

"But so is Mr. Eisenberg, so are you!"

"That's different. Mr. Eisenberg is the boss. Everybody knows that he can fire them. And as far as I'm concerned, I'm keeping to myself when I'm not in the laboratory where I am the boss. I'm friendly, but I don't fraternize with anybody except with Jack, another Jew by the way, who is my friend. Frank, don't ever forget that there is a lot of anti-Semitism in this country, in Chicago, in our company. You are not like everybody else."

I promised to watch myself from then on, and I did. But more than anything else, this conversation opened my eyes to my greatest shortcoming: I didn't see what I didn't want to see. Teri wasn't all that surprised when I told her what Charles had told me.

"I'm terribly sorry, of course," Teri said, "but you must understand that we are still new in this country and don't always know how to behave."

"No," I interrupted. "That's not it. Look, we came from Hitler's Europe, you and I. This country is fighting Hitler now. Isn't it safe to assume that Hitler's ideas should be unpopular?"

"I should think so, but it isn't necessarily so," Teri said. "And here is something else: almost all the advice

Charles gave us was excellent with just one exception: he said that we should not associate with people like us, meaning refugees. Rather, we should try to make friends with American-born couples of our own age. But you and I know what happens when we call your second cousins, and there are a lot of them, they seem to be so nice, but when I ask them to come and visit us, there's always the same answer: "By all means, we should get together sometime soon." You know what that means: "after a week of Sundays."

So, we tried to find friends of our own kind: newcomers to this country who had an accent similar to ours, and it wasn't difficult at all. Soon, we were part of a group who liked each other, enjoyed each other's company. All made a living, but just barely. For instance, there was Elly and Felix. He knew he'd soon be drafted (he was), but he wanted his wife and the baby that was soon to come to live as comfortably as possible. They rented a small apartment, but of course, there was no money for furniture. Never mind! They got a mattress from the Salvation Army and a lot of bricks. The mattress was mounted on some of the bricks. For night stands, orange crates were used, but you would never know it: colorful fabric from the five-and-ten cent store covered the crates, whose insides were used as bookshelves. A few pictures and a clock finished the decor. A table and a few chairs – also from the Salvation Army of course – made their two rooms quite livable.

Compared to our friends – most husbands would soon be drafted – Teri and I were rich.

"I can't help feeling terrible," I said to Teri. "Yes, I'm working 10 hours a day, and I'm going to school at night, and nobody is shooting at me. I sleep in my own bed every night; we are saving money. But our friends, they are struggling."

"Never mind about the money we have in the bank," Teri said. "After the war, my parents and my sister will need all the support we can give them."

Sadly, they didn't. All of Teri's family were killed, as were most of her uncles, aunts and cousins. Except for one aunt and her children who barely survived the concentration camp Bergen-Belsen, Teri was the only survivor. But she would believe for a long, long time that at least her younger sister Magda must have survived.

"She was so strong," Teri would say. Until many years after the war, she would cry out: "Magda, Magda!" whenever she saw a tall blonde woman walking ahead of her. She often ran ahead, only to look at the face of a stranger.

In March of 1942, we got terrible news from Cuba: my father had suffered a stroke and died soon afterwards. Certainly, many of us have this feeling of abandonment when their parents die; suddenly, there's nobody above us, nobody to turn to for advice or even to show off our successes.

Charles said to me, "I would have liked so much for father to see us here. I know what he would have said to me: "You did well." He would've been so proud to see us working together."

My mother (53-years-old at the time) was alone in Cuba now. Luckily though, it was possible to get her into this country in spite of the war. I hadn't seen my mother since 1939. She certainly looked older than her years. She joined us on October 12, 1942 (Columbus Day). Charles had arrived here on Columbus Day 1938. Teri and I on Columbus Day 1941.

There was no doubt as to where our mother should live: with us, not with Charles and his wife, who didn't know a word of German. We moved to the South Side of Chicago into an apartment hotel; it was quite impossible to find a regular apartment in Chicago during the war.

We now had a small bedroom where my mother slept and a large living room containing a couch that could be opened into a double bed for Teri and me. There also was a bathroom, kitchen and a large hall.

My mother wanted to do all the cooking. Teri loved that. The two ladies got along quite well in spite of all the stories one hears about mothers and daughters-in-law.

Of course, we had to speak German with my mother or occasionally Czech. We subscribed to a Czech daily newspaper for my mother; a German paper, which also existed in Chicago, was out of the question; Charles and probably I too would have objected.

There was rationing during the war, of course; it was difficult to buy tires, and only a small amount of gasoline was allotted to those who didn't need it for the war effort, but that didn't concern us since we didn't own a car. Food stamps were needed to buy certain groceries like flour and sugar. One day, I looked at the shelves in our kitchen and saw more sugar than we could use in a year. My mother explained: "You never know, maybe tomorrow there won't be anything to buy. With sugar and flour, I can always cook something to eat." She was still thinking of the rationing as she had seen it in Austria. Luckily, we didn't have a freezer that could be filled up with meat (also available with coupons).

My mother ran into a strange sort of discrimination. We had introduced her to a few elderly Jewish ladies in our building who seemed to be glad to see her until they started talking. They spoke Yiddish, my mother didn't understand most of what was said, and tried to answer in German. One of the women screamed at her:

"You German Jews haven't learned anything yet! You refuse to speak our language! You should be ashamed!"

Well, these ladies had come from Russia (now Poland or Lithuania), countries which hadn't existed at the time of their immigration 30 or 40 years earlier. They knew that English was the language of this country, but if you were a Jew, you must know Yiddish, they thought. Luckily, we found other acquaintances for our mother: parents of our friends, all refugees like ourselves.

Shortly before my mother joined us, Teri received a telephone call from her union.

"Won't you PLEASE come back to work? We have a very attractive position for you!"

Indeed, Teri was offered a job in a small company with guaranteed wages and a bonus for piecework. And there was an additional inducement: anybody who would come to work every day for a whole week, without being late a single day, would receive another ten percent. Because of the labor shortage, all kinds of creative means had to be found to attract workers. Teri accepted and soon made a lot of money. All was deposited in the bank.

"After the war, we can bring my parents over," she would often say.

The labor shortage was so severe that many of us were given additional jobs that had nothing to do with our regular work. I had to "supervise" an assembly line: ten or twelve girls were embellishing water glasses with decals. (Actually, I thought that the glasses looked better without these decorations, but who was I to say?) More than once, I was "invited out" by some of the girls. One was rather aggressive. "Honey, how about taking me out tonight? I'll be good!"

"But I'm a married man!" I said.

"That don't bother me no how," she answered. But honestly, I was never really tempted.

About this time, the Chicago Tribune reported that, starting immediately, the number of different flavors of ice cream would be reduced from seventeen to only eight. The money that was saved would go to the war effort!

By the spring of 1942, much had happened. Most important for our family: my father, who had wanted so badly to see his son's work in America, had died in Cuba. My brother brought his ashes to Chicago.

Then, in 1944, our forces invaded France and Italy, and it looked like the war in Europe might soon be over. Teri and I discussed having children, maybe soon. But then came the "Battle of the Bulge" and the firing of missiles into England.

(Editor's Note: The Battle of the Bulge, December 16, 1944 to January 25, 1945, was a major German offensive launched through the densely-forested Ardennes region of Belgium, France, and Luxenberg. The surprise attack caught Allied forces completely off-guard.)

All of a sudden, having children didn't look so good.

Let's wait a little, we thought. But when the Battle of the Bulge was over in December and the Allies had pushed on across Europe, we decided to wait no longer. On September 25, 1945, our first daughter, Frances, was born. (*Editor's Note: Frank and Teri's second daughter, Linda, was born on June 29, 1949.*)

Of course, I have to thank my brother (*who passed away in 1998*) for getting me a job at American Decal and Manufacturing Company, where I stayed for 39 years in various capacities until my retirement in 1980. But also, I must thank him for helping me climb the corporate ladder there. I never had to look for a job, never in my life: in Europe, I worked for my father, in America for Mr. Eisenberg, the owner of the business.

I have certainly spent the greatest part of my life in America; working and then in retirement. I think of myself as a good citizen, a good American.

But unfortunately, I'm still speaking with a foreign accent.

POSTSCRIPTS

The following postscripts to "With a Foreign Accent" include the final letter sent from the Vidor family in Hungary to Frank and Teri in Chicago in April, 1944. Also included here are Frank's remembrances of his sister-in-law, Magda Vidor Bettleheim, his brother, Charles Weinman, and his aunt Kamilla Laufer.

This is a translation of a letter sent by Rudolf Vidor, Teri's father. The letter is dated April 23, 1944, the day before Teri's family were presumably deported from their home in Kassa to a Nazi concentration camp. They did not survive. The letter was left with a previous servant of the Vidors, who mailed it on October 2, 1945. It arrived in Chicago on October 26, 1945.

April 23, 1944
RUDOLF VIDOR, Kassa (Kosice)

My beloved Teri, my dearest Frank!

Until this moment at least I could hold myself together, but now that I have to write a farewell letter to my dearest children, my heart is getting very heavy. I must stop after every word and collect myself in order to continue writing. Well, we are about there! When Frank filled his rucksack, he could at least hope to be with his Teri soon. But when we fill this rucksack, which he bought in Prague, for ourselves, we are confronted with utmost uncertainty. Will we ever find an anchor to sink into secure soil?

My Teri!

I left my last will with Dr. Joseph Pilat, attorney. Be sure to visit our Ilus (*a former employee*) who knows all about the content of this last will. We placed Ilus with Mrs. Steven Palcso, textile shop, Szent Isvan korut 6, next to Hausmann's shop, Szepsi korut. By talking to Ilus, you will know how we spent the last five days of excitement and where our life insurance is. You will find your mother's very good photograph with Janos Papcun (address: Srobarova 23, Kosice, this is the Czechoslovakian address). We sent you this picture through Curt Kaiser *(a Swiss intermediary, who was kind enough to receive and forward letters, even during the first years of the war).* (We hope) that you receive it. Both in January and in February we sent you long letters through him, but we must assume that you never received them. Teri! Find out all about two of my best Christian friends, who will receive you, as former corresponding secretary, with open arms! *(This is probably a hint that these two friends are Freemasons.)* They will not let you go empty-handed!

(Frank's Note: This is probably a hint that some of his valuables were with some of the above-named Christian friends) One of them was your good friend; in spite of the fact that he would not marry his beloved, the pharmacist's daughter, he did not forsake her in her different religion.

The bravest of the three of us *(Rudolf Vidor, Teri's father; Matilde Vidor nee Stein, Teri's mother, and Magda Bettelheim nee Vidor, Teri's sister)* is Magda, who is of course 30 years younger and this is important. Her husband, Dr. Martin Steven Bettelheim, from Satoralja Ujhely, was sent to the front after a marriage of only two months, as a non-armed and not-fighting Jewish member of a special working battalion. Imre, now in Israel, was in a similar unit. *(Frank's Note: The lives of many thousand Jewish young men were thus saved by the Hungarian government. Martin Bettelheim survived and went back to Hungary or Czechoslovakia. He is not in Israel. Teri could not find him.)* The poor boy, a graduate physician, works in the mud, chopping wood, makes bunkers, everything except as a doctor. He loves Magda since early and, like our dearly loved mother, enjoyed few good things. It is a miracle that he is still alive!

We are praying to the Almighty that the three of us will stay together and not, like the Aladár's, whom we hardly can hope to be alive anymore, were torn from each other! We can bear all suffering if we can just stay with our dear mother! *(Frank's Note: Rudolf Vidor's brother, Teri's uncle Aladár, with his wife, daughter and son, lived in Bratislava. None survived.)*

We are often talking about you, dear Teri, what you are doing now, if you are hearing anything about our fate? Frank, my dear son, continue to be good to our often-obstinate Teri and love each other always. Always fervently and sincerely.

Be well, my dear children. Be happy with each other. Give our regards to your parents and to Charles' family. I kiss you many millions of times. I love you very, very much.

Your Father *(written in Hungarian as)* Apuca.

The following lines were written by Matilde Vidor, Teri's mother.

My dearest Children!

I hope with great confidence to our dear God that we will see each other again in gladness and will spend many happy hours together. I kiss you, dear children, with great love.

Your loving mother *(written in Hungarian as)* Anyuka.

The following line is written by Magda Bettelheim, Teri's sister.

I kiss you.

Your loving Magda.

(Frank's note: we were later told that Magda survived in a concentration camp but died a few days after its liberation).

Further notes about this letter by Frank Weinman (Skokie, December 23, 1980):

The letter is written in German, the Vidor's third language (after Hungarian and Slovakian). This was probably done so that I could read it and that Jan Papcun, the servant who mailed the letter in 1945, could not read it. The letter was sent registered mail and arrived in Chicago on October 26, 1945, about one month after Frances was born.

In spite of many hints of valuables left at several addresses, Teri decided not to follow up. This seems hard to understand now, but at the time it made sense. We had saved money in order to pay for the passage to America of Teri's family, and this letter, together with the information received shortly afterwards that the parents, at least, could not possibly have survived, hurt so much that Teri just wanted to get the whole past out of her mind. This was the main reason for doing nothing. Furthermore, Teri was a new mother. And conditions in Europe (Czechoslovakia) were turbulent.

The optimism expressed in Matilda Vidor's lines was entirely out of character for her. She had always been a pessimist. On the other hand, Rudolf, who did not find a single hopeful line to write, was an eternal optimist. That is probably the reason why the Vidor's did not go into hiding, as many Hungarian Jews did, more than half of them successfully. Rudolph Vidor felt that as a man who had only friends and never did anything wrong in his life, he had nothing to fear.

Rudolf Vidor had two brothers and one sister. The oldest brother, Aladár, is mentioned in the letter. He and his family lived in Bratislava. Teri stayed with them when I met her. None survived.

Rudolf's younger brother, Zigmund, lived in Budapest and died several years before the war. He had a wife and two children. His wife died, only this year (1980), in Switzerland. Their daughter and son-in-law live in Geneva, Switzerland, 56 rue de Montchoisy, 1207 Geneve. The name of the son-in-law, who is considerably older than me, is Zoltan Fedritt. Zigmund's son lives in Australia.

Rudolf Vidor's sister's husband changed his name (from Schwarz) to Vidor (his wife's maiden name). He, an old frail man when I met him in 1941, survived the war and lived for many more years in Slovakia. Their daughter is Valli Farkas, you know the family, now in Montreal. Valli somehow survived the war in France.

There was another brother of Rudolf Vidor. He immigrated to America around 1910. Although he and his family later returned to Hungary, his two children were U.S. citizens and thus *(either prior to or when war broke out)* had no difficulty coming to this country. You know the children: Julius Vidor, whom you met in Cleveland, and Margit Horovitz, who you, Frances, met in Connecticut and who now lives in Florida. They have a son, slightly older than you.

MAGDA VIDOR BETTELHEIM

This is a memorandum about what I remember of my sister-in-law Magda, Teri's only sister.

First her name: she was known as Vidor Magda (in Hungarian, the family name comes first) until later 1941. Her marriage to Dr. Martin Bettelheim must have occurred shortly after Teri and I departed Europe in September of 1941. Magda was born in Kassa, then already known as Kosice, in Slovakia. But before her birth, Rudolf Vidor was still in Szeged, Hungary (where Teri was born) in his capacity as director of a factory which had something to do with textiles, probably weaving (he was a graduate of a special school in that line).

Immediately after the end of World War I, there was lawlessness in Hungary. The Communists (Bela Kun, a Jew) were nominally in charge. Many factories were destroyed, burned down. One day a horde of hooligans appeared in front of the factory where Rudolf Vidor not only was in charge, but also where his family lived. The situation was very serious, threatening.

Matilda (Teri and Magda's mother), a usually shy woman, stepped in front of the building and faced the hooligans (this story was told to me both by Rudolph and Matilda) and talked to the hostile crowd. Pointing at her belly, she said:

"You wouldn't kill a pregnant woman and her unborn baby?" Or something like that. The crowd dispersed. The still unborn baby was, of course, Magda.

But it must be said, there was a violent streak in Magda, as I remember.

Shortly afterward, Rudolph Vidor moved his family to the new state of Czechoslovakia. Since he was born in Slovakia, he had the right to opt for citizenship in that country. Both Rudolf and Matilda were fluent in Slovakian, as well as in Hungarian and German, not Yiddish. Just why he chose to settle in Kosice (pronounced KO-shiz-a) I do not know. It was then a prosperous town of about 30,000 people, not far from the Hungarian border. The language spoken in town (but not in the surrounding hills) was HUNGARIAN, not Slovakian.

This was important for Magda's upbringing. While her parents were fluent in Slovakian, Magda, unlike Teri, never learned it, but spoke only Hungarian. Because of this fact, many professions and opportunities were closed to her.

Teri and her two-years-younger sister were very close. I don't believe that there was any sibling rivalry. They loved and respected each other. Teri told me that on many cold evenings she told Magda that she had a secret to tell her, but only if Magda would come to her bed and warm it. Of course, Magda soon caught onto this, but the two sisters still spent many cold evenings in bed together, not only warming each other but also telling each other stories, girl secrets. Even later in life, this intimacy never stopped, although their lives soon took quite different paths.

I think that had something to do with the schools they attended. For a few years, their schooling was the same: a kindergarten taught in German (not Yiddish), though it was a religious school. I believe that it was there that Magda learned her very rudimentary German. Afterwards, the girls attended Hungarian grammar schools. This fact is very important: while Teri, to the end of her life, would count, add and subtract in that language, for Magda, Hungarian essentially was the only language she could communicate in.

The reason for this is important. Magda was a very obstinate girl. Even early in life, she was rather obstinate, certainly disobedient to her parents (her father being the dominant figure). Magda's life, from age 10 on, was shaped by this fact. While Teri, at her parents' suggestion, attended a Slovakian school (we would call it Junior High or Middle School) at age 10 and soon became fluent in that language, Magda refused to do so. She did not want to work so hard to subject herself to a new language.

This meant that although she spent the first 19 years of her life in Czechoslovakia, she never learned the language of the land! She also did not learn about Czech or Slovakian culture and music. Those things, which meant so much to Teri, were unknown to Magda. Nor did she study French (Teri took private lessons at the insistence of her parents).

Thus, Magda was, at least for the first 20 years of her short life, very much a person unto herself, with one, very important exception. Very early, probably at the age of 13 or 14, she fell in love. (I'm sorry I forgot the first name of the boy; his last name was, I believe, Prinz, or similar; I met him once, probably in 1937 when I visited the Vidor family. He was tall and Jewish, but I can't remember that he impressed me one way or the other.)

However, Rudolf Vidor disliked him immensely. This fact split Magda and her father, who never seemed to have been very close. Two strong personalities collided and Magda was in the middle between her boyfriend and her father, himself a rather stubborn, proud man. Both her mother and her sister did their best to mediate, but were not very successful.

From June to September 1941, I spent time with the Vidor family in Kassa. There was an interruption of three weeks when Teri and I had been detained and spent time in a Hungarian concentration camp. But this is not part of my story about Magda. Important for her was the fact that she and her boyfriend of many years broke up (I have a hunch that he broke up with her). His family had not liked the friendship with Magda any more than Rudolf Vidor had.

I believe that it was on the "rebound" that Magda met Dr. Martin Bettelheim, whom she married in late 1941. Her father, who had heartily approved, sent us a picture of the couple (via Switzerland) to Chicago. I certainly hope that the young couple was happy in the short time they spent together, until he was "drafted" into the Hungarian army.

Now, a description of Magda, as I remember her. Please realize that there was a language barrier between us: I had learned only a few words of Hungarian (from Teri) and Magda, in turn, knew very, very little German. But there was enough communication between us to make it possible to assure each other that we liked each other.

"You good for my sister, she good for you. Love each other, always." That was essentially what this proud young woman, who loved her sister very much, said to me. Magda was tall, probably 5 feet 11 inches. She had long, dark blonde hair that she allowed to fall freely over her broad shoulders. She walked very straight, in what I'd call a "defiant" way. Her features were very strong, more so than Teri's. I don't think that she was beautiful. "Stunning" may be a better description. She had an excellent figure and she knew well how to take care of herself. She wore the clothes best suited for her, with the right makeup. Any man who saw her would look at her again. She conveyed a picture of strength. (That was the reason why Teri, while she accepted the death of her parents when we received the wire from the Jewish community in Kosice ("the Vidors have not returned"), couldn't believe that her sister was also dead. Teri often said to me: "She'll turn up, someday, she was so strong."

Strength, outer and inner strength, that was Magda, who, it turned out, died shortly after the concentration camp she'd been held in was liberated.

Editor's Note: It is believed that Magda, along with Rudolph and Mathilda Vidor, her parents, was initially sent to Auschwitz, but later was either marched or transferred to the Stutthof concentration camp, located in a secluded, wet and wooded area west of the small town of Sztutowo (in German: Stutthof). The town is located in the former territory of the Free City of Danzig, 34 kilometers east of Gdansk, Poland. Stutthof was the last camp to be liberated by the Allies, on May 9, 1945. More than 110,000 people had been deported to this camp. 85,000 of them died.

Holocaust records at Yad Vashem in Israel indicate that Magda perished at this camp, shortly after its liberation. The precise circumstances of her death are unknown.

CHARLES H. WEINMAN

My brother, Dr. Charles H. Weinman, died on September 30, 1998. The following should serve as a memorial to him, which will be sent to all who knew him well. My sources are, of course, my own memories but also what my parents and others told me. While I will try to be accurate, mistakes might happen.

Charles was born on October 27, 1911 in Vienna, in our apartment in the eighth district, Josefstaedteratrasse 56. There can be no doubt that his birth had been anticipated with great joy by my parents, who got married on November 10, 1910. My mother mentioned to me how unhappy she was that it took her three months to conceive. She thought she might be barren because it took so long and offered to divorce my father, as much as she loved him, if she couldn't give him a son.

Charles (Karl in German) was named after my father's best friend, Karl Klein, then the owner of a prosperous shoe manufacturing plant. The middle name (rather unusual in Vienna at that time) of Herman was given to my brother after our grandfather Herman Weinmann, who had died in 1908. Our father, Heinrich Weinmann, was at the time of Charles' birth already the co-owner of a small paint factory located in the 16th district of Vienna.

We were a typical Jewish middle-class family. My father was a strictly self-made man, born in lower Austria, the son of Moravian Jews. My mother, Marianne, was the oldest daughter of Fritz and Paula Newmann, Czech Jews who could afford to give their oldest daughter a handsome dowry. My father refused to invest it in his business; too risky he said. Rather, he bought gilt-edged Austrian government papers with it. All of it was lost in 1918, after World War I.

Although a marriage broker may have brought my parents together (I'm not sure of that; I was also told that a newspaper ad placed by my maternal grandfather and answered by my father's mother may have played a part), my parents' marriage was from the beginning to my father's death in 1942 one of great love and devotion. The fact that my brother Karl looked very much like my father made him especially loved by both my parents.

Charles had a very happy childhood! I remember pictures of him, rather strange-looking at age three or four, wearing strong eyeglasses, which were needed to correct an eye problem at birth.

Whatever it was, he didn't need them anymore when he went to school. His vision was always excellent. At age 10, he was already a handsome boy. I, born in 1914, always had a "big brother" until the day before yesterday. Charles often told me that his earliest clear memory was the death of Emperor Franz Josef *(Emperor of the Austro-Hungarian Empire)* in 1916.

"Father held my hand as we walked on the Ringstrasse to see the funeral celebrations. There were so many people."

Charles also fondly remembered our paternal grandmother Auguste Weinmann nee Bauer, a brave woman as well as a poet who died during the same year. Our maternal grandparents also adored Charles, their first grandchild. When World War I broke out in late summer, 1914, our father, as a Second Lieutenant in the reserves, was immediately called up and was supposed to be sent to the Russian front. Luckily for him, and for our family, he suffered a mild heart attack and was sent home for the duration of the war.

In 1916 our father moved his family from Vienna to Pressburg, Hungary (now Bratislava, Slovakia) because he had a factory there that needed supervision. This move was no doubt traumatic for five-year-old Karl, but was made easier because our nanny moved with us and remained with our family for several more years.

Why did we two boys need a nanny, since our mother was always with us? She never had any kind of a job. I don't know the answer, except that our mother seemed to be sickly from time to time. I believe that it was important for Charles to feel that mother was always somebody to be protected, rather than somebody who would physically care for him. Not that mother didn't love us boys as dearly as she loved her husband (later she would always refer to my father, my brother and me as "my dear three men"). Charles and I always loved and honored her, but it was my father who was respected; there was never any doubt who the head of the family was.

Charles had a hard time in Pressburg because he didn't know Hungarian, then the language of the land. As my parents explained to us later, it would have been unpatriotic to send their oldest son to any but a Hungarian school. But by the age of seven, Charles had become perfect in this difficult language.

The war was over in 1918 and in January, 1919 Bratislava became a part of the new Czechoslovak Republic. Our family moved back to Vienna and Charles would attend German schools from then on. It wasn't easy for him, but he never had to repeat a grade and soon forgot Hungarian. After completing the fourth grade of grammar school, Charles (as I later did) chose the option of entering high school immediately, rather than to attend grammar school for a fifth year, as most children did at that time. It seems that there was an ambitious urge in our family to move forward whenever possible, not to hesitate.

Most Jewish children attended high school in Vienna, although less than 20 percent of the general population did so. Most children only attended eight grades of school, until they were 14 years old, then entered into some kind of apprenticeship. However, not to go to middle school would forever disqualify these youngsters from ever attending any university, and few Jewish parents would agree to that. This was the reason why, although only 11 percent of the Viennese population was Jewish, some 30 percent of our classmates were of the "Mosaic Faith" (as Judaism was referred to in Austria), enough for Charles to have only Jewish friends.

He made friends easily and was always popular. His two closest friends were Adam Reischer and Kurt Ackermann. They formed a kind of triumvirate called "KAKWAR," formed from the first letters of their names (Kurt Ackermann, Karl Weinmann, Adam Reischer), who were well-known throughout their school. The three would remain friends for the rest of their lives, not only in Vienna, but also later in America. They remained in close touch until just a few years ago, although Kurt lived in Kentucky and Adam in Michigan. This was so characteristic for Charles: unlimited loyalty to friends as well as to family, which was always reciprocated. Charles never forgot a friend and no friend ever forgot him.

When Charles was thirteen years old he had his Bar Mitzvah, an important event but not celebrated in any way with enormous parties, as is so often done in America. The boy had to read a few verses in Hebrew from the weekly Torah portion, as well as the blessings, and that was often the extent of it. There was a small party, of course, with a few presents: mostly books, always a fountain pen. Our father's best friend, Karl Klein, presented Charles with a gold watch that he would cherish for many, many years.

The eight years Charles spent in middle school passed without any important events, except that, during his last few years, Austria suffered a major economic depression. It came much earlier than the Depression in America. With the scarcity of jobs came a re-awakening of anti-Semitism and a wish by many Austrians to be united with Germany. Somehow these people believed that all that was needed was a "Greater Germany" to set everything right. Only much later did this feeling crystalize in Austria to become Nazism.

This meant a siege mentality for the Jews, who had to be Social Democrats because this was the only party that accepted them. This would be important for Charles. He had to be a Socialist. It was the party that not only accepted Jews in leadership positions, but also stood for justice, for equality. (Once in this country, Charles would transfer his loyalty to the Democratic Party.) But Charles also got along well with people of other political stripes. He was always respected: "If only all the Jews were like you," he was often told.

The relationship between Charles and myself (we never had any other siblings) was very good, though he would often tease me. Being three years older, he was, of course, not only physically stronger than me, but also more adept at sports. He may have been 14 or 15 years old when he became a good table tennis player and wanted a sparring partner at home. But I wasn't quite good enough. In order to make me do my best, he invented an interesting ploy:

"If you ever beat me," he would say, "in any single game, I'll tell everybody, really everybody, that my little brother is the better player." I have no doubt that Charles would have done that, because he never lied, always kept his promises, although he carefully calculated just what he could promise so he'd be sure he could deliver.

During the last year of middle school, we had to select a subject for a major project. Charles chose to write about a novel by Emile Zola, *L'Assommoir* (The Killer). It had to be written in French and be about thirty pages long. Charles studied the novel, as well as the life of Zola. This effort would foreshadow what he did later in life with any of his scientific work: be absolutely thorough, leave nothing to chance. He always assumed that he was wrong until he could prove otherwise.

Charles's education, both formally in school and informally at home, was excellent but one-sided, geared to mental stimulation and knowledge but deficient in manual dexterity. He didn't have to know how to use a hammer or a screwdriver. I remember an incident involving a table that wasn't standing firmly; maybe one leg was shorter or the floor may have been warped. Charles suggested putting a little piece of wood underneath the shorter leg in order to prevent the table from wiggling. My mother disapproved. "Don't do that," she said. "You don't know how to do it right. Wait for the cleaning woman. She knows."

Somehow, this kind of education took hold in him. Charles would always mistrust himself when it came to using any tools or machinery. This probably turned out for the best: he would always ask for extra help. He did the thinking, the investigating, the research. And he saw to it that all went well. Nobody could supervise a project better than Charles. If anything went wrong, he would be the first to report it. No deceptions, no lies, ever. And he always assumed full responsibility for failures. As far as credit for success, he didn't ask for it. He didn't have to because it came naturally.

We were exposed to foreign languages during our middle school years. In school, we studied French and Latin, but we also had private lessons in English (which seemed easy) and also in Czech, a very difficult language to learn for German-speakers. My father insisted we boys study that language because he felt that we might work in his factory in Bratislava, Czechoslovakia one day. But that wasn't enough: Charles and I also decided to study Italian on our own. We had fun doing it.

After Charles graduated from middle school in 1929, there was no doubt that he would go on to study chemistry. After all, our father's paint factories in Vienna and Bratislava required knowledge of it. My father's partner, Dr. Winter, was a chemist. Charles worked hard, very hard in his studies. "I want to finish in the shortest possible time," he would often say. "Father needs me in his business!"

He was right. The financial situation in Austria had become very bad. It was next to impossible for any young man, especially for a Jew, to find a job, unless you worked for your father. But even while working hard at the university, Charles found time for other activities. First, he wanted to make money. He did that by tutoring boys. And Charles liked girls and they liked him. He was never shy; somehow, he always knew what to do and what to say. When he was about 18-years-old, Charles joined a Zionist youth organization called "Hyrcania," modeled after the German "Burschenschaft," a student organization whose main purpose was to drink, to fight, and say stupid things. He had to learn the Jewish national anthem, in Hebrew. Actually, this was somewhat out of character for Charles because he detested being told what to do or how to behave; he didn't easily subject himself to any group discipline. But his short membership in this organization served him well, because it got him in touch with Zionism. While he had no patience for organized religion, including Judaism, a certain nationalist Jewish feeling stayed with him throughout his life. He became an ardent friend of Israel. Together with his wife Marilee and his son John, he visited Israel in 1955. In later years Charles would always remember the image of Israel as a country of young pioneers, mostly living on a kibbutz and dancing the "Hora."

Charles was a born leader. Our father was a Freemason, a very secretive organization whose only prerequisite was to be "a good man of good reputation." And our father was certainly that! Because of our father's membership, Charles and I were allowed to belong to the Mason's youth organization. I think we got an excellent education there. Frequently some of the most prominent Austrian scientists, lawyers and politicians (all Freemasons) would lecture to us. We were not only encouraged to ask questions but also to give speeches ourselves. Maybe that's when we learned never to be afraid to speak in public, always to hold our own. Charles was an excellent speaker, always well-prepared.

To be the president of our youth organization was a very prestigious job. There was much lobbying for it before the biannual election. Somehow, Charles was in the running. When the secret ballots were cast, there was a tie between him and another young man. It was decided that they should both give a speech stating their qualifications. The other young man spoke first, telling us what a good job he would do, much better than my brother would do. As befitting the occasion, he mildly attacked Charles. When Charles's turn to speak came, he agreed with everything his opponent had said, and called him a good friend who would no doubt make an excellent president. But, said Charles, if just possibly he himself would be elected, he promised to do as good a job as he could. Charles had found exactly the right words for this audience, made up of friends who trusted each other.

Charles was elected with a huge majority. Later, in America, Charles would always find the right words for any occasion; never attacking, never pleading and always with a lot of self-confidence.

Charles earned a PhD in chemistry, in record time. As he explained, it was difficult not to "get stuck" with the dissertation, a research project dear to the professor who initiated and supervised it. It was important to be thorough, but not to "get lost," not to open up new avenues of research which could lead to more work, more time spent at the university, something Charles certainly didn't want to do.

It was during this time that Charles experienced a major defeat, as far as I know the only one in his life. He had fallen in love with a nice girl from a good family. She was in love with him. There was a huge engagement party. Everybody was happy, except me. I had "bad vibes." The girl's family was rather overpowering. It seems that his prospective father-in-law wanted Charles to enter <u>his</u> business, which was much more prosperous than my father's. But for Charles, family loyalty always came first; it always would. The two young people remained friends, but the engagement was called off.

After graduation Charles worked for a while in our Czech factory where he had a chance to experience Czech chauvinism. It seems he tried to make a sale with a Czech-speaking customer who criticized my brother's poor command of the language.

"You are a doctor of chemistry?" This man said. "You don't even know how to speak good Czech!" I don't know exactly how badly this stupid comment hurt Charles, who had made every effort to do right, even rehearsing a sales pitch in Czech. But I know that Charles never cared for "selling" again, not in Europe and certainly not in America.

Soon, Charles transferred to our factory in Vienna where he was badly needed. Things were very bad there. My father's partner wanted to get out, fearful that the business was failing and that he would be personally liable for any debts. So he quit. The company was re-named "Henry Weinmann and Sons." My brother was in charge, at first under my father's supervision, but soon he took over completely. He managed to do the nearly impossible, a turnaround! By 1937, our Viennese factory became profitable!

Since he had been a child, Charles wanted nothing more than to please our father, not that this was difficult. Our father adored him. There was a relationship between the two of them which ran so deep that nothing could have hurt it. But still, Charles was proud that he could show father how able he was.

The year 1938 promised to be a good one for Charles. He had many good friends in Vienna. And he did not lack female companionship either. Then, on March 11, everything came to an end! Hitler's hordes marched into Austria and were received with open arms. Charles wasted no time with doubts or regrets; he wanted to get out of Austria as soon as possible. Luckily, we had relatives in Chicago who gave him an Affidavit of Support. Charles sold the Viennese factory for one schilling to his bookkeeper, who didn't even want it. Before emigrating, Charles made a quick stop at our factory in Bratislava where my parents now had a small apartment. My father tried desperately to hold Charles back.

"There is enough room for all of us, don't leave us!" He pleaded. But this one time Charles was not the obedient son.

"I wish you all the luck in the world, "he said, "but I want to get out of Europe. I don't think that you are safe in Czechoslovakia either! I'll do my very best to prepare for all of you to join me in America as soon as possible!"

Charles arrived in the U.S. on October 12, 1938, Columbus Day, which he considered to be a good omen. He wasted no time in New York because he didn't feel there were any prospects for him there. In Chicago, he found a warm reception from my relatives, descendants of my maternal grandfather's brother who had immigrated to America in 1885. They loved him instantly, and why not? He was a handsome, personable man, 27 years old, who couldn't possibly become a burden to them. And he was unattached.

In spite of the Depression, Charles had little difficulty finding a job. After about a week, he answered an ad in the *Chicago Tribune*, looking for a paint chemist. A Mr. Eisenberg, owner of the American Decalcomania Company, wanted the paint he was buying for his silkscreen plant to be checked for quality and price. Charles accepted the job in late October, 1938, for $25 a week. He stayed with the company until 1988.

Obviously, Charles did a good job, not only doing what he was hired for, but much more. Soon he told his boss, George Eisenberg, that he thought the company could manufacture its own paints, rather than buying them, thus saving a lot of money. Mr. Eisenberg agreed and gave Charles a raise. Charles did much more for the company, raising the quality of merchandise and making it possible to enter new markets. He quickly established a warm personal relationship with Eisenberg, becoming his confidant. That was not an easy thing to do because the boss was mostly feared, not loved, by his employees.

Then, as Charles later told me, he accomplished the most difficult task in his life. While he had told Eisenberg about his family "in the old country," he hadn't asked for any help in getting them out. Rather, Charles had hoped to get the necessary affidavits for my parents, myself and my fiancé Teri from our Chicago relatives. But it seems the family always found a reason to delay coming up with the necessary documents.

Charles was still a relatively poor immigrant. While he had a good job, he couldn't possibly prove that he had the means to support all of us, as was required in the affidavits. Meanwhile, back in Czechoslovakia, we had lost our other factory. My parents and I were living in a tiny apartment in Prague, waiting to hear from Charles.

Charles knew that, of course, and in February, 1939 he mustered all his courage to ask Mr. Eisenberg if he would provide affidavits for us to come to America. This meant that a certain sum of money had to be pledged to support all of us, in case we couldn't take care of ourselves. Mr. Eisenberg instantly agreed to my brother's request. He had to co-sign the affidavits and deposit money as proof of intent to support us.

Charles later told me that there were probably several reasons Mr. Eisenberg agreed. First, he really liked Charles and wanted to help him. Second, he would gain the everlasting gratitude of a young man who would stay loyal to his company. And finally, Eisenberg, a Russian Jew, wanted to show the "stuck up" German Jews, meaning our Chicago relatives, that he would do what they hadn't done for their own flesh and blood.

Charles's efforts to bring us over were by no means finished when he sent us the affidavits. With the help of Mr. Eisenberg, he established a connection with the senior senator from Illinois, Scott Lucas, then one of the most powerful men in the country. When I finally got my American visa, there was a letter in my file from the senator. It may have helped, we'll never know.

Then Charles had to pay for our ship tickets! In 1941 there was very little transportation available from Europe to the U.S.; no American, Italian or German passenger ships were operating. Only neutral Spain still allowed a few small vessels to cross the Atlantic, and charged the passengers enormous prices. Furthermore, Charles had to pay a commission to some Dutch agents, who only sold first class tickets, a real racket. So, Charles borrowed money from his boss and paid the expenses, in addition to what amounted to a $10,000 bribe to Batista's government in Cuba *(Editor's note: Fulgencio Batista was the president and dictator who ran Cuba at the time)* to allow my parents to land there; their visas only took them that far.

On December 19, 1941 Charles married Marilee Bernstein. She must've loved him very much to agree to his condition: wait until he had brought his family out of Europe! They had met years earlier, I believe through one of our relatives, and quickly agreed that they were made for each other. They stayed married for nearly 57 years. Always a family man, my brother was very, very close to his wife and to his son John, as well as his daughter-in-law and his granddaughter. And Charles had the additional good fortune to have his two best friends, Adi and Kurt, in this country.

When I came to the U.S. in October 1941, I had a job waiting for me, thanks to Charles. He had found a position for me in his laboratory at American Decal. So my brother was now my boss. I, too, advanced fairly rapidly, though not nearly as fast as Charles, who soon became the number two man in the company. I don't know how and when he repaid Mr. Eisenberg all the money he had borrowed.

Charles always lived modestly; only when it came to spending money for others was he generous to a fault. In 1948, during Israel's War of Independence, he telephoned our cousins there, Dr. Dolfi Brunner and his wife Tamara, and offered to bring their children to America for safety. They declined the offer.

At American Decal, Charles was the chief chemist, and later he was also made the head buyer. His method of handling salesmen who called on him was first, to get any and all possible information about the product they were trying to sell, and only then to give them an order, not all the time, but frequently enough to keep them on their toes, as he explained to me. I think the salesmen dreaded him, but they also liked him for his friendliness and fairness. Even stronger was the respect and loyalty of all those who worked for Charles. He never fired anyone. He was able to attract good people, allowed them freedom in their activities, and saw to it that they received credit for their work, as well as raises in pay. He always managed to look out for those who worked for him, was always on the side of those who were weaker, who needed help. But he could be ice cold to fakers or anybody who tried to undermine his position.

My brother managed to get out of life almost everything he really wanted, with only one exception. When he was 30 years old, newly married, and had just helped me come to this country, he said to me:

"When I'm forty, I'm going to sit down in a car and drive west, slowly. It should take at least a month. I want to be a bum for a while." I reminded him of his wish when the time came.

"I still want to do it very much, but I can't get away right now. But when I'm 50…" Well, he never found the time to fulfill his dream, not when he was 50 or at 65 when he did NOT retire. He finally stopped working when he was in his 70's, but then he was an old man, it was too late for the trip. But I, his little brother, took the trip for him when I retired at 65. The trip took me three months, and I thought of Charles every day.

About 10 years ago Charles was greatly honored by the Mayo Clinic, the favorite charity of George Eisenberg. A professorship was founded and named after Charles. Mr. Eisenberg died soon afterwards, leaving Charles that token of appreciation to his most trusted employee.

Well, Charles was not only trusted but loved by all who had the good fortune to meet him, most of all his family: His wife Marilee, his son John, John's wife Rodica and their daughter Samantha. How can Charles best be described? Just like our father, who he resembled. Simply put, he was:

CHARLES WEINMAN, A GOOD MAN OF GOOD REPUTATION.

KAMILLA LAUFER

When Kamilla Laufer, nee Neumann, died in September, 1988 at age 94, there was no funeral. Her remains were cremated, her ashes put into a vault. All this was according to her wishes.

Thinking of Kamilla, the idea of "goodness" comes to mind. I do not know that she lived a successful life. She had no children and among her generation this was no doubt important. Her marriage to Otto Laufer was a failure and ended in divorce after a few years.

Yet as I remember, she was a happy person for most of her life because she was good and caring.

She was born in Belcice in Bohemia, but I do not think her Czech roots were very important because the Neumanns moved to Vienna while she was still a child. As the youngest of four siblings, she was no doubt overshadowed by her brother Pepa (who died at age 100) and her sisters Marianne and Anny, both supposedly "prettier," although Kamilla was certainly good looking.

There was money in the family. Her father was a successful businessman. Kamilla received what was considered a good education in Vienna, but was oriented toward being a good housewife and a suitable partner for a Jewish husband. Her life at home was happy, as she remembered it. There was much music and dancing.

But she must've learned early in life that it was best for her to not assert herself, that it was important to "get along," even if that meant to "give in." Her mother was a domineering woman who thought that her son was much more important than her daughters simply because he was a male. Furthermore, there seemed to have been a close bond between the two oldest siblings, which left both Anny and Kamilla somewhat isolated and rivals to the others.

Kamilla was he in her middle twenties when she met Otto Laufer and was, more or less, talked into marrying him by her brother. At least that is what she remembered. She had a good dowry, very important in those days. Unfortunately, Otto Laufer invested Kamilla's dowry in his business, which failed after a few years. Since there were no children, the family decided that a divorce was indicated. Though it was probably not her idea, Kamilla agreed. But she did not remember her marriage as unhappy, probably because she did not expect much.

The couple did a lot of hiking together. As a matter of fact, this is how they first met. Otto was a nice, well-disposed fellow. Twice the couple took care of us boys for extended periods of time and that was probably the only occasion Kamilla had to function as a mother. She did well.

After her divorce, Kamilla worked in her father's business. Many attempts were made to get her married again and she certainly wanted that, but somehow the right man could not be found.

When she came to Chicago in 1939, without any means and looking for work, her good appearance, pleasant manners and good general education pointed the way to the kind of job she would have for the remainder of her working days: companion to an elderly, extremely wealthy woman. Kamilla had a fair command of English, knew how to play bridge and mah-jongg, was a very good dresser and was not overly awed by the very rich. Most of all, Kamilla had the wonderful gift to be loved, probably because she was always interested in other people and others liked her in turn.

For many years Kamilla lived with Mrs. Eichengreen. I find it hard to say she "worked" for this lady, who was the mother-in-law of Joseph Block, the chairman of the Inland Steel Company. It may well be that those were among the happiest years of her life. The job was certainly not too demanding. I remember Kamilla once telling me about some travel itinerary she was supposed to work out for a long trip she was to take with Mrs. Eichengreen, then a very old lady.

When Kamilla had the journey all prepared, she showed it to the old woman, who looked at it, smiled, and then proceeded to do the entire itinerary over again and improved it considerably.

"I wonder," Kamilla asked me, "who works for whom? Whatever I do for Mrs. Eichengreen, she could do better herself and the Blocks treat me like a member of the family."

After Mrs. Eichengreen died, Kamilla found herself in a very secure situation financially. Her earnings may not have been very substantial, but she had kept all of it, spending virtually nothing for decades. Furthermore, she had been well-advised about how to invest her money, both by the Block family and later by her brother-in-law Stuart Pollay.

Kamilla decided to move to Los Angeles around 1960 and never left that city. Just why she moved there is not clear. True, she had her sister Anny there, but she also had her brother Pepa in New York. Her sister Marianne (my mother), who lived in Chicago, had died much earlier. Perhaps it was because Kamilla's best friend, Mrs. Rosenberger, whom she had known earlier in Vienna, had moved to Los Angeles a little earlier.

Kamilla found a little apartment in Los Angeles, made new friends, joined a temple, and was happy there. Both my brother and I visited her frequently. But more importantly, our cousin Heidi Pollay Baum kept an eye on her and was extremely helpful when needed.

A few years ago, it was time for Kamilla to move from her apartment into a retirement hotel. Not only had her neighborhood deteriorated over the years, but also she had just had a difficult operation, which turned out to have been unnecessary. Her health was not very good anymore. Lotte Ehrlich, Kamilla's second cousin, and her husband Joe, helped Kamilla enormously. All of Kamilla's old friends had died and the Ehrlichs were the only relatives living near Los Angeles. Finally, one of Kamilla's legs had to be amputated. She had to move to a full-care home and was truly miserable there, even though she was looked after well. Unfortunately, much of the time she was in pain. Her will to live was gone. Death came as a relief.

Kamilla may not have lived the most distinguished life but, except for her last year or so, was happy because she loved and was much loved by others. The Block family stayed in close contact with her until her death. My cousin Heidi, my brother Charles and I visited her frequently, as did the Ehrlichs. She also received visits from the next generation: John Weinman, Frances Schwartz, Dr. Linda Wolf, the Baum boys (Heidi and Jost Baum's sons), her grandnephews, as well as from grandnieces and other members of her extended family.

At least on the telephone, Kamilla could also talk to her niece Marietta in Austria and to her sister-in-law Mitzi in New York. Kamilla and Mitzi loved each other dearly.

Kamilla will always be remembered by all who loved her. May she rest in peace.

ADDITIONAL WRITINGS

The following stories were written by Frank Weinman over the years 1959 through 2006. They include reflections on turning 45, a Yom Kippur speech he gave at his synagogue in Walnut Creek, California, an account of his sentimental journey in 1996 to Central Europe with his two daughters, two of his grandchildren and his son-in-law, and his recollections of his 90th Birthday cruise, an event celebrated with his entire family, in 2004.

<u>AFTER 45</u>

One should make the last change of jobs before age 45, if at all, or so I had been told. Everybody, I guess, has his "druthers." I was no exception. Teaching, for instance, might be nice. I had done that for a while in the Sunday School of our congregation and might have liked it. Most of my students – an impossible bunch of 14-year-old children whom only their mothers could've loved – actually told me that I was a good teacher. But I could not handle the class clowns. These are usually intelligent but insecure boys out to make the teacher's job difficult by trying to be funny. I soon found out that the majority of the class didn't like their jokes, but laughed anyway.

I had another idea: owning a travel agency. I might be good at that, having knowledge of foreign languages; even my (German) accent could be helpful with customers who wished to travel abroad. I liked to talk to people and knew how to collect information.

But having a wife and two children made me appreciate my weekly paycheck that was, after all, not too low. And I did not actually dislike my job. I just wasn't crazy about it: formulating paints and adhesives, trying to come up with new products; writing specifications for our customers in such a way that our competitors would have difficulties meeting them. There was no possibility for advancement. My direct boss was my brother who was a much better chemist that I, a better manager and, most important, willing to work much harder than I was. Constant studying, be it the newest publications or voluminous books about organic chemistry, was not my idea of life. Since high school, I had always been a little lazy, preferring intuition to hard work.

One day in 1960, two Frenchmen contacted Mr. Eisenberg, the owner of our business. One, Mr. Duval, had a factory quite similar to ours: manufacturing decals, pictures or messages printed on a temporary surface. The other man, Mr. Simsi, was the supplier of paints to Mr. Duval. Both agreed that their products were not up to American standards. This was in 1960 when the whole world still thought a lot about the quality of U.S. products. Furthermore, several huge American companies, such as John Deere and Caterpillar tractors, had opened manufacturing plants in Europe, and had sent specifications for decals they needed to Mr. Duval, the owner of the largest French maker of decals. But Mr. Duval was not able to meet the American specifications. When he turned to his paint supplier for help, Mr. Simsi shrewdly suggested a trip to Chicago to ask for our help. Mr. Eisenberg was flattered.

"You see, Doc," he said to my brother, his right-hand man, "they know about us even over in France. But I wonder, what's in it for us?"

"Not much," said Charles. "We could supply them with the paints, at a good price, but they wouldn't know how to use them. It's too risky for us. They will, of course, let their customers know that they use our paint. And if they fail, that would reflect on us."

"True. Still, Doc, I'd like to help them. Let's have a meeting."

So, the four gentlemen met: Mr. Eisenberg, the successful man with very little formal education but an excellent head for business; my brother, the "Doc" who was, after all, responsible for the quality of our products; Monsieur Duval, the aristocratic Frenchman and last, but certainly not least, Mr. Simsi, probably the most interesting man of the four. He was a Sephardic Jew, born in Salonika, Greece, had fought in Israel in 1948 during their War of Independence, but then decided he didn't like the country ("Too Socialistic. They don't let you make any money!") and had emigrated to France. He got into the import business and called himself "Comptoir Franco-Britanique." He explained to me later: "Franco-Britanique" means that I am a Sephardic Jew. Most French companies use the name of their owners."

I don't know how Simsi became a manufacturer of paints; probably he imported paints but thought it might be cheaper to make them. He spoke French, Spanish, German, Hebrew, and English – all languages fairly fluently and with the same Greek accent. Duval, the conservative, tall, blonde Frenchman and Simsi, the short, swarthy Jew, made quite an interesting pair. They got along very well.

During the meeting, Simsi—the spokesman since Duval's English was poor—addressed my brother directly:

"Dr. Weinman, perhaps you could be persuaded, with Mr. Eisenberg's consent, of course, to spend some time in Paris with us."

My brother, who hated traveling as much as I liked it, interrupted with an icy smile: "I'd love to, of course, but unfortunately I happen to be in the middle of a project." Simsi wondered: "Could you, perhaps, suggest somebody in your organization who..."

It was Mr. Eisenberg who came up with an idea. Turning to Duval, who he seemed to respect more than Simsi, he said:

"Doc's brother, Frank, is in charge of formulating our paints. I could spare him for a month or so. Maybe he could be persuaded to work with you."

My brother, who was sure that I'd love to go, seconded Mr. Eisenberg's suggestion and said to Mr. Duval: "Il parle Francais, Messieurs" (he speaks French, gentlemen).

And that's how I came to be sent to Paris. Here was the deal: I would teach Simsi's people how to manufacture the paints he'd sell to Duval. For this service, Simsi would pay to American Decalcomania a thousand dollars, certainly a very small sum. Plus, however, five percent of the value of all paints made with our formulas. Duval, on the other hand, would pay us five percent of the invoices of finished goods he'd sell to European plants of American companies he would be able to satisfy, with the know-how he had learned from us.

In June 1960, I was on my way to Paris. Simsi had a room rented for me close to his plant, in a place called "Hotel Des Artistes." I'm sure not a single artist lived there. It was simple but adequate; my only problem was that it contained a bidet and I had no idea how to use it. Simsi greeted me on my arrival, but immediately made sure to let me know that I wouldn't see him often.

"I'm a very busy man. Of course, you'll be very busy too. I assigned a man to work with you. If something important should come up, contact my secretary for an appointment, then knock on my door and I'll see you."

"I'll be glad to keep you informed about our work, Mr. Simsi," I answered, smiling, "and I'll know how to find you." Mr. Simsi understood me: I'm the American expert, not his servant.

"Very good," he said, "and while you are in Paris, you'll want to see something of our town. Tomorrow, Mr. and Mme. Vedun, a very nice couple who work in my office, will take you to dinner at the Moulin Rouge."

At the Moulin Rouge *(Editor's note: The Moulin Rouge is the most famous cabaret in Paris)* I was surprised to find myself in a box next to the stage. It must've cost a small fortune. I was prepared to see one of those fancy reviews with many scantily-dressed ladies, but I certainly did not expect to become involved myself.

During one of the acts, a lady whose total garment would have fit into a thimble, slowly walked to our box, pointed at me, and with the bright lights shining on us, said:

"Mr. L'Amercain, viens ici! (come here)" What could I do? I stepped on the stage of the Moulin Rouge!

"Now," she continued, lifting her left breast with her right hand to make it look at me, "if you give me a kiss, I'll give you an orange!"

Again, what could I do? I planted a timid kiss on the grease paint that covered her cheek.

"Bon." She made a face at me, indicating the quality of my kiss to be inferior.

"Allez-vouz en (get out)!"

While I walked back to our box, the bright light was following me. Obviously, Mr. Simsi had arranged the whole thing; the Veduns laughed.

My work went pretty well as I had planned it. The man assigned to work with me, the foreman of the paint department, was a clever young Spaniard whose French was about as good as mine; he only spoke it with a different accent. "I had to run away in 1941, Franco would have me killed. But as soon as he dies, I'll go back! Spain is more beautiful!"

During lunch, as well as after working hours, Mr. Derchin, the man assigned to "take care of me" saw to it that I ate well (he paid, always) and told me that his name had been Derjinsky. He was a "White Russian" living in Paris since 1919. He even introduced me to his fiancée, easily 30 years younger than he.

The pretty, plump Frenchwoman and the Russian with his deeply lined, Slavic face made for an interesting couple, obviously devoted to each other.

Once, when I wanted to take them out and pay for the dinner, Mr. Derchin instructed me:

"Don't be silly. Simsi is paying, and well he can afford it!"

During long summer evenings and on weekends, I visited museums and theaters. But most of all I walked and walked. There is no city on earth where walking can be as much of a pleasure as in Paris. I took a Metro to the center of town and just walked in any direction, admiring what I saw. When I got tired, all I had to do was to find a Metro station, push a button with the name of the station closest to my hotel and voila, a light switched on a map instructing me how best to ride home. Oh, these clever French!

The "Comptoir" (that's how Simsi's place called itself) had a small department where rush orders were printed for local Paris customers of Mr. Duval, who's plant was in Limoges, 150 miles to the south. One day, the foreman of Simsi's printing department invited me to visit his place. I couldn't help noticing that the room was poorly ventilated; the fumes of the paints used – nitrocellulose lacquers – were rather strong. And several workers were smoking! I ran out, directly to Mr. Simsi's office and with no appointment, began knocking on his door.

"Your people want to blow up the place to kingdom come."

"What's the matter?" Simsi got a little excited too.

I explained to him that any spark from a cigarette could cause an instant explosion. The next day there were signs all over the plant:

DEFENCE DE FUMER! ABSOLUTELY NO SMOKING!

A few years later I visited the "Comptoir" again. Several workers were smoking, others had a lit cigarette dangling down from their lower lip. As far as I know they are still alive. God must love Frenchmen.

Towards the end of my stay in France, I was invited to Limoges to see Mr. Duval's factory. Limoges is a beautiful old French town. There is a ruin of a castle on the hill above. Most streets are still paved with cobblestones. Mr. Duval's plant, on the other hand, was quite modern, well-equipped with new machines. He gave me quite a buildup.

"This is the American expert who will help us to improve the quality of our products!" he said to his key employees who had assembled in his office.

"From now on, with Mr. Weinman's help, we'll be able to meet even the toughest specifications of our customers."

Actually, I could make only a few suggestions on how to improve their printing methods. Their main shortcoming had been the quality of the paint they used. (A few years later, their finished products were better

looking than ours. I guess more care was used in printing.)
Mr. Duval explained:

"We measure in millimeters in Europe, you in America use inches. Of course, we are more accurate because a millimeter is much smaller than an inch. (C'est la vie! Such a life!)

Before I left Chicago, my boss had asked me to visit three places for our company. In Germany and Italy new printing machines were made, possibly cheaper and better than the American ones. And in Belgium one of our customers had a plant manufacturing outboard motors that used our decals.

"I'll be happy to travel to these places," I said to my boss, "and I think I'd like to take my three weeks' vacation in Europe, following my work in France. But instead of paying three different railroad fares, it might be cheaper to buy a three-week Eurail Pass."

"Certainly." My boss immediately understood that I had in mind to travel all over Europe.

"Just don't forget to come back. By the way, isn't Israel fairly close to Europe? You could find out for me how this "gonef" (thief) is doing, the guy who bought machinery and paints from us but doesn't pay the bills. I'll pay for your airline fare from the nearest point in Europe." My wife agreed that I could extend my trip.

"Of course you should stay longer once you are in Europe. Afterwards, you'll appreciate us even more."

I couldn't help but feeling bad for missing my family for such a long time and spending a lot of money. I needn't have worried about the last point. When I said goodbye to Mr. Simsi he presented me with a check. "You spent thirty days with us, at $20 a day, this comes to $600."

"But," I said, 'you already paid for all my expenses, hotel, food…"

"Never mind! That's how I do my business."

I could see no reason not to take his money. That's how I came to be one of the few Americans who had a good time in France for a month, then spent three weeks traveling all over Europe and Israel but had more money when I came home than when I'd left. Six hundred dollars went a long way in the Europe of 1960.

Wanting to get the business calls behind me, I made Brugge (Bruges), Belgium my first stop. I had no idea of the eerie beauty of this town! The old city has little changed since the Middle Ages when it was an important harbor and trading center. The town is crisscrossed by canals with old stone bridges over them, so low that the passengers in the boats must lower their heads or bump into the bridges. Swans swim in the water; no cars are allowed in the old part of town; all is quiet; it seems unreal. Luckily, the modern hotels and all industries are kept apart from the old town. In the evening, when I ate in a good restaurant, I was to get a lesson in the European problem of ancient feuds between language groups.

The menu was printed in two languages: Flemish (similar to Dutch) on the right, French on the left. Not speaking Flemish, I placed my order in French. I was not prepared for the waiter's reaction. He screamed at me in English:

"You are obviously not a Frenchman. How dare you speak French in here! Don't you know that we in Brugge are Flemish?"

"But I don't know Flemish, and the menu is also in French."

The waiter, calmer now, explained: "You are a tourist. You don't know that we must print the menu in both languages. But please, speak English or German here, not French! We don't like that language."

My next stop was Wupperthal, an industrial city in Germany. I was ushered into the office of a man who introduced himself in the following manner:

"I am Chief-Diplom-Engineer Guenthet Wittels."

As he said this, he clicked his heels and bowed his six-foot frame, as he extended his hand to me. I had forgotten how title-happy the Germans are and had a little difficulty not laughing. Anyway, we got along well, although I had to report back to Chicago that the Italian machine was better and cheaper.

From Wupperthal, I took a train to nearby Cologne and had a sightseeing tour through the city. It was late evening now, and I wondered where to go next. It started to drizzle. My Eurail Pass entitled me to travel first class to any point in Europe, and studying the timetable of departures at the railroad station, Interlaken in Switzerland looked best to me. When I woke up after a restful night, I was the only passenger in my compartment. The majestic Swiss Alps greeted me in brilliant sunshine! I hadn't been in Switzerland since my Boy Scout days as a poor Austrian; now I was a "rich American" who could afford to spend money. I walked up a green meadow, listened to the cowbells, admired the snow-capped mountains, and knew that something was wrong. It took me a while to find out just what made me feel uneasy. Then I understood: there's no point in seeing anything beautiful without being able to ask somebody close to you: "Isn't it wonderful? Just look at this mountain, did you ever see such…"

I knew it then and still know it now: I'm not fit to be alone.

Taking advantage of the beautiful weather, I traveled up and down the famous Jungfraujoch (*a "saddle" between two mountains, the Jungfrau and Mönch*), revisited places I had seen as a scout, including the Vierwaldstaettersee (*Lake Lucerne*) where William Tell once roamed. After seeing more of Switzerland, I took a night train from Zürich to Vienna.

In the Austrian parlor car, I listened to a conversation. "The Americans are not only stupid but also cruel," a young man, an Austrian, explained to anybody who would listen to him. "Just because my father was a guard in a concentration camp during the war and not very nice to the Jews, they hanged him."

"Terrible," another passenger agreed. "to kill a man who only did his duty? After all, we were Germans at that time."

"Oh, how we Austrians suffered!" a woman chimed in. "Not only did the Nazis occupy our country, but later the Russians were so beastly to us, they even cut down some of the trees in the Vienna Woods."

Well, Austria is a lovely country, Vienna may be one of the most beautiful cities, but I still don't like the Austrians very much.

It takes nearly 24 hours to travel from Vienna to Rome. Wishing to arrive there in the morning, I left Vienna with the early luxury train. I almost had my compartment to myself; but at the last moment a lady with a big suitcase arrived. I helped her stow it away and of course we started to talk. Now, more than 30 years later, I can't remember what she looked like or what her name was. I'm only sure that she was around 40 years old, the age at which I always found women most attractive. She had a good figure and a pleasant voice. We spoke English, but I detected an ever so slight Austrian accent.

Yes, she had left Vienna as a little girl and was living in New York, working for a travel magazine, now writing about Austria, especially covering theaters. We both had seen the opera *Der Rosencavalier* the night before.

"A beautiful performance," I said, "they still know how to do operas in Vienna."

"Not only was the orchestra and the singing outstanding," she agreed, "but also the acting. I could really feel the Marschallin's sadness knowing she could not hold her young lover anymore."

"Well," I interrupted, "the opera was written two generations ago and the action was supposed to take place 200 years earlier. I wonder if, nowadays, a 39-year-old beautiful woman would feel too old to have a lover?"

"Don't be too sure," she said softly. As we kept discussing opera, literature, even politics, we couldn't help noticing how similar our views were, as if we had known each other for a long time. I liked this woman.

"I'm leaving this train in the evening, when we get to the lakes in southern Austria," she said. "How far are you going?"

"All the way to Rome. I'll be on this train until tomorrow morning."

"Must you be in Rome tomorrow? Is anybody expecting you?"

"Not really. In the morning I'll have to attend to some business, then I'll just do sightseeing. I've never been in Rome before."

"Rome has been there for a long time. It'll wait another day for you. Why don't you interrupt your trip, get out with me this evening?"

Well, I did. Why not enjoy the beauty of the country I knew so well from my Boy Scout days? We checked into the same hotel, in adjoining rooms. It was soon obvious to me that she knew many people in the hotel.

There was a party going on. I was invited as her guest. During dinner I wondered what to do. There was no question what she had in mind: she must have liked me as I liked her. She asked me to leave the train with her and I had done just that; didn't that imply consent? Still, I had never had such an adventure before. Should I really? I ate a lot that evening; we danced, and between dances I drank quite a bit of the delicious sweet liqueur they served. At midnight I was very, very tired. Well, equality of the sexes may be with us, but it is still true that if the man does nothing, nothing happens. I retired to my room.

The next morning, we took a little trip on the beautiful mountain lake in a small electric boat; there was none of the noise of American powerboats. We didn't talk for a long time. Suddenly she asked me: "Did you ever cheat on your wife?"

I felt I should tell the truth. "No, never."

"You are a lucky man," she said softly.

I'm quite sure that she did not say: your wife is a lucky woman. What a smart lady I had met on the train. We said goodbye that evening, not even pretending we might see each other again. Today, all I remember of her is a pleasant voice. I'll never know what she really thought of me.

Arriving in Rome early in the morning, I bought my airplane ticket to Israel for the next day, then quickly took care of the business my boss had asked me to do: visit a shop that manufactured printing machines similar to the ones we used. What I learned was quite interesting because it taught me how business was done in Europe, or at least in Italy.

"Isn't your machine rather similar to the American model?" I asked the plant manager who demonstrated his product.

"Of course it is," he admitted. "Only we made quite a few improvements. Our machine is really better. Furthermore, since our wages are lower, we can sell it to you at a very attractive price."

"But the American manufacturer has a patent on his machine. Aren't you violating it?" I wondered.

"Certainly," he said. "But so far we only gave our product to a few Italian friends; they won't squeal on us. And they suggested improvements we should make! Next spring the American patent will expire. We'll be ahead of our competitors because only we will have had our machines already tested!"

In the afternoon the manager took me sightseeing all over Rome. A bribe? (Upon my return to Chicago I reported all this to my boss. He bought five Italian machines at $8,000 each for delivery next spring. They were of superior quality and thirty percent cheaper than the American model.)

I don't think that I was in the perfect mood for sightseeing in Rome, especially since all the time I had was one afternoon and a few hours the next morning. Still, I dutifully visited the Vatican. Even more than the Sistine Chapel, I admired St. Peter's Square in front of the building. When I looked towards the Vatican, it seemed to be quite close. There are many columns on both sides. All one had to do is walk between them in order to get to the door. But, as I walked and walked, I hardly came closer. The enormous square where the faithful assemble who want to hear the Pope seemed to be endless.

I remembered I had a similar feeling in the Canadian Rocky Mountain National Park, standing on an ice field: the mountains looked so close, but they were many miles away. One understands, standing on this square, that when the Pope speaks "urbi et orbi," to the town and to the world, his voice carries far.

On the Forum Romanum (*the Roman Forum*) it was the Arch of Titus I especially wanted to see. Because it celebrates the destruction of Jerusalem in the year 70, Jews are not supposed to walk through it. But if my cousin in Vienna could forget what happened there just a few decades ago, I might well be excused from mourning about an event 1,900 years in the past.

Next day to Israel!

I am certainly not a very observant Jew; my commitment to Judaism is more one of intellect than of feeling. And yet, when our airplane approached the coast, I felt my heart beat a little faster. The Roman Empire, which destroyed Jerusalem, has long disappeared, but the Jews are back in the land of their ancestors.

Israel in 1960 was a very small, somewhat shabby-looking country. The traveler cannot help but form his first impression at the airport: it looked so primitive, especially coming from Rome. There was dust all over. The first thought that came to mind: "this is a poor country."

My cousin Dolfi greeted me at the airport; he had hardly aged since I saw him more than 20 years earlier; much less than my cousin Otto in Vienna, or me, for that matter.

"When we were children, you didn't believe me when I told you I'd be living in Israel someday. Well, here you are, too. You are staying in the country, of course; you will have your wife and children come soon."

"Not so fast," I said. "Right now I'm on a business trip."

"Anyway," he said, "right now you're coming home with me. Tamara and the children are expecting you."

We had been very close when we were children in Vienna. "Dolfi" (short for Adolph) was my father's sister's son, a few months younger than me. As a child, he had been very short; for many years, the clothes I had outgrown just fitted him. But when he was about 15-years-old, he didn't stop growing as I did; at 20 he was much taller than me. But, somehow, I still remembered him as "little Dolfi."

He had his car – a late French model – at the airport and drove me to his apartment in Yafo, now part of Tel Aviv. It was a hot day in June, but not nearly as uncomfortable as in Chicago. I guess once you have lived in Chicago you can live anywhere.

"The street we live on is called "Donolo" after a Spanish physician of the Middle Ages," he explained. "Very convenient because our place is right next to the hospital."

"YOUR hospital?" I asked. Dolfi laughed.

"No, I don't own it. I only run it. Donolo Hospital is owned by the government." This was my introduction to the fact that my little cousin Dolfi, now Professor Daniel (you can't be called "Adolf" in Israel) Brunner was a real big shot now.

"I was lucky," he explained to me much later. "As a young doctor, I realized that Israel couldn't compete with America or even Europe when it came to big investments in medical machines. So, I was looking for something new that didn't cost any money but would still help people! The first thing I studied was the influence of running – jogging, the Americans call it, I believe. It's good for the heart. I wrote a paper about it. Your President Eisenhower's physician, Dr. White, picked it up. Then I noticed that the Yemenite Jews had hardly any heart diseases, many fewer than the taller and better nourished European Jews.

Guessing that this had something to do with their diet, I started a controlled experiment: 100 Yemenites were given good, fat, European food and 100 other Yemenites were left to eat their usual vegetable diet, with maybe chicken once a month. All 200 received a bottle of wine every week. That made them come and be examined. After a few years, the fat-eating Yemenites had the same amount of heart problems as the Europeans, although they thought they were the lucky ones because they had gained weight and became stronger. I only hope they went back to their old diet after the study was over."

"How did you get to be in charge of a big hospital?" I asked.

"During the War of Independence in 1948, I fought in the 'Palmach,' the elite troops of our new army. I had the good luck to survive; not too many officers did. In Central Europe, before coming here in 1940, I had been rather well known as one of the leaders of the Zionist movement, mostly for helping to bring many thousands of young Jews here, illegally, of course. This is a small country. Among the "old Zionists" everybody knows everybody. In 1949, I was offered an ambassadorship, but I asked rather to be put into a large hospital, working under an excellent heart specialist. A few years ago, I was put in charge. A little 'networking' doesn't hurt, not even in the State of Israel. Of course, it helps, but being promoted at such a young age leads to jealousies, especially in Israel, where jealousy is a national vice."

My cousin also told me how he met his wife, Tamara.

"(Moshe) Sharett, the second prime minister of Israel, was, during the war, in charge of the health of the Jewish settlements. He asked me why I wasn't married. 'Every Jewish man should marry and have children. Don't you know that, he said.'

'But I have no time to meet anybody,' I answered. That was in 1942. I had the job of checking the water supply of the Jewish settlements; we still had a lot of malaria at that time."

Tamara, my cousin's wife, took up the story. She would have been beautiful had her face not been already deeply lined by the merciless Israeli sun. (But now, more than 30 years later, she looks young. She's hardly changed.)

"I was working in a kibbutz, picking oranges when the manager approached me: 'A young doctor is coming over to make sure that our water is not contaminated,' he said. Sharett asked me to get somebody to show him around, but it should be a girl who speaks German. The doctor's Hebrew is still bad. He comes from Vienna. You are from Berlin, so talk to him in German. You know we Russians and 'Yeckes' don't always get along." ("Yeckes" is a mild cuss word the Eastern European, Yiddish-speaking Jews used for their "German" brothers. It comes from the word "Jacket," meaning German Jews are so formal—or stupid—that they wear a jacket even when it is hot.)

"I guess our water was OK. Anyway, the young doctor and I liked each other enough to get married and have three children. Even after Mr. Sharett became Prime Minister, he was still bragging about having brought us together."

"The best thing he ever did," my cousin admitted.

Well, Tamara is the best thing that ever happened to my cousin. He may be very intelligent and industrious – he can study most of the night after having worked all day – but he is impulsive and headstrong. Without his wife's moderating influence, her common sense, he wouldn't be where he is now.

"Nobody ever slept with a better secretary," my cousin often said.

Unfortunately, I had only five days to spend in Israel, and one of them was reserved for business. I had to look up the man who had bought paints and machinery from our company but didn't pay his bills. I could only confirm my boss's suspicion: this man lived above his means, had a poor reputation as a businessman and his own plant was hardly functioning. My boss could never forget his "bad investment" in Israel, and though good opportunities came his way later, he said to anybody who would listen: "I don't trust these Israelis. They are thieves."

With my cousin's help, I tried to pack as much as possible into my short stay in Israel.

My biggest disappointment was the city of Jerusalem. Right through the middle of town, like a black, obscene snake, ran a wall of barbed wire, at least 10 feet high and just as wide. Next to it was a whole city block with nothing but rubble; the nearest houses still standing were pockmarked with bullet holes. I couldn't even see the old, walled city. There was quite a bit of building activity but nothing seemed to be finished.

"Why do you waste your resources?" I asked my cousin. "This place looks so dreary; it will never amount to anything!"

He strongly disagreed. "Don't you ever believe that! Things will change. Jerusalem is eternal, it will be beautiful again!" (Today the terrible scars have healed. Thanks to excellent planning, Jerusalem is indeed one of the most beautiful cities I've ever seen.)

We drove to the Kineret ("Harp," in Hebrew), the Lake of Galilee. It was a hot day and we went swimming. My cousin, a much better swimmer than I, swam far out into the lake. Soon I couldn't see him anymore.

"Your friend is crazy," a bystander who had watched us enter the water, said to me.

"Doesn't he know that the Syrians are shooting down from the Golan Heights, just for the fun of it?"

This didn't make me feel very good; luckily, my cousin showed up half an hour later.

"I always survive," was his only comment. On the other hand, I wasn't sure I would survive my cousin's driving. Physicians have a poor reputation as drivers. Israelis, at that time at least, were notorious for their inability to handle a car. The driving of an Israeli physician, especially one like my cousin, whose mind is always somewhere else, can be rather frightening. Once, we rounded a hill, on the wrong side of the highway, and suddenly there was a truck. Luckily, we could both stop. The truck driver got out, a huge man, tall and brawny.

"You are a jackass!" he said to my cousin. "A big jackass."

Later, I asked my cousin: "Doesn't he have any better words?"

"The Hebrew language is poor as far as curses go," he said. "The Bible doesn't have any. But we are learning from the Arabs and our children will soon teach us."

We were to spend the night in the kibbutz where my cousin had "found" his wife. As we walked down the lane towards the assembly hall, I heard the sounds of Beethoven's Ninth Symphony coming from one of the cottages.

"How come you sang only Hebrew songs in Vienna, but in Israel, you play German music?" I asked my cousin.

"Now we have our own state. We can afford to play anything we like!" My cousin introduced me to German-speaking members of the kibbutz and we had a lively conversation. An old lady – she must've been close to 90 – said, "I used to be strong, a long time ago. Until last year I could darn socks, but now my hands are not steady enough. But I'm still working. I decide which socks can still be done and which should be discarded."

A young man explained to me: "We had a lot of malaria because the brook running through our kibbutz formed a swamp, a breeding-ground for insects. We drained the swamp, of course, and we made it flow straight into the sea. But that was not a good idea! We were losing the water. Now we collect the water for fish ponds; we can use the protein."

I couldn't help asking myself: what am I doing in America, making decals that our competitors could make just as well? In Israel, there's real work to be done. But my family is in Chicago. When I left Israel, I promised to come back, even if only as a tourist. I've done it ten times so far; so have my children and my grandchildren.

Later, on my way back to Paris from Rome, I decided to stop in Cannes, on the French Riviera, arriving there in the morning.

After seeing a little of the town, I took a small steamship to one of the nearby islands. It was time for lunch; but as I entered a restaurant, I could not find an empty table.

Observing me looking around, a group of people asked me to join them. When I introduced myself – you have to do that – and my foreign accent was obvious, a discussion immediately started about what I was to order and even more important, which of the local wines I should drink. I followed instructions, had a good meal with good wine, said goodbye and went swimming at the nearby beach, admiring the beautiful ladies with nothing on above their belly buttons.

When I took the boat back to the mainland in the late afternoon, I noticed a good-looking lady was glancing at me, slowly approaching me. Finally, she spoke to me, modestly lowering her eyes.

"Excusez-moi, Monsieur."

"Madame?" What am I in for now, I asked myself.

"It is a shame, a national disgrace, what they told you when you had lunch. I happened to be sitting at the next table and heard it all."

"But they were so friendly, they asked me to join their table."

"Of course. But, Monsieur, they advised you wrong! You should have taken a different wine, one that goes well with your meal! But excuse me now, we are arriving in Cannes and my husband is over there expecting me."

Well, MY wife and children were expecting ME back home!

CAN WE FORGIVE?

The following was delivered by Frank Weinman at Temple Isaiah in Lafayette, California on Yom Kippur, 1993.

Today, before we can ask God, the Supreme Being, to forgive our own sins, we must forgive other fellow mortals who sinned against us. But can we? Should we? Must we? Always?

Suppose somebody spilled ink on our carpet. We are furious at first. But after we have the ink stain cleaned – the wrong-doer may even have paid for it – we can forgive, although a slight shadow still persists. That's easy. But what if the ink was indelible, the staining done on purpose, with the clearly stated intent to ruin our carpet forever?

Well, the carpet stained with regular ink is my life. The Nazis—I am talking about them, of course—hurt me and all the European Jews. Most of the survivors are in Israel now, but many are scattered in this country and all over the world, even in Germany. We have been uprooted, damaged perhaps, but we <u>live</u>, still able to praise God.

But what of the indelible stain, the six million killed, be they children or adults, and not by accident, but on purpose with the intention to kill, because they existed? Worst of all, what of the Jewish children who were never born because the parents who should have conceived them were not allowed to live? Some of us want to say Kaddish for loved ones, but we don't know the precise day when the Nazis killed them. We've had to select one day. The day we select is usually the day when the uprising in the Warsaw Ghetto occurred, 50 years ago. Let us remember: Fifty Years Ago!

This means that when I meet a German, say age 68 or over, he could be the one who pushed my loved-ones into the gas ovens or who shot them with a bullet in the head. How can I shake his hand? How dare I forgive him, even on Yom Kippur?

And yet... As I am asking for guidance, looking for words in our own ancient Holy Scriptures telling me what to do, I came across the number 50 in a very significant context. We are reading in Chapter 25 of the Book of Leviticus, that every 50 years, on the blowing of the Shofar on Yom Kippur, a Jubilee would start. All Hebrew slaves must be set free. ALL HEBREW SLAVES MUST BE SET FREE.

Well, can one be like a slave although physically free? I think so. Yes, we can be enslaved by hatred, even though we feel that this hatred was justified by what was done to us; many wars were based on such hatred. But could it be possible for me, upon the hearing of the Shofar on this Yom Kippur, to become free of the slavery of hating?

To be sure, our Scriptures tell us many times to remember: we are never commanded to forget. But maybe, just maybe, on this 50th anniversary of the death of Jewish heroes in the Warsaw Ghetto, we might at least be trying to emancipate ourselves from the SLAVERY OF HATING, a slavery that only hurts ourselves. Well, some can do this. Others cannot and they should be understood too. But as for myself, I'll try – I will try. There is a German man in a club I belong to, about 70 years old. I know nothing of his past. The next time I see him I will try to shake his hand.

A SENTIMENTAL JOURNEY
MAY- JUNE 1996

I. THE SUITCASE CARRIER AND THE PRODUCER.

Let me start with the suitcase. As long as I can remember, I've always carried my own! Well, it may have been a backpack, a long, long time ago when I was a Boy Scout. I was very proud to carry it then. I would show anybody how grown-up, well, almost grown-up I was already: "Look, I'm not a child anymore. I don't need anybody to help me."

Some 10 years later I could have used a little help, but not necessarily with carrying my suitcase, although it contained all my belongings, all my possessions: six shirts, six sets of underwear, one pair of shoes, one suit. My baggage was light. My problem was not how to carry it, but rather where to? To what destination? Not how to lift my suitcase up but where to put it down. But after a few years of wandering, I did find myself settled in Chicago, safe and sound and married. Luck had been with me. To handle a suitcase was certainly the last thing on my mind. I was happy to be where I was; no traveling for me, not for a while.

Many years went by. We had two daughters, they would go to summer camps, but first we had to get them to a train.

"Help me with my suitcase, daddy!" Of course, I was elected to do just that, to lift up the suitcase through the train window. Who else to perform this easy task? Wasn't I the only man in the family? (As the late author Franz Werfel put it so succinctly: a carrier of the spear.) Still later, when my girls went to college, I was allowed for the first time perhaps, to carry their luggage to the dorm where my wife would unpack the suitcases and see to it that all sweaters and underwear would be neatly placed in the proper drawers, knowing quite well, of course, that in a day or two a more familiar sloppiness would take over.

Well, a few years later, there were sons-in-law. It was their duty now to provide the necessary muscles for carrying suitcases for my daughters! There are now only the two of us, my wife and myself, just as it was many years earlier. We were still young enough to travel with me in charge of our luggage. That's how it was, that's how it should be. I wouldn't have it any other way.

Many more years ran through my life. Years formed decades, several of them. But traveling is still in my blood, as long as I can manage. I want to see more than my immediate surroundings; I want to revisit places where I've been before and see new sites. So, when my children and grandchildren suggested a "sentimental journey" to Central Europe, I was happy to participate, maybe act as a tour director. A last hurrah for me, perhaps?

We rented a van, the six of us: my two daughters, one of my sons-in-law (the other had to beg off at the last minute; too much work, he couldn't get away), my two oldest grandchildren (two more were too young) and me. Although we traveled light, especially me, there seemed to be more luggage than the van could hold. But miraculously, all our suitcases did fit into the back of the vehicle!

Another miracle: I wasn't involved; my expertise wasn't called on.

"Just sit down, Grandpa, next to the driver's seat!" I was told.

A new experience: I didn't have to drive. Navigate, yes. I can still read maps rather well, even in foreign countries and, moreover, I had been there before. And when it came to checking in at hotels, I went ahead with the driver in order to negotiate for the best rooms available. If they didn't know English, I was there to translate. Since we rarely stayed in big hotels (let's not spend a lot of money for sleeping, we decided), there was never anybody there to take care of our luggage. But never mind.

WHEN I GOT TO MY ROOM, MY SUITCASE WAS ALREADY THERE!

Even if my room was on the third floor, without an elevator, I didn't have to worry.

My grandson had taken care of my luggage! And not only mine. He would grab two or three suitcases (including my daughters', which were rather heavy) at the same time and, without even groaning, carry them where they were supposed to be. I couldn't have done that, never, not even when I was his age. As a matter of fact, nobody else in our family is endowed with especially strong muscles. But David has them.

David, age 22, wasn't allowed to drive during our European trip; the insurance premium for boys under 25 is prohibitive. But when we came to Hallstatt, a small town close to Salzburg, his time had come. Our family rented a small powerboat on the lake next to town. Our family voted democratically, the vote was unanimous: David was selected to be the captain and driver. He took us out onto the lake, perhaps the prettiest I've ever seen! The lake is small; it covers only a few square miles. Although the weather was perfect with not a cloud in the sky, the sun couldn't reach the water because high mountains surrounded it. The town of Hallstatt clings to a ledge next to the lake; there is room for two churches but not enough room for a real cemetery! The dead are buried in a small plot of a few square yards, but only for 25 years. Then the bodies are exhumed in order to make room for newcomers. The skulls are saved and displayed in an ossuary.

There is no parking in town, which is not a great hardship because except for emergency vehicles, motor traffic is not allowed. We had to leave our car in a parking lot, which looked from our view on the lake like a hole in a mountain, some hundred feet up, with steep stairs leading down into town. This is a place that has hardly changed in hundreds, perhaps thousands of years. It was already inhabited by a Celtic tribe when the Romans discovered it. They were mining the nearby salt deposits, the "Hall" of Hallstead means "salt" in the Celtic tongue.

We didn't hear a sound as we sailed on the lake. There were no wakes because only electric boats were allowed. To David's chagrin, we couldn't go very fast; this gave us lots of time to admire the darkly wooded mountains stretching up to the sky. The word "majestic" couldn't be held back from our minds.

Before we went on our trip, I tried to lay out our itinerary in such a way that there should be an equilibrium between seeing great cities, and admiring ancient, picturesque castles or ruins (by the way, personally I could do without castles and ruins but my family, all good Americans, admire these sort of things). They also admire nature, if possible unspoiled nature, of a kind that should be different from what we see in America. Hallstatt in Austria and its lake had been one of those places I remembered; I had visited it when I was a Boy Scout, in my early teens.

Another was the High Tatra Mountains in Slovakia. I had visited them for the last time in 1937 when I was living in Bratislava, Slovakia's capital.

There were four of us on that trip: my best boyfriend and his girlfriend and, most important, my fiancé as well as I. Was it just our happiness, our young love, that gave me such fond, melancholy memories? My friends perished a few years later under the Nazis. My fiancé, later my wife, the mother of my daughters, has been dead for 20 years. I wondered: is this place, the High Tatra Mountains, really as beautiful as I remembered it?

Well, it is. Our party, in late spring of 1996, had spent the night in a charming, ancient walled town some 38 miles away, avoiding the ugly high-rise tourist traps the Communist regime had built near the mountains from the 1960s through the 1980s, where most unfortunate German, Italian, French or British tourists are sent by their travel agents or tour guides.

When we arrived at "Strbske pleso" (don't even try to pronounce it unless you know Slovakian or a related language) near the foot of the mountains, I was disappointed. The weather, beautiful until an hour earlier, had become overcast and foggy. We couldn't even see the mountains I had praised so much to my children and grandchildren. Nevertheless, we set out, on a rocky, sometimes steep path, to climb to the place I remembered so well.

"Don't worry, grandpa," David said. "As we get higher, it will clear up! Anyway, the trees are beautiful!" He was right. No more than half an hour later and a few hundred feet higher, we first saw a few patches of blue sky. Unfortunately, my older daughter, David's mother, had been "under the weather" for a few days. Possibly higher altitude didn't agree with her. She felt bad and looked pale. We considered turning back.

"You just keep going!" David said. "I'll take mom down, get her to a restaurant where she can wait for a few hours. I'll catch up with you before you know it!"

"But that will be an hour..." David's dad objected. "Maybe we should all..."

"Maybe nothing!" David could get a little angry when he was contradicted. "You're walking so slowly. I'll be with you soon!"

Sure enough, David showed up an hour later. "Mom wants you to be sure not to hurry!" He said. "She's fine!" Well, so was the weather. The few patches of blue sky had spread until there was only a wisp of clouds left! We were now in the middle of high mountains, just at the line where the trees get stunted and flowery meadows take over. High above us we saw craggy mountains, waterfalls, and just half an hour's walk ahead of us, one of these little lakes which make this landscape so uniquely beautiful.

These lakes are called "more oci" in Slovakian, or "the eyes of the ocean." People say the water is so deep that it connects directly to the sea.

"Thanks, grandpa, for leading us here," David, the boy from New Jersey, said. "This must be the highlight of our trip!"

David had been rather small for his age when he was very young. Not only was he short, he also wouldn't talk, at least not to me, until he was more than three years old. Once, I was driving him and his older sister to a swimming pool. She wondered:

"Grandpa, we should be there already. Are you taking a longer way, not like daddy always does?"

"No," little David entered the conversation. "It's the same route. It only seems longer because daddy drives faster than grandpa."

Well, not only did David utter a perfect sentence, but also, he had his facts right (by the way his daddy still drives a little too fast, or so his wife, my daughter, has been heard to say). I had to wait two more years for David's next sentence. He was a cute little boy, five years old, when we took him to a zoo. He stopped in front of the lion's cage.

"You are the king of all the animals," David addressed the huge beast. "You are the king because you are strong!"

In high school, David must have decided that if his short, light body was a lemon, he might as well make lemonade: he joined the wrestling team! Since he was obviously in the lowest weight class, he had as good a chance as anybody else to win! So, he started training and because he had a very well-proportioned body, he soon grew muscles in the right places. He didn't always win but did prevail often enough to be encouraged to continue his training. He kept on growing until he's now 5 feet 5 inches tall; still on the short side, perhaps, but nobody who sees his huge biceps would call him a shrimp. At the same time, his little boy features became strong, very manly. After getting his degree in communications from Syracuse University, he got a job at a talent agency. He looks at the audition tapes and interviews applicants for jobs in broadcasting news, sports or commercials. Then he helps find them jobs. Recently, at age 22, David's picture was in Cosmopolitan Magazine as one of the most eligible bachelors of New Jersey. There are two from every state of the union. He had to rent a post box in order to accommodate letters from ladies who might write to him.

"How many letters did you get so far?" I asked him.

"Oh, about 25."

"How many did you answer?"

"One. It was funny."

David is still not a man of many words. Last summer he was "bumming around" all over Europe with a girl.

"Do you still see her?" I wanted to know.

"Naw. We had fun together, but after a month I said goodbye to her."

"What did she say?"

"I don't know."

Well, David, the strong man, my oldest grandson, should learn that some girls should be treated gently, with care. Because of their sex, they are said to be weak.

Girls? Weak? Not David's older sister Dana!

Dana won't win any competition in weightlifting: 5 feet 2 inches tall, perfectly proportioned, 25 years old. Yet, she's one of the strongest women I've ever met. She's also very pretty. And she knows what she wants!

She always did. When she was three or four years old, I took her to the park. We played in the playground, we admired the flowers and the ducks swimming in a pond, a little waterfall; finally, we walked back towards the parked car.

"Grandpa, carry me!" Dana wailed suddenly.

"It's only 50 feet from here to the car," I explained.

"But I'm sooo tired!"

"Dana, we've been playing for two hours now. Surely you can walk for one more minute." Whatever the logic of this statement was, it escaped her.

"Carry me!"

"No."

"If you don't carry me, I'll sit down right here."

She did just that. A contest of wills.

"And I will never, never get up!" She added. I wasn't going to let this little girl beat me! "Ok, stay here, I'm going home." I walked a few feet, carefully monitoring the situation by looking back, hopefully without her noticing. She was sitting on the asphalt path. I walked another ten feet. Still, she didn't move. Wondering how I should handle this situation without losing face, I kept walking, very slowly. Suddenly she was running, skipping past me to the car. Then she turned around and hollered:

"Grandpa, I beat you! You're so slow. You must be tired!"

I can't prove it, but it's a fair guess that this was the last time she didn't prevail. Certainly, she managed to manage her parents. She attended George Washington University and decided to stay in D.C. after graduation. Following in her daddy's footsteps, she chose a career in television.

"How did you find a job?" I asked her.

"By interning for anybody who would have me." I had to show my ignorance.

"What's interning?"

"Actually, for a student or any other beginner it means hanging around, working without pay. By the time I was a senior in college, I had interned at ABC, NBC, CBS and CNN. I didn't know much, but I tried to help out wherever I could. I guess I made a little nuisance of myself; but I wanted to make sure they would remember me. After graduation, I found an opening at CNN. It was a terrible job, but I got my foot in the door."

"What did you do?"

"Sit in the tape library, which is really a room in the basement, looking at tapes and finding old material that would relate to reports somebody was working on. After half a year, I couldn't stand this any longer and pushed for a job where I would have more contact with life, and with people, rather than with tapes. Luckily, somebody took pity on me and I was made a 'gofer' (this means someone who "goes for" just about anything) in the main office. I got to know reporters who are really important; Wolf Blitzer, especially, who gave me some real work to do."

"Like what, for instance?"

"Contact people he wanted to interview; get hotel reservations for them, make sure that they showed up on time and in good condition, kid around with them until it was time to be on camera. For instance, there was Texas Senator Phil Graham, who was then running for the Republican nomination for president. I complimented him on his well-fitting gray suit; I told him he looked handsome. He, of course, had to tell me that my blue dress was nice. Now, you know, Grandpa, that Senator Graham has a thick Texas accent and I, well, I'm from New Jersey."

"Gray and blue, Senator," I said to him. "I'm glad we're not fighting the Civil War anymore. He was amused. He laughed and laughed until it was time to go on camera. My boss, Wolf Blitzer, found him in good spirits, easy to interview."

I asked Dana what other shows on CNN she was connected with?

"Well, several. For instance, *Evans and Novak* is one." *(Editor's note: Evans and Novak was a weekly public affairs show on CNN that aired for twenty years.)*

I may have made a sour face because she added quickly: "Oh, Mr. Evans is really a nice man. I must prepare myself very well for his interviews."

"YOU must prepare?" I wondered.

"Yes. You know, Mr. Evans and others, of course, has a little earpiece, a bug, in one ear. I am on the other end of this bug talking to them. Whenever I notice that Mr. Evans needs a follow-up question, I whisper one into is ear, then it's funny to hear my words come out of his mouth! Here I am, a little "pisher," telling this man old enough to be my grandfather what to say."

"How's Mr. Novak?" I asked her.

It took her a while to find an answer.

"Mr. Novak?" she said, "You get what you see, you know…"

At that moment Dana reminded me of my father, her great grandfather. He, too, would never say anything bad about anybody. I once asked him about a man who was said to be a drunk and a poor provider for his family. "He does the best he can," was my father's answer.

Dana likes what she does, but she always wants to do more. "I got a new job recently," she told me. I'm a field producer now. I've wanted this job for some time, but they told me that I was too young. Of course, I pushed and pushed until I got it. I guess I was promoted over others who've been with CNN much longer."

"Aren't you afraid that somebody might step on you?"

"No, not at all. You see, I'm nice to everybody and helpful if it's necessary and if they want me to do it, I'm covering for my bosses. They like me, I know. They are really great people at CNN in Washington. By the way, as a field producer, I now have to travel quite a bit. I must prepare for interviews, figure out if it's cheaper to hire local camera crews or bring our own, make sure the photographers stand in the right place during the interviews."

"What is the most difficult part of your new job?"

"That's an easy question to answer, Grandpa. Before I can start with any project, I must get the budget approved. That takes a lot of preparation because I must be on solid ground when the big shots who hold the purse strings ask lots of tough questions."

"Aren't you afraid sometimes, you, a rather young little lady with all kinds of men around you?" I wondered.

"Me? Afraid?" Dana laughed. And her mother, my daughter, assured me. "My Dana can always take care of herself." *(Editor's Note: Dana is currently (2017) the Chief Political Correspondent for CNN.)*

It didn't take long for Dana to start bossing me around a little, and I enjoyed every minute of it. In Salzburg, when I gave a little lecture (I'm prone to do that, I'm afraid; a congenital disease) on the town's history under the rule of various bishops, good ones and not so good ones, she made me repeat it while standing on the walls of the fortress overlooking the city. It was a beautiful, clear day, a rarity in Salzburg, where it often rains. We could see the whole town on both sides of the River Salzach with its baroque domes, its beautiful gardens. While I was talking, she kept her camcorder running, panning out across the city, now towards the surrounding mountains and sometimes, I'm sorry to admit, having me in the picture. Later, in front of the Mozart Houses (there are two in Salzburg; one where he was born and another where he spent most of his younger years) there was a repeat performance: she filming and me talking.

I can make a good case for my guess that without Dana's prompting and pushing, our trip might not have come to be. Sure, I wanted to do it, but more on a theoretical level.

I may have asked: "wouldn't it be nice if we could travel to Central Europe, all of us, together?" Dana thought so too but added: "OK. Let's find a date that's convenient for everybody. We must adjust our vacation times. I want to see exactly where grandpa grew up."

Well, when we came to Vienna, she wanted to know everything: where I went to school, how the park looked where I played, and the theaters I visited most often. And she was impressed at how close they were to my parents' apartment where I grew up.

I took my family to the house where we lived until 1938. Dana, the producer, made me stand in front of the house. I had to tell my story to the camcorder.

"Until the 1850s, there had been walls around the inner city of Vienna, although most people lived already in the suburbs. The emperor, Franz Josef, decided that the walls had to come down; they served no more purpose. During the next decades, the famous "Ringstrasse" Boulevard was built, replacing the walls. The Opera House, the Parliament, the City Hall, the Palace of Justice, the Burgtheater, many gardens and parks were built at that time, as well as many great hotels. All are still standing in perfect condition."

"Now just outside this ring street, but before the existing suburbs began, there was a vacant space. We are standing there now. This was high-priced property. Expensive buildings, built according to the best standards of the second half of the 19th century. This house, built probably around 1880, was one of them."

My family was impressed.

"So, you lived in one of the best neighborhoods of Vienna?" Dana inquired.

"Probably. An address starting with "Wien 1" (the first district of Vienna, the "inner city") was, and still is, prestigious. But you must realize that rents were cheap when my parents moved us here in 1924."

"There was strict rent-control in already-existing buildings. As you can see, the properties were well kept up. These houses, as well as the other five-story buildings on the street, are in perfect shape. Right after World War II, everything looked dirty, black with grime. But fairly soon the houses were washed, repainted."

"Just think how our inner cities look!" my son-in-law said. "And our buildings are certainly not 120 years old!"

"And who put the Austrians back on their feet after the war?" I answered my own question. "America's Marshall

Plan." *(Editor's note: The Marshall Plan was an American initiative to aid Western Europe after World War II. The United States gave over $12 billion in economic support to help rebuild Western European economies.)*

Dana wanted me to show her the windows of what had been our apartment. I pointed out that several more rooms faced a courtyard inside the building.

"Fine. Let's go in and look," Dana said. The door was locked. "I guess we can't go in," I said wisely.

"We can too. All we have to do is ring the bell where it says 'concierge.'" Dana wasn't easily discouraged. "Somebody will answer. I'll say, with a smile, of course, that I want to see the house where my grandfather lived sixty years ago."

That's exactly what happened. The concierge was a young, good-looking man, much too young to have served in Hitler's army or, even worse, to have been a guard in a concentration camp were so many of my friends were murdered. I still have problems shaking the hand of an Austrian who is older than 65.

Dana told the concierge what she wanted, and she had to interview him, of course. He said that he had lived in the U.S. for several years but came back to Vienna because work was too hard there, and he was homesick, and he's glad that he found this job which is OK. Why does he keep the door locked?

"You know, there are so many foreigners in Austria now, all kinds of people, you can't trust anybody nowadays. Isn't it horrible? Not how it used to be, you know."

Well, I thought, the Viennese haven't changed very much. Give them half a chance, and they start to complain. Actually, they never had it so good!

"Now, if the old gentleman," he motioned to me, "wants to see the house where he grew up, of course, come right in. Isn't it a shame that so many nice people like you," he addressed me, "left Vienna before the last war." Obviously, he had us all figured out: Jews. "And you were so right to leave," he continued, "my parents told me many times how much we Austrians suffered during the war, not enough to eat, you know."

I addressed the good man, in German.

"I'm glad I could get to America. I love it there! You see, I had a good job; I raised a fine family; they are eager to see where I grew up. I thank you very much for letting us into the house."

He accompanied us into the courtyard, which used to be paved in old times. Now, it looked like a miniature park. Dana admired the flowers.

"You have a beautiful garden," she said to him with one of her famous smiles. "It must be a lot of work to take care of it."

"Yes, it is," he answered her. "But I love to do it! Because…" He was trying to find the right words, then turned to me and said, in German:

"Nur die besten Herrschaften leben hier (only the best ladies and gentlemen live here)!" He added a moment later, still in German: "Just like before, of course."

Now our gang wanted to get up to the fourth floor and look at the apartment where I had lived. This was a little too much for me.

"It's just an apartment like all others in this house!" I said.

"But I want to see it! Dana insisted.

"I'm going to stay here, I like the sunshine," I quietly informed her.

Sure enough, they all took the elevator up and returned a few minutes later. "Did anybody let you in?" I asked.

"There was a little problem," Dana said." A lady, she even spoke a little English, asked us what we wanted. When we told her, she may have been afraid that we wanted to get the apartment back. Anyway, she wouldn't cooperate."

A young woman showed up. We introduced each other while Dana had her fun with the camera. She said that her husband was out with the children, but she certainly would tell him about the nice people she met. Then Dana made me tell her where the formal dining room was in our apartment, where the piano stood, in which room my parents slept. Finally, I had to describe exactly the "kinder zimmer," (the children's room) where my brother and I grew up. "In the same room, and we thought nothing of it," I said, looking straight at my daughters who still can't forgive my cruelty for making them share a room.

"You made quite a production," I said to Dana afterwards.

"Of course," she admitted. "I'm a producer and I know I'm good at it. But now I want to learn how to be a reporter."

"Quit your job? Start all over?"

"Possibly. I couldn't work in Washington as a beginner! I've got a lot to learn. I'll have to find a job as a reporter in a small market, something like Peoria, Illinois. Later, when I get good, I will return. Only by that time my fiancé will be through with law school and soon I'll have to quit whatever job I have."

"Why?" I wondered.

She looked at me as one would look at a nice, but not very bright fellow.

"I'll have babies, of course! I'm almost 25 years old! When mom was my age, she was already pregnant with me!" (I couldn't help thinking: my mother had two boys at your age, but she had no college education.)

"How many babies will you have?"

"Three. I know that mom had only two, but I think I want one more."

May my granddaughter get what she wants! Whatever she does, she'll always be the producer.

(Editor's note: Dana did go on to become a correspondent for CNN without having to go to Peoria first. She has one child, Jonah Frank King.)

II. A RECENT SCHOLAR

There are only a few four-lane freeways in Central Europe. Most other important highways, while having only two lanes, are fairly good and would conform to most American specifications: well-paved shoulders, center lines indicating where passing is allowed and where it isn't, speed limit signs when there are restrictions. Trucks are not allowed to travel nearly as fast as passenger vehicles, which means that when you are driving behind a truck, you want to pass as soon as possible, as soon as you are sure that nothing is coming from the other direction! I was sitting in the "honor seat" next to the driver, my son-in-law Stuart.

While he believes in obeying all traffic laws including, more or less, the speed limits, he doesn't feel that staying behind a truck longer than absolutely necessary is a very good idea. Once, when he passed a truck and made it just in time before a huge eight-wheeler came from the opposite direction, I heard a loud female voice behind me crying out:

"CAREFUL!"

Whether I'm the driver or not, I don't like backseat driving very much. Some wives, like my older daughter Frances, are often doing just that, helping their husbands with good, if unsolicited advice.

"Fran!" I said, raising my voice a little, though sounding not even half as loud as the shrill voice we'd heard before. "Your husband is a good driver. Leave him alone, PLEASE!"

I wasn't prepared for what followed next.

"Dad, I didn't say a word. You are always harping on me!"

"It was me who screamed," my younger daughter Linda explained. "From where I'm sitting, it looked a little dangerous."

"Fran, I apologize, I said. "You girls have similar voices."

"Apology NOT accepted."

I wasn't worried too much. There is a very close bond between my "girls" and me.

My daughters share more similarities than their voices, which, by the way, are very pleasant, even musical, if used in a normal, non-shouting mode. Both are intelligent, generous, pretty women, good wives to their husbands, but they have their own ideas. It's easy enough to account for the differences between the two girls. For one, there are four years between them. When Fran was born, my wife and I were so unsure of ourselves that we followed our pediatrician's (may she remain nameless forever) orders. This lady, who must have been of Prussian descent, was strict, to say the least.

"You must feed her every four hours, no sooner nor later, day and night" she ordered.

"What if she cries?" my wife wondered.

"Let her cry. Furthermore, you must know exactly how much milk she takes. Write it down and report to me at your next visit."

"How do we know how much she takes?"

"Easy. You must weigh her before she drinks and afterwards. Obviously, the difference in weight can only be the milk."

I could visualize a difficult situation. "What if she fills her diaper while she drinks? We want to keep her clean, don't we?"

"You may change her. But be sure to weigh the diaper with its contents."

Now, more than 50 years later, I still can't believe that we suffered this situation for several months. My mother was living with us at the time. "This must be the American way of bringing up children. I didn't do all this and you survived." And we didn't do all that when Linda came along.

As for Fran, we got ourselves another doctor who told us about Dr. (Benjamin) Spock (*a widely-read author on how to raise a baby*). But by that time, Fran's character must have been shaped; she is the most orderly person anybody can imagine. She never forgets to do what ought to be done.

Moreover, whatever she does, it's done on time! And she puts her whole heart into it! In high school, when she had to write a report, she would research it thoroughly, sometimes bringing half a dozen books home from the library, barely able to carry them.

Her writing style became crisp and clear. Soon she was the editor of her high school paper.

Later, when she studied journalism at Northwestern University, she was taught the tools of the trade of writing for a newspaper. Now her sentences, her grammar, her syntax are all perfect. Her style is as good as anybody's. After graduation, Fran worked for ABC News for a while, but these were the days when a woman didn't have much of a chance. She was made a "secretary." Still, she stuck it out for a while until she found a much better job with better pay and more responsibilities, which included reporting the news on a small local cable station. While she was still with ABC she met Stuart Schwartz, the man she would soon marry. The couple moved to New York because Stuart was transferred. Fran got herself all kinds of jobs there until the babies came. As soon as practical, Fran went back to work and then, four or five years ago, she made THE decision.

"Stuart is making a good living. The children are away in college. I'm going back to school!"

She knew well what she wanted to study: Judaica. As a child, we had sent her to Sunday School, and she had gone to Jewish camps during the summer months.

At that time, our Reform congregation did not have Bar or Bat Mitzvahs (the coming of age at 13-years-old, when a Jewish boy or girl is considered an adult). Since Fran had missed this ritual, she (and others) decided to have it as an adult. As is customary, the ceremony includes a speech, explaining the personal significance of the event.

Fran chose to read a translation of a letter her grandfather had written on the eve of his, his wife's and his younger daughter's deportation to a concentration camp in 1944 from Czechoslovakia. All were killed. In the letter, my father-in-law, a tall, proud, good-looking man, wrote about his premonition of death; that he never did anything wrong to anybody and was therefore well-liked. He blessed us and admonished us to be good to each other. The letter reached us after the war, in October of 1945, just after Fran was born.

In May, 1996 Fran finished at Hebrew Union College with a Master's Degree in Judaic studies. At this time, she is co-writing books with a rabbinic scholar from HUC (*Dr. Eugene Borowitz)*. Now, on our trip, she wanted to see as much as possible of the houses of worship her ancestors attended, in the neighborhoods where they lived.

Our first stop was Prague, the capital of the Czech Republic. My mother's family had been Czech Jews; I had many relatives in Prague before the war. All had been killed by the Nazis with the exception of two men who escaped just in time to join the Czech army in exile, fighting the Germans.

Essentially the old Jewish community of Prague has ceased to exist. There are about a thousand Jews living there now, but they are mostly survivors of concentration camps who settled in Prague after the war.

The Jewish community of Prague has an old, proud history, going back to the 11th century. In the 16th century, the famous Rabbi Judah Loew lived there, the creator of the "Golem," a statue made of clay, which supposedly came to life when the good Rabbi wrote the name of God on its forehead! There are a number of synagogues, all in good repair, still standing in Prague, the most famous among them is the so-called "Alt-Neuschul" (Old-New Synagogue) built in the 12th century, one of the oldest Gothic buildings in Europe. The "Golem" lived in the attic, we are told.

"Why must we step down when we want to visit this old temple?" my granddaughter wanted to know.

Her mother knew the answer, of course. "There was a law at the time that no Jewish building, certainly not a Jewish house of worship, could be taller than the closest Christian building. In order to gain the necessary height for the synagogue, the Jews had to dig down, starting from lower ground."

By today's standards, the building, by far the oldest synagogue in the world still in use, is fairly small. It might hold about 100 or 200 worshipers, but I doubt that many would show up for a regular Sabbath service. Actually, the building is as much a museum as anything else. Right next to it is a cemetery, rather unusual in the Jewish religion.

"A house of worship is for the living," my daughter explained. "It is not only for praying! It's a house of study, a house of assembly. A cemetery should be nowhere near it. Obviously, the Jews of Prague were short of space."

Obviously. Although the cemetery is quite small, there must be thousands of people buried there. Only a few gravestones, among them the good Rabbi Loew's, are more than a couple of feet tall. All are so close together that it's impossible to walk between them. One cannot help thinking how crowded must living conditions have been.

There are three more synagogues close by, all in good repair.

"How about Kristallnacht? Didn't the Nazis destroy all Jewish buildings in November of 1938?" my son-in-law wondered.

"Prague didn't become part of Germany until a few months later, in March of 1939," I explained.

"During the war, the Nazis sent the Czech Jews to concentration camps. Almost all died there," my daughter said. "But the Nazis didn't destroy everything. Quite the contrary, Jewish ritual or art objects were collected from the Czech lands and sent to Prague. Two eminent Jewish scholars were put in charge of cataloging and describing everything, down to minute details."

"Why would they do that?" my granddaughter asked.

"They were quite sure that all European Jews would be killed. The ancient ghetto of Prague would be the only witness of a "cursed" race, which just managed to produce a few objects of interest for later generations."

One of the synagogues (Pincas) was converted to a museum showing drawings and paintings from Jewish artists who were obviously quite active in Terezin, a fortress town some 100 miles from Prague. Terezin served as a "model" concentration camp, which was shown during the war to journalists from the neutral countries Sweden and Switzerland *(and to the Red Cross)* to show the world how well the Jews were being treated; how all the gruesome stories coming out of Poland were nothing but lies. The Jews of Terezin were well-dressed for the occasion, even sang and performed plays for the journalists.

The day after the visitors left Terezin, the actors and musicians were sent to Auschwitz. Most of the performers and artists died; many of them were children. One of the most touching paintings was one by a 10-year-old boy who drew himself sitting in a small, crowded room, looking through a barn window at a bird flying outside, way up in the sky. Below every painting is a brief history of the artist: name, place, date of birth, and date of death. The boy who painted himself shut inside and the bird outside, flying freely, did not survive the concentration camp.

The old synagogues of Prague are so close together because they are standing in what used to be the Jewish ghetto. There never were any walls around it; rather, the Jews lived in their own district immediately adjoining the oldest part of town. They had their own city hall with a clock with Hebrew letters instead of Roman numerals. The hands of the clock ran backwards, counter-clockwise, probably because Hebrew is written from right to left.

There is another strange sight, and tourist attraction, connected with local Jewish history.

On the oldest and, until modern times, the only bridge across the Vlatava (Moldau) River, there are several life-size statues. One of them is a crucifix, adorned in pure gold with the Hebrew letters: kadosh, kadosh, kadosh (holy, holy, holy).

I explained: "Sometime during the 16th century a Jew said or did something very offensive (we don't know what it was) to Christians. As a punishment, all Jews were to be banished from Prague. However, the harsh edict was revoked because the Jews agreed to pay for a statue of Christ. They had to add, in their own secret language, the word 'holy' three times and it had to be in gold."

Relations between Christians and Jews were better in Prague than in neighboring Poland, Slovakia or Germany, but still often strained. The reason, especially in the 19th century, when nationalism became an important issue, was not so much religion as language. The great majority of the citizens of Prague, including the Jews, spoke Czech, although there was always a German minority. The Czechs sent their children to Czech schools, of course, and the Germans to German schools. The Jews had their own school system, which was taught in German! All during the 19th century, the Jews of the Czech lands spoke Czech, the language of their neighbors, not Yiddish, as in Poland.

The Empress Maria Theresa, who died in 1780, disliked Jews profoundly. But she was for a general education and insisted that every child should be taught, if possible, in German.

"You Jews can have your own schools," she decreed, "but only in German!"

That policy prevailed for more than one hundred years. For instance, Franz Kafka, the famous writer of the early 20th century, who lived in Prague, would write in German, although he spoke only Czech with his family or friends. The Czechs can't be blamed very much for resenting this. Today however, everything connected with Kafka has become a major tourist attraction, much like Mozart in Salzburg. By the way, both disliked their hometowns.

Before our family started our Central European trip, my daughter Fran had advised me that she'd be especially interested in Jewish themes. Easily understood. After all, she had spent several years studying at the Hebrew Union College in New York, writing her master's thesis on the history of adult Jewish learning in America. Last summer in Israel she attended a seminar on how to teach about the Holocaust.

I asked myself: why did Fran, when she wanted to go back to school in her mid-40s, decide on studying Judaica? Neither her husband nor her parents nor any of her grandparents were particularly observant. True, my wife and I were always involved in the affairs of our temple and attended services at least twice a month. Fran went to Sunday school and to a Jewish summer camp.

But so did thousands of others whose religious curiosity wasn't aroused.

An explanation comes to mind: the "third generation" syndrome. The first generation of immigrants have funny accents, if they can learn English at all. They don't know how to dress. They never make a decent living. They don't associate with "real" Americans very much because they don't really understand them. The second generation, the first "American-born" generation, wants to be utterly different from their parents. Forget all this old country stuff. Blend in with your surroundings. The third generation is the first to feel secure. They don't have to pretend. They don't have to "melt into the pot." Yet, some in this third generation who are inquisitive want to know, "where do I come from?" Is there anything special about me? Anything in my background worth knowing, or studying about?

In our case, the experience of the Holocaust plays a major role. Hitler didn't like Jews (an understatement, of course). Hitler was evil; everybody knows that. The conclusion must be that there is something "good" about Jews or at least something interesting. And since Hitler wanted to kill all Jews, both physically and spiritually, it's our duty to not give him, as Rabbi Fackenheim has said, a posthumous victory. Let's keep Judaism alive. Let's be fruitful. And let's not have any of our descendants go through another Holocaust.

Chronologically, my children, Fran and Linda, are second-generation Americans. But my generation itself wanted to quickly "transfer" ourselves to the status of second-generation by integrating quickly. We wanted to forget the tragedies that were behind us. Furthermore, we knew enough English to make a living, the key to the success of many refugees. Our European educations made us employable, and we weren't afraid to look around. Thus, effectively, our "second-generation" children actually became "third-generation" Americans.

So, my daughter Fran had good reason to be interested in her background and certainly a well-organized intellectual curiosity to pursue her interest. There was, I am almost certain, an additional cause for her "feeling so Jewish." It's a complicated story, going back to an event in the summer of 1956 when she was 10 years old.

It was a Sunday in August, the weather in Chicago was just warm enough to go to the beach but not too hot; an almost perfect day except for a little wind coming from the east, somewhere from the middle of Lake Michigan. Our family was spending the day on the sandy shore having a good time, together with friends who had boys the same age as our girls.

"Let's go swimming!" somebody suggested.

"The water might be too cold," somebody else objected. "Let's try."

"There's the black flag! You know that a green flag means fine for swimming, a yellow flag means caution, a black flag: don't even go near the water."

"They must have forgotten to change flags. Yesterday the weather was stormy."

So, we decided to go in, but certainly no farther than the end of a pier, which extended a hundred feet out into the lake. The ladies objected, but the older boy and Fran, who may have wanted to impress him, prevailed. I also thought that fooling around in the shallow water, near the beach, was a good idea. The three of us had fun jumping in the waves, which weren't even very high.

"Just a few feet farther out in the lake it won't be quite so shallow, we can swim a little," Fran suggested.

The water felt fine, the waves were no more than a foot high until, suddenly, a bigger one came which raised us up quite a bit. When we came down on the other side, the ground had somehow disappeared! Still, we saw no reason to be afraid; the pier was right next to us.

"Let's swim to the pier," I suggested, "just to be careful."

The boy, a very strong swimmer, just made it and climbed out of the water. But both Fran and I missed the pier by a few inches and were carried out into the lake. The water got suddenly cold. I saw my wife and my younger daughter standing on the beach, staring at us, waving to us to come back. We certainly tried, but we couldn't.

"Help! Save the girl!" I shouted as loud as my breath would allow me. (Later, Fran told me that when she heard my cries for help, she suddenly realized that her daddy wasn't all powerful; he needed outside help! An illusion gone.) Actually, Fran, a faster swimmer than I, wasn't carried out too far by the undertow. Somehow a lifeguard appeared from nowhere and reached her, and I saw a man help her climb out of the water. Although I did my best trying to get back to the shore, I was far out in the lake by that time and felt myself getting tired. 'Stop fighting, just do enough swimming to stay afloat,' I remember thinking. Sure enough, a boat reached me after a while and I was pulled aboard.

"Didn't you see the black flag?" The young man, who had just saved me, shouted. "This is Lake Michigan! You are not a kid; you should know better than to fool around!"

Of course, I should have. I must have looked pretty bad when I joined my wife a few minutes later because she took me directly to our family doctor.

"Act your age! You are over 40 years old!" was the only prescription he gave me.

This was by no means the end of the story, only the beginning. When my wife had seen us being carried out by the riptide, she had tried to make a pact with God. "Please don't let me lose my oldest child; don't let me become a widow at age 39 years! I promise I'll light Shabbat candles every Friday night!"

She hadn't done that before.

I'll never know if her promise to God or the young man in the boat saved us.

Maybe they worked together. Anyway, my wife never broke her word. Until her death 20 years later, she would say the blessing when she kindled the Shabbat tapers. And Fran? Could it be that a strong bond with her faith was forged by her mother's pious act? Did she realize that somewhere there must be a force much more powerful than her own daddy, who could fix her toys but couldn't save her by himself?

Well, whoever was in charge, on our trip the weather certainly favored us now. During the only long stretch of our trip, from Salzburg, in the center of Austria, to the eastern border of that country, we made good time. Late in the afternoon we reached Eisenstadt, the capital of the eastern-most province of Austria, very close to Hungary. Actually, this province had been a part of Hungary until after World War I, but had been detached and given to Austria because its inhabitants spoke German. Eisenstadt, a city of perhaps 30,000 people, has one claim to fame: the great composer Josef Hayden wrote most of his symphonies there during the second half of the

18th century, while he was employed as a court musician by the powerful Count Ferdinand Estherhazy. The Count owned tens of thousands, perhaps hundreds of thousands of square kilometers of real estate, with lots of people on it.

This was, and still is, excellent farmland served by only a few small towns, which were, until the Holocaust, populated by many Jews. It is said that these Jews had come with the Romans, probably as traders, in the fourth century. Many famous rabbis had lived in this part of the country. It seems that the Jews were relatively undisturbed there, possibly protected by the Count who used some of them as tax collectors, until the Nazis took over Austria.

In Eisenstadt, Fran and I went for a walk in the city, searching for any signs of Jewish inhabitants. We didn't have to look very long; at the edge of town we found a well-kept building with an inscription over its door: "The Jewish Museum of Austria." The place was open. It contained only a few ritual objects made of silver, all neatly labeled. No doubt the Nazis had stolen most of what was valuable and an enormous number of pictures, testifying to the important Jewish communities which had existed in Eisenstadt and surrounding towns.

"I feel like an American Indian must feel who sees the remnants of structures once inhabited by his ancestors," my daughter said. "It was an interesting culture, all right, but it's all gone now."

"But why did the Austrians build this museum? Why do they maintain it?" I wondered. "Out of a feeling of guilt, perhaps? Or because they think it will attract tourists with money?"

We asked if any Jews were still living in Eisenstadt or in the surrounding towns. Had any of them returned who survived the concentration camps?

"Yes," we were told. "There are still two Jews left, both are over 80 years old. One is quite sick."

We found a large Jewish cemetery nearby, all overgrown with weeds. It wasn't possible to read any of the gravestones because we couldn't get over a fence surrounding it. There was nobody who could open the rusty door leading into it. We first thought that there must have been some kind of festival in Eisenstadt; there was music all over town. We soon found out why there were so many people in the streets: elections were coming, several parties tried to get the voters interested. Orators were standing on soapboxes. I listened, halfheartedly, to a good-looking blonde man with a booming, well-trained voice.

"We don't want any foreigners here! Austria is for the Austrians, for those of us who have been here for many generations! Out with the riffraff." I inquired as to which party this particular chap belonged.

Since there is very little difference between the local accent and the Viennese accent I spoke, I was obviously taken for a resident voter and received a storm of rhetoric, trying to convince me to become a member of the "Freedom Party." The arguments presented by the speaker sounded familiar to me, in a bad way.

"Do you perhaps have any connections with the National Socialist party of old?" I asked innocently.

"Absolutely not!" was the answer. "But anyway, the Nazis weren't so bad." The speaker addressed my daughter. He couldn't know that she didn't understand a word of German.

"Don't believe the terrible rumors you hear!"

I had to think of the local Jews who had also been here for many generations and were deported to concentration camps, killed. I motioned to my daughter to go on.

In all of central Europe, Budapest, the capital of Hungary, has the only Jewish community that is active, vibrant, numerous. After all, "only" half of the 200,000 Jews of Budapest were killed by the Nazis, before the Russians liberated the city. Today, about 80,000 Jews are living in Budapest, many of them children, and unlike in Prague or Vienna, practically all of them are the descendants of those who'd been living there before the last war. Since the fall of the Communist regime in 1990, there has even been a fair amount of religious activity.

On Sunday morning, when our group arrived at the main synagogue in Budapest, we were lucky: An English-speaking docent was just starting a tour. We received her permission to join and to listen to her explanations.

"You are standing in front of the second largest synagogue in the world, holding three thousand worshipers; only Temple Emanuel in New York holds more. The building has been completely renovated on the outside, and more than half on the inside."

"Did the Nazis destroy it?" Somebody asked.

"No. But during the Communist regime there was no money for upkeep. Nor was there any interest by the regime in any religious buildings, either Christian or Jewish. What few funds our own community could raise were barely enough to keep the most elementary services going. Without help from outside Hungary, we couldn't even have done that. But now, there is some money from the city and also from the state available. Our budget is low, that's why it's taking us so long to finish the renovation. We couldn't have done it at all without the generous help from two American benefactors: The actor Tony Curtis (real name: Bernard Schwartz, whose family is Hungarian) and the Estee Lauder (the cosmetics mogul) Foundation."

The building is huge, high, and expansive. Obviously, when it was erected during the last decade of the 19th century or shortly thereafter, the Jewish community of

411

Budapest was not only well-to-do, it felt secure. The Hungarian establishment was liberal on many issues and fiercely nationalistic on others. To enjoy full rights as a citizen, one had to be a "True Hungarian." It helped to be a Catholic, even better to be of noble birth, but it wasn't absolutely necessary, as long as you spoke Hungarian and only Hungarian. The situation was quite different from that in the Czech lands, where the Jews showed a strong affinity for the German language and German culture. The Hungarian Jews spoke and wrote Hungarian and frequently changed their names to sound Hungarian.

My father-in-law's name had been Weiss (German for "White") when he was born, but he and his brothers changed their names to the Hungarian-sounding "Vidor." One may safely assume that the situation of the Jews was better in Budapest during the turn-of-the-century than in Vienna, which had a freely-elected anti-Semitic mayor. It wasn't until after the First World War, when Hungary lost half of its territory, and a short-lived communist regime, headed by the Jew Bela Kun, was overthrown by Count (Miklos) Horthy, a semi-fascist dictator, that Hungary turned anti-Semitic. But even then, and until 1944, when the German Nazis ousted Horthy (he didn't fully cooperate with Hitler) and installed their own puppet regime, one could live fairly well as a Jew, sharing the ups and downs of the general population.

That changed abruptly in March of 1944.

"First, the Jews of the provinces were herded together, deported to concentration camps and then killed there," our docent explained (my wife's family among them). "In October of 1944, 15,000 Budapest Jews were locked into this synagogue. Almost all of them froze to death during the winter. There was no heat and practically no food. Thousands of others were sent directly to the gas ovens; they didn't even get inside the labor camps. There was no more pretense of using Jews as workers, not even as slave workers."

"How come so many of the Budapest Jews survived?" we asked.

"You know the story of the Swedish Count (Raoul) Wallenberg, a diplomat who gave Swedish papers to many Jews? It's true. But more important is the fact that the Nazis simply didn't have time to finish the job. The Russians threw them out in January, 1945."

(Editor's note: Wallenberg was a Swedish diplomat in Budapest who saved tens of thousands of Jews in Nazi-occupied Hungary during the latter stages of World War II. As Sweden's special envoy in Budapest between July and December 1944, Wallenberg issued protective passports and sheltered Jews in buildings designated as Swedish territory. After the war, he disappeared; widely believed to have been abducted, jailed and then executed

by the Soviets. Not until 2016 was he officially declared dead by Swedish authorities).

The docent showed us a huge bronze plaque in front of the synagogue, describing these events in Hungarian and in Hebrew. The inside of the synagogue isn't quite restored yet, but it shows an opulence of style, a certain grandeur I haven't seen in any Jewish building in America. There is not one, but two galleries for women, although we were told that for regular services the men sit on one side of the main floor and women on the other. Contrary to strictly Orthodox custom, there is an organ! It seems that during the last decades of the 19th century, a typical Hungarian style of Jewish worship developed: Orthodox, but with modern amenities. These were people with money who weren't afraid to show it. A few blocks away is another synagogue, this one for strictly Orthodox worshippers.

Attached to the big synagogue is a Jewish museum that shows not only artifacts but also a lot of history. We found it interesting to learn that there were Jews in Hungary (the Roman province of Pannonia) since the fourth century. The Hungarians (Magyars), a war-like people related to the Huns, left Asia 500 years later and arrived in Europe in the ninth century.

A gift shop is part of the museum. "This is where we will do our shopping," Fran said. There was a big selection of embroidered needle work, all done by volunteer ladies who brought in a lot of foreign currency to help restore the synagogue. We bought heavily. Luckily they took VISA.

We crossed the border to the Slovak Republic the next day, a fairly long trip from Budapest, arriving in Kosice (pronounced: Ko-sheet-zeh, accent on the first syllable) in mid-morning. This was the town my daughters were looking forward to seeing because it was the place where Teri, their mother, had grown up; also, the last residence of my wife and myself before we left Europe in 1941. It was also the place from which my children's grandparents and aunt had been deported to their death. I didn't look forward to our coming to the city. As a matter fact, I had tried to talk my daughters out of traveling to Kosice, but they insisted. My memories were too painful, so painful that I actually forgot where the Vidors lived! I had been a guest in their apartment for many months but couldn't even remember the street, or even the neighborhood of their residence.

"Dad, you said your father-in-law picked you up a few miles north of here; you traveled together for a few minutes and got out at the railroad station. Was it far to walk to the apartment?"

"No. About ten minutes."

"OK. We are at the station now. Which direction did you walk?"

"I don't remember. All I know is the HUNGARIAN return address given on my father-in-law's letters that reach me, via Switzerland, during the war. But I think this was a business address."

At a police station, I tried to find out where the Hungarian street "St. Istvan Korut" was. The policeman tried to be helpful, but he simply didn't know the present, Slovakian name of this street.

"Sir, this was fifty years ago!" the sergeant in charge said. "None of us here at the station was even born at that time!"

I found it strange that nobody in town spoke Hungarian now, only Slovakian. In 1941, when I was last in this town, it was just the opposite: nobody spoke Slovakian, only Hungarian.

"Daddy, you are dreaming. You MUST remember where mother grew up. Please, try!" my daughter Fran pleaded.

"I know it was on a quiet, residential street. The building may have been three or four stories high. And I think we could see a church tower from the window."

Not very helpful. There are lots of churches in Kosice. Finally, my daughters realized that we were not getting anywhere. I think it was Linda, my younger daughter, who suggested: "Maybe the house isn't standing anymore. Or let's pretend that it was this building, right here. It fits your description. Let's go on."

"I know the Jews in this town were collected in a synagogue before they were sent to Auschwitz," my daughter Fran said. "It shouldn't be hard to find."

The synagogue was easily located on a map of the city. "Well, there must still be lots of Jews living here," my granddaughter observed.

This sounded logical, only it wasn't true. Sure enough, in a residential street near the center of the town, we spotted the building. It was fairly large and seemed to be in good repair. We decided to go in but found the front door locked, as was the side door. Quite a bit of dust was visible around the doors, also debris deposited by the wind, even fallen leaves from last year. Obviously, this synagogue hadn't been used for a long time. I asked a woman across the street if anybody ever entered the building?

"Not that I can remember," she said. "Who would go inside? There aren't any Jews around here."

Then we noticed a bronze plaque, covered with dust, on the corner of the building. It stated, in Slovakian and in Hebrew, that 12,000 Jews were incarcerated in the synagogue for several days in 1944 and then deported to their deaths in Auschwitz. We stood there for a while, nobody had anything to say, knowing that my daughters' grandparents had been among the 12,000. This was as close to them as we could come.

I had a profound sense of failure, of not having done my homework. We should have simply looked in the telephone book for the Jewish Community; I understand that there are still 200 Jews living in Kosice now. Possibly there might have been records about the Vidor family.

Why didn't I insist on pursuing some of the clues in my father-in-law's last letter? It contained a number of hints where to look for "hidden" memorabilia. I can only explain my negligence by saying what happened in Kosice had hit too close to home. Sure, I had distant relatives in Prague who were killed, also many friends. The same holds true for Vienna and for Bratislava. But the Vidors were the parents of my beloved late wife, the mother of my daughters, as well as wonderful people. I just couldn't go on. (I must now insert a footnote to this report about our trip, which took place in May and June 1996. It is now August, two months later. Suddenly the address I couldn't remember comes to my mind: Kovacka Ulica number 26.)

It's about as far as one can travel in the Slovak Republic to get from Kosice to Bratislava, the capital, situated on the extreme southwestern corner of the country.

"This looks like a lively town!" my son-in-law Stuart said as we looked for a place to park our van. "Isn't this where you met Teri?"

"Certainly. This was way back in 1936, when Hitler was far away in Germany."

"Did you feel secure at that time?"

"Absolutely. This was a prosperous town in a strong, democratic country. Czechoslovakia wasn't even suffering very much from the worldwide Depression, certainly a good country to love and to live in. Of course, when we were living here last, in 1940 during the war, it was a different story."

"Was there already a ghetto?" Fran wondered.

"In a way, yes. Those Jews who resided in choice neighborhoods were forced to move to the part of the city that was already predominantly Jewish. There were empty apartments to be had because the Gentiles who had lived in these apartments were told to move out! So, it was actually a population exchange. There was no wall around the Jewish part of the city.

"How did you find a place to live?"

"An elderly widow, a very pious Orthodox Jewish lady, had a fairly large apartment and was looking for a couple to occupy one of her rooms. Had she not found us, she would have been forced to rent to a family with many children, and she didn't want to do that. Our problem, and hers too, I assume, was that she didn't like us because we weren't pious enough. We insisted on turning on the lights on Friday evenings and even used a small electric hot plate! Of course, we were never allowed to enter her kitchen."

"What happened to the Jews later?" My son-in-law asked.

"In 1942 and 1943 all were deported to Poland. Very few came back after the war. Teri's uncle, her father's brother, and his whole family perished. None of my many friends survived."

"Couldn't the Jews get out?"

"In 1939, quite a few young people got out on transports, down the river Danube, to Palestine; illegal transports from the point of view of the British who controlled Palestine. The Nazis and their Slovak friends didn't care one way or the other. Starting in the winter of 1940, when the Danube froze over, there wasn't any way out for any Jew. No country would let them in. There was a war on. Teri and I realized in early 1941 that there was no realistic chance of us surviving in Bratislava, although it didn't look all that bad yet. We took our chances in Hungary, hoping to get an American visa."

"Can you show us where the Jews lived in Bratislava?"

"No! during the Communist regime, in the 1960s, a new bridge was built across the Danube. The ramp to this bridge was built in such a way as to destroy almost all the buildings which had once been inhabited by Jews. So, the Communists managed to destroy any physical evidence of where 15,000 Jews had lived for many centuries."

"I read that there are a few hundred Jews living in Bratislava now," Fran said. "Mostly descendants of concentration camp survivors and that there's a Jewish museum worth seeing."

We did indeed visit this museum. Yes, it was very well done, like the museums we had seen in Prague, in Budapest, even in the small town of Eisenstadt. There were pictures of famous Jews who had lived here; there were photos of Jews who had perished in the concentration camps. There were also many Jewish religious artifacts, beautiful silver candlesticks, cups, ornaments from Torah scrolls and prayer shawls.

But I'm afraid there isn't any viable Jewish community here anymore. Only a museum.

III. A TOWER OF STRENGTH

My daughter Linda and I had arrived in Vienna on May 26, 1996 after a long, exhausting flight from San Francisco. We had a nine-passenger van reserved, big enough to hold not only our party comfortably but also our luggage. When we presented ourselves at the Avis counter in the early afternoon, the vehicle wasn't there.

"My computer says that your car is here, but it isn't." A friendly Austrian lady told us, speaking English. "Too bad. Anyway, I'm expecting one tonight."

I felt myself getting hot under the collar. "We MUST have the van now!" For good measure, I repeated in German: "Wir muessen den Wagen jetzt haven!" It's possible that I spoke in a rather loud voice.

The lady smiled. "I'm sorry, but there is really nothing I can do! You see, these computers are sometimes wrong."

Linda took over, motioning to me to stay out of it.

"You see," she said, "we are expected in Prague this evening. There are four more people in our party. It's a long drive I understand. So we should be on our way, don't you think so?"

"It will take you not much more than four hours. Anyway, here's what I can do for you: I'll give you two four-passenger cars for the same money. How about that?" Again, this ingratiating Austrian smile. Linda and I looked at each other; we both took our heads.

"No," I said, very emphatically. "Our party wants to stay together. We contracted for a van and we want to have one. Call your supervisor in America!"

"Daddy, that won't get us a van," Linda whispered to me. "Miss, please look in your inventory," she said to the Avis lady. "Maybe you have something."

"You said that you have six people in your party?" the clerk said, looking at Linda. I don't think she liked me very much. "I have this beautiful minivan. It would hold you very nicely."

"And our luggage?"

"Well, if you don't have much…"

I couldn't help thinking of my daughter Fran, and especially my granddaughter Dana. Both don't usually travel very light.

"Can we look at the car?" Linda asked.

"But of course. We aim to please."

It was a nice enough Ford minivan with only a few kilometers on it, with very little luggage space. Linda looked at her watch.

"The Schwartz's will leave New York for Prague in six or seven hours. They must re-pack. Absolutely not more than one suitcase per person, and not a very big one. I'll call them immediately."

While she made her call, I started to sign the necessary papers and noticed that the price was higher than what I had contracted for.

"How can you charge us more for a minivan then for a regular van?" I wondered. "It should be less money, not more!"

"But this one is a special beauty. Only Americans take it. You'll love it. It has air-conditioning!"

I was too tired to start a fight which I felt I would lose anyway. A week later, when we drove through the Hungarian plain in 90-degree heat, we were glad indeed to have air-conditioning. The luggage did fit, barely; it was a challenge for my grandson every time to squeeze the suitcases into the car. It would have been impossible if my older daughter and my granddaughter hadn't left many of their clothes (which they never missed, of course) at home. So everything worked out. It usually does when Linda takes over.

Only Linda and I, the "West Coast Contingent," started our trip in Vienna. My older daughter's family – the Schwartz's – would join us in Prague; they had direct flights from the East Coast: Dana from Washington, the others from New York. Linda did the driving since she was less tired than I was from our long flight, but also used to driving a minivan with a stick shift. That left me with the job of navigator, which I did poorly. Will anybody, in any country, on any continent, ever learn how to mark the exit signs from airports in such a way that even a stranger can find them? It took us quite a while to find the highway to Prague, more or less bypassing the city of Vienna. Only then could we start a conversation.

"I'm missing my family already," Linda said. "My children, my husband. Alex was the first who suggested this trip, and now he had to stay at home."

"Was it necessary?" I asked. "Couldn't the great big Kaiser Permanente organization do without him for a couple of weeks? After all, you could take off."

"I am only a 'healthcare provider' as they call us physicians now. I'm entitled to a vacation just like everybody else. When I'm not available, another doctor will take over. There are four more ear nose and throat specialists in my department. But since Alex became the head of pediatrics in our facility, he feels he has special duties, since his department is just moving into new, larger quarters. He said that he'd feel uneasy being away just now; he'd worry too much. I can understand that. So he's staying at home with the boys."

We had agreed from the beginning that her sons, Ricky, age 11 and Jon, age 9, were much too young for this trip. "This is the age of 'instant gratification,'" Linda had said. I put it more simply, if less scientifically: when they are hungry, they want to eat "right now" and when they are tired, you can't explain to them that they should enjoy what they are seeing. "I'll make it up to them," Linda continued. "I'll spend every free minute with them. Of course, I always did. But right now, I feel bad."

"You have your housekeeper to take care of them," I tried to comfort her.

"That doesn't mean a thing. Luckily, my mother-in-law is staying with us for a while. The children get along very well with her. By the way, so do I."

"Here we are at the Austrian border," Linda said. "I want to have my passport stamped."

I asked the border policeman, who just waved us to go on, to oblige my daughter.

He seemed to be mildly annoyed. Why should we make him work? Crazy Americans, he probably thought, looking at our passports, but he did what I asked him. A minute later, when we arrived at the Czech border, it was the same non-event. Actually, both the Austrian and the Czech hurt my feelings. They weren't the slightest bit impressed that I, the holder of an American passport, spoke their language. They just didn't care. We could have smuggled in a minivan full of gold.

"Tempora mutantur," I said to my daughter, who still remembered enough of the Latin I made her take in high school to understand: times change. (By the way, why is it quite permissible, even in chic, polite society, to utter platitudes in a foreign language, preferably an ancient one?)

But Linda and I couldn't help remembering the time, 30 years earlier, when the four of us, Teri, my wife, my two daughters and I, sat around the dinner table and Linda and I tried to carry on a conversation in Latin. As with talking dogs, it isn't very important what we said but that we did it at all.

The two girls had their plans all mapped out even then. Fran would become the philosopher, the master of the King's English; Linda, the linguist, the scientist. We practiced democracy: when it came to any decisions to be made, each of us had 25 percent of the vote except in the case of a tie; then Teri's opinion would prevail. If there were any loud arguments between the girls, Teri would quietly take one of her shoes off and carefully aim it at the nose of whoever had raised her voice. Then she would throw the shoe, always missing by at least five feet. Everybody laughed. And Teri would say: "If there is any shouting in this house, I will do the shouting!" Only actually, she never did.

Shortly after we entered the Czech Republic, we found ourselves on a four-lane freeway and got to our hotel in Prague before it was dark.

"I had no idea that Prague was so romantic," Linda said. "It looks unreal: the narrow, steep streets paved with cobblestones, right under the castle, above the huge Gothic cathedral." The hotel with the three violins on a shield had a narrow entrance just wide enough for us to get in. "Now I'm sure we're not in America."

"Well, this isn't a Howard Johnson's!" I assured her. "The hotel is at least 200 years old. The rooms, they have a total of five or six of them, won't be as comfortable, though we have our own bathroom. But there's no doubt that the food will be excellent and plentiful, very Czech. Actually, as far as I can tell from the pamphlet they sent me, it is a restaurant, which operates a small inn."

"I love it already!" Linda said. "I only wonder where I can park the van?"

A waitress from the restaurant gave me a small card with the shield of the hotel printed on it, signed and dated it, and advised me to put it underneath the windshield and park across the street.

"In front of the Romanian embassy? There's an important-looking sign."

"They have three parking places," the waitress said. "They only use one of them. It's OK. They eat here sometimes…"

Our van would rest comfortably underneath the Romanian flag for three days and three nights while hordes of tourists were desperately looking for a parking place.

"Your room is on the third floor," the waitress said, and continued, looking at me: "I will help you with your suitcase. After you wash up, come down for dinner."

"Can you really understand what she saying?" Linda asked. The waitress had spoken in Czech and I was happy I understood her.

"A language has a way to come back," I assured her.

"Daddy, what would I have done without you?"

"You'd have gone to a big hotel where they speak English. That wouldn't be romantic."

Well, the inn was romantic all right. What it lacked in width, it made up for in height. There were 64 steps up to our room! Once we had climbed up, we found it surprisingly large and comfortable, just as the pamphlet had described, with a view down to the street with its old baroque buildings.

The food was excellent, as expected, and much too much. Beef, a kind of sauerbraten, with dumplings and red cabbage was the main course, followed by "palachinky," similar to a crêpe, filled with marmalade. And the beer! Bitter and sweet at the same time, a dark brew so different from the "Bud" we knew from the U.S. It came in half-liter glasses, about 18 ounces, and the waitress looked at us as if we had hurt her feelings because we didn't want another glass.

"This dinner was good for 2,000 calories," Linda said. "But what the hell!"

"Long live capitalism!" I exclaimed. "This is the food I remember from 60 years ago."

We got up early the next morning. The breakfast, which was brought to our room, was enormous. All kinds of sausages, cheeses, three different brands, coffee and the inevitable "kolacky," sweet rolls with preserve in the middle.

"Let's go down," Linda said, "the Schwartz's won't be here until 11 o'clock. I want to see all I can!"

We were happy to see our car still standing where we had left it right underneath the "no parking" sign in front of the Romanian embassy. The street was already filled with tourists going up to the castle. We walked in the opposite direction, down to the huge square called "Malostranske Namesti," (The Square of the Little Side).

"We are across the river from the main part of the city of Prague," I was happy to explain. "On the side below the old castle where the Kings lived and the alchemists and more recently Franz Kafka."

The huge cathedral in the center of the square had been all black and grimy when I had last seen it 10 years ago, but it was all washed and shiny now. Since it was Sunday morning, there was a Mass going on, but signs informed us that there would be a concert inside the dome later that afternoon: Vivaldi, Handel, Bach, Mozart, Telemann.

"Today is Sunday and May is the month of the Prague music festivals," I said. "There are always some kinds of festivals in Prague, I guess that's good for the tourist business."

"Daddy, we are the tourists! There's music, good music, I want to hear it. Find out if there are tickets available!"

There certainly were, I was told: "The dome is so huge that it would hold almost any crowd; just come at 5 o'clock this afternoon, sit any place you want, the acoustics are perfect anywhere in the church."

Well, it was only nine in the morning; we had plenty of time to walk around until my older daughter and her family would join us. Prague, like so many European cities, is a town best enjoyed on foot. Descending just a few blocks from the dome, we reached the Vltava River and the ancient Karl's Bridge, the only connection between the city and the castle until the 19th century.

"Every street, almost every house looks... well... I can't think of a better word... romantic," Linda said. "I understand that the movie *Amadeus* was filmed here because the city still retains its baroque atmosphere."

"Yes," I answered, "and the Czechs make a lot of money for allowing the American filmmakers to use their streets."

"Daddy, you're such a cynic. I want to enjoy the city as I see it now. Let's admire the river with the little island with houses on it; it looks just like Venice!"

"As a matter of fact, it's called 'Little Venice.' There was a big flood over 100 years ago and afterwards they built a dam. You can see it, right under the bridge. And these islands were created."

We picked up the Schwartz family at our hotel; they had arrived on a direct flight from New York and were not a bit tired, they said. A few minutes' worth of climbing up fairly steep streets and stairs brought us to the huge castle (the Hradcin) overlooking the city of Prague. There were tourists all over. I received compliments for selecting a hotel close to the tourist attractions. We didn't have to look for a place to park or look for cabs.

We arrived at the castle just in time for the changing of the guard.

"Do you know how old the fancy uniforms are that you are seeing? A couple of years ago the president of the Czech Republic, Vaclav Havel, decided that a little pomp and circumstance might be good for the tourist business. After all, he had been associated with the theater. So, he had the people who created the *Amadeus* film design these uniforms."

"I still like the ceremony," Linda said. "Now listen to the beautiful music."

The soldiers all moved in perfect rhythm. I only felt a little sorry for these lads, clad in their heavy uniforms while we tourists stared at them, wearing shorts in the summer heat. The castle has several courtyards with many buildings; in one of these there was to be a concert in an hour or so: Czech, German and Italian arias.

"I know that we'll hear a concert in the dome this evening, but I want to hear as much music as I can," Linda said. So, while the rest of us had lunch in a beautiful café overlooking the city, Linda listened to an intimate presentation of arias accompanied by an ancient piano from Mozart's time.

The castle is huge, a sprawling building more impressive by its size than by its beauty. It is built in a mixture of styles, the oldest parts going back to the Gothic era. Later, many rulers of the Czech lands added what they thought to be timely architecture, quite a bit in Italian style. As a matter of fact, the citizens of Prague didn't like it very much because it was a symbol of the Habsburgs, the Kaiser in distant Vienna.

Only a few of these emperors were loved by their Czech subjects, especially Rudolf II, who ruled during the 15th century. He actually resided in Prague, possibly because he was interested in alchemy, trying to turn base metals into gold. Prague was the headquarters of these somewhat weird-looking (if we can trust old pictures) scientists, who actually performed an excellent service for the understanding of chemistry, because they were not afraid to perform all kinds of experiments and kept good notes. The "Alchemists Street" has survived as part of the castle compound; it is only a few hundred feet long, narrow, paved with cobblestones. The houses are small with doors so low that its inhabitants must have bowed their heads when they entered. Franz Kafka lived there for a while; some of his stories are more easily understood when one sees this street.

Later that afternoon Linda and I had no difficulty convincing the Schwartz family to join us at the concert in the great dome. Once inside, the enormous dimensions of the Basilica were apparent. There must have been several thousand people present, with room for many more. We were sitting somewhere in the middle, rather far from the orchestra.

"Will we be able to hear anything?" Linda wondered. No need to worry. The first notes of Vivaldi's Concerto for Four Violins seemed to come from all sides, practically hitting us, engulfing us. We looked at each other in disbelief.

"Do they have such a good loudspeaker system?" I whispered.

"I think they have none at all. It's all in the acoustics of the building," Stuart said. "The orchestra is placed in exactly the right spot."

Later, when we listened to a cantata by J.S. Bach and a sonata for trumpet and orchestra by Telemann, the great sound quality was even more apparent. (I can remember having heard such sound only once before: in Harlem, near Amsterdam, when my wife Frances and I listened to an organ concert in a church where J.S. Bach used to practice.)

My family would see on this sentimental journey how the capitals of Central Europe look, especially the inner cities, which do not decay and where history can easily be traced. The architecture of the buildings, secular as well as churches, with strange-looking sculptures or pictures, is part of history.

In America, old buildings are removed and replaced by new structures. This is only reluctantly done in Europe, where there is a tendency to preserve.

Our trip would be balanced by looking at nature: mountains, lakes and rivers different from what we can see at home. Not an easy task to achieve for my daughter Linda, a resident of California, where we seem to have everything. Then there is the exposure to languages. We listened to four different ones during our short trip, which often stand for different cultures. Of course, the sentimental part of our journey was important: my children and grandchildren wanted to see where my wife and I grew up.

"Of course, I want to see fortresses, castles, and old cities with walls around them," Linda said when I asked her, before we started our trip. Her tone said she was interested but could take them or leave them.

I soon found out that the rest of my family felt the same way. (Alex, Linda's husband, my son-in-law who couldn't come with us on our trip, might have dissented. He was born and brought up in Poland, studied medicine in Italy, and was a first-generation American, just like I am.) Still, we satisfied my children and grandchildren's curiosity. In the southern part of the Czech Republic are several marvelous castles, really fortresses where noblemen managed to keep themselves removed from their subjects. We visited the Schwarzenberg Castle, a huge, white-walled building that looks exactly like Walt Disney's idea of a castle. It might be the place where a knight in shining armor would come from, only it's all genuine. Inside, we were shown paintings, some pretty bad, but also quite a few excellent pictures by Dutch and Italian masters.

"How did the Schwarzenbergs get these?" I asked the guide. "Why, they bought them, of course."

"How did they get all their money?"

The guide eyed me suspiciously. Was I a Communist perhaps?

"They inherited it. They were honest, very generous people; the present Count lives in Vienna and helps to pay for the upkeep of the castle. You don't think, sir, that the entrance fee you're paying covers the upkeep of the gardens or these magnificent rooms?"

We spent the next night in Cesky Krumlov, a walled city near the Austrian border. The town was built on a high bluff during the Middle Ages and has hardly changed in hundreds of years. The Vltava River winds around it in such a way as to make it impregnable to any assault from enemies! Even I had to admit that the city is a truly magnificent sight with its old houses, narrow streets and, of course, a huge castle overlooking it.

Unfortunately, the good burghers who planned this city couldn't think about providing parking places for automobiles, as we found out later to our chagrin. The next morning, we toured the castle by ourselves since no English-speaking guides were available, a fortunate event which allowed us to concentrate our interest less on old pictures and more on the magnificent surroundings and the building itself. A three-story bridge across a steep valley connects the castle with a bluff, which can be climbed only by visitors, friends or foes, in full view of the inhabitants of the fortress. The structures have survived all these centuries with little need for repairs! Be it churches or fortresses, they knew how to build way back then.

We arrived in Budapest in mid-afternoon and checked in at a very good hotel, one of the few where we had made reservations because we wanted to be sure that English would be understood. For the six of us it was cheaper, and certainly more convenient, to hire our own guide for a three-hour tour of the city. The weather was perfect for seeing this magnificent capital of Hungary, built on both sides of the river Danube. "Buda," with the castle on the hilly left bank and "Pest," the bigger half of the city with most of its inhabitants, on the flat right side. The Parliament, the most prominent building as seen from the hill, is situated right on the river and seems to dominate the view as if to let the king in his castle know that the ordinary citizens are important.

We wanted to eat well in Budapest, but only in a restaurant with good music.

Close to our hotel was the Opera Café where, we were told, some of the singers of the opera would show up after their performances and sing some more. We were not disappointed. A good orchestra supported the stars and between courses the waiters congregated and sang loudly and in harmony. Obviously, all that was geared to foreign, international visitors! Our table was located on a balcony overlooking the performance, and when the musicians started to play Hebrew songs, Linda wasn't timid about joining in. She had spent a year in Israel a long time ago and still knows Hebrew fairly well. A successful evening!

For the next evening, I had something different in mind. "Let's not forget that we are in Budapest, the capital of Hungary. We should eat Hungarian, not international food, "I said.

"And hear Hungarian music!" Linda quickly added.

It wasn't difficult to find just the right place. The menu was only printed in Hungarian and in German, so I had to translate. But as in most Central European restaurants, it's a good idea to have a conversation with the waiter and follow his suggestions.

Hungarian food is somewhat less heavy than Czech food, a little spicier than Austrian and a little richer in cream than Italian food; the wines are a little less dry and fruitier. Maybe it's an acquired taste. I loved it, and it brought back memories of the time I had spent with my in-laws. But even more important than the excellent food was the music! The quartet, all gypsies of course, consisted of a violin, a viola, a bass and, most important, the typical Hungarian instrument, the cymbal.

These musicians were not just as good as those we had heard the day before in the Opera Café. These were virtuosos!

"The violinist is as good as Yitzchak Pearlman!" I said.

"Well, almost…" Linda, the American and perhaps Israeli patriot, added.

After we left, I found myself in possession of a tape of the orchestra. My children had bought it when they saw my enthusiasm. Luckily, the manager of the establishment knew enough English to negotiate the purchase.

I wanted to leave Budapest early the next morning but Linda objected.

"Daddy, you need your surgical stockings! Your feet are badly swollen."

She was right, of course. Ever since the long airplane ride across the Atlantic, I had had problems with my feet, but I was sure the swelling and the pain would just go away in due time. I could walk without too much trouble, but I had to avoid standing for more than a few seconds. Linda noticed that, looked at my feet and insisted that we stop at a surgical store.

"You don't want an embolism!" She scared me into submission. The stockings I bought really helped; moreover, I was commanded to keep my feet high whenever possible. This meant that during the drive, always sitting in the passenger seat, I had to put my feet up high, practically in the front window. If I neglected to do that for just a moment, there was a family chorus:

"Grandpa! Put your feet up!"

I asked Linda when she first decided to become a physician.

"Daddy, you and mother brainwashed me, ever since I was a child."

I could remember no such thing. Maybe we bought her toys of the human body, especially a plastic one called "The Visible Man," which showed the organs and the skeleton and could be taken apart and reassembled. Maybe we mentioned to her that the medical profession is interesting and fulfilling. But to become a doctor was her own decision. She started medical school when she was already 25 years old, after finishing undergraduate school with a degree in biochemistry from Cornell, spending a year in Israel and then getting a master's degree in nutrition from Harvard's School of Public Health. She entered Einstein Medical College in New York, which at that time allowed students to finish in three years, provided that they took summer school. There was practically no vacation time.

Since the beginning of 1975, while Linda was still in her first year of medical school, my wife hadn't felt well. Our family doctor dismissed her complaints. "You're a hysterical woman, there's nothing wrong with you."

In May of that year I noticed that she was losing weight and suggested that she be admitted to a hospital for observation. Her doctor first was against it, but I may have been somewhat forceful. We were scheduled to go on a vacation, to Prague and Vienna, of all places, and I wanted to be sure she was up to it. We described her symptoms to Linda over the phone. She consulted her textbooks and seemed quite concerned.

After a few days' tests in the hospital, we received the probable diagnosis, and not a good one: cancer of the pancreas. All a prominent surgeon would tell me before the operation was: "We'll do our best."

Linda flew in from New York and confessed to me that what I had told her on the telephone, exactly what Teri had described to her doctor, made her suspect this very ailment. The cancer was inoperable, as this particular cancer almost always is. There were some medications, of course, so we were told; there's chemotherapy. It was during this time that her mother conferred on Linda the title, "Tower of Strength." It was Linda, more than I, who did all negotiations with the hospital, with the doctors, with our pharmacist, making sure we'd always have a source of the necessary medications. She also talked me out of being rough with the doctor who had missed the earlier diagnosis.

"That won't help mother now," she said. Teri had a few good months left, but died suddenly in November of the same year. On our trip, I mentioned all this to Linda again.

"Had mother been operated on a few months earlier, she might have lived a little longer but under terrible conditions. She died before the pain set in."

"Linda," I said, "when you first received your medical degree everybody congratulated you."

"I was terribly scared," she said. "I would be called to work on real people and make decisions, knowing that I was incompetent, that I really knew nothing. It's an awful feeling every new doctor has, and rightly so. We really start learning during our time of residency, our specialization, and our fellowship."

"Linda," I asked, "are you competent now? Are you a good doctor now?

"Yes, I think so."

When we left Hungary and crossed the border to Slovakia, I again had a good feeling of understanding what people were saying. I know perhaps one hundred words of a Hungarian; I can count in that language, ask for directions: "where is..." But I don't understand the answer. On the other hand, I had once known Slovakian fairly well.

"It sounds just like Czech to me," Linda said after listening to a few words I exchanged with a border guard.

"The two languages are quite similar; there's no more difference between them than, let's say, the standard American English spoken by a television anchor person and a Texas drawl. When the Czechs and the Slovaks were still sitting together in their common Parliament, before the two countries separated in 1993, both would speak their own languages, and they had no difficulty understanding each other."

A few days later we were back in Vienna, the last stop on our trip. Our trusty van was returned to Avis. Only public transportation would be used from now on, except for our own feet. Our hotel, small and inexpensive, was centrally located, within easy walking distance of the Stefans Platz, or Stevens Square, the center of Vienna.

"There seems to be music all over!" Linda cried out when we encountered an orchestra playing in one of the main squares. It sounded absolutely awful!

"Look," I said. "They've got nothing but accordions, about thirty of them, and they are playing the *Blue Danube Waltz*. There is a sign: 'Our contribution to the Viennese Music Festival. The Luxembourg Accordion Players.'"

Luckily for Luxembourg, the Viennese are tolerant when music is involved. They applauded politely. On a different square there was not one, but two orchestras playing, not at the same time, but as soon as one was finished, the other one started.

"One is from Finland, the other one from Turkey." Linda read the placards advising us of the orchestras' home towns. "What's going on here?"

"The June music festivals. International, of course, and non-controversial," I said. "Actually, the Finnish orchestra is quite good. They are smart to play their own music."

"Well, music is one of the reasons why we came to Vienna," Linda said. "We want to hear more of it!"

We spent a long morning in a museum; somehow Linda and I stayed together most of the time. Our tastes must be similar when art is involved. However, I rebelled when my family wanted to see Schoenbrunn Castle, the famous residence of the Habsburgs, built to imitate Versailles, the home of the French kings.

"I've seen it many times, and I don't particularly like castles," I said. "Attach yourselves to the English-speaking tour; enjoy yourselves!"

Indeed, I also enjoyed myself alone in Vienna. But on our last day, I made sure to take my family to the "Wienerwald," the Vienna Woods, the forest surrounding much of the city.

"I used to spend my Sundays here, first with my parents, then with the Boy Scouts, finally with girlfriends. We hiked in those days. Now we can take a bus all the way up to the mountain with this good restaurant on top," I said to my family as we admired the beautiful view of Vienna while we ate our lunch. We had traditional Austrian food: Wiener Schnitzel with new potatoes and stewed carrots, and for desert, Apfelstrudel. We finished with a demitasse of strong Turkish coffee.

"Actually, this spot is important for the history of Vienna, of Austria, of all of Europe."

"What a mixture! What happened here?"

"What did NOT happen is important. In 1683, the Turks had conquered all of Eastern Europe and besieged Vienna. The city was about to fall. The Kaiser had asked the Christian kings and princes for help against the Moslem infidels, but they were all afraid of the Turks. The only exception was the Polish King Sobieski. He came to the aid of the city, assembling his army on the very spot where we are now. The Polish army stormed down from this hill and put the Turks to flight. Vienna, Austria, Germany, Europe, all were saved."

"How about coffee?"

"Coffee had been unknown in Europe up to that time, but it was the favorite drink of the Turks. When they fled, they left many bags of coffee behind. One of the Polish officers asked for this coffee and a grateful emperor gladly granted his request. The Pole started a coffeehouse and, presumably, lived happily ever after."

"There's certainly a lot of history around here," Linda said.

IV. A GOOD DRIVER, HUSBAND, FATHER AND PROVIDER

There were six of us on the trip, three women and three men. But this division by sexes would be useful only if we slept in two rooms, as we often did, of course. But other divisions were possible too. For instance, by generation: I was the only senior. Three of us, my two daughters and Stuart, my son-in-law, were in the so-called "sandwich generation." And then there were my two grandchildren, both in their 20s. Finally, among the six travelers there were four (a clear majority) whose name was SCHWARTZ: my older daughter Fran and her husband Stuart, as well as their children Dana and David. Thus, in a way, my younger daughter Linda and I were the outsiders! We never felt that way, of course. Still, Stuart, the only one without Weinman genes, was the man in the middle, the driver, the parker, the one who couldn't fall asleep at the wheel.

Sometimes Stuart and I would go for a walk together. His interest was not as much in Judaica, as was Fran's. Nor did he care quite as much about music, history or old romantic buildings as Linda did. He wanted to get the overall impression of the cities we visited, including the tourist attractions, of course.

But more than anybody else, he was especially conscious of the beauty of our surroundings. Stuart has a special gift for appreciating visual art. For instance, when he, David and I walked near the Vltava River in Prague on a beautiful early summer night, he would point out to us how the Prague skyline was dominated by the city's castle, brightly illuminated by the lights directed at it and the dome where we had heard a beautiful concert the day before. A full moon and just enough clouds to make the sky interesting completed the picture.

"What a production! It all works so well together," Stuart, the producer, said.

He would, of course, notice better than anybody else the harmony of the city with the landscape, set in just the correct setting.

As a television news producer, Stuart has worked in a leading capacity on just about every important show on his network, ABC, including *Good Morning America*,

Nightline with Ted Koppel, *This Week* with David Brinkley, and *World News Tonight* with Peter Jennings. He's currently working on some so-called "specials."

On our last night in Prague we decided to eat again in our hotel as Linda and I had done after our arrival from Vienna. But when we presented ourselves at the restaurant, the waitress, a pretty Czech girl, reproached us:

"I'm so terribly sorry, but all our tables are occupied. Why didn't you make a reservation?"

"What did she say?" Stuart asked. "Is there a problem?"

After I translated for him what the waitress had said, he quietly walked to what looked like the lady in charge of the restaurant and said to her in perfect American English that we (he pointed at the six of us) wanted to eat here. I don't think she understood a word, but a whispered conversation between her and the waitress followed. Then the waitress took me by the hand and led me up a few stairs to a secluded room where a table for eight guests was set with a white embroidered tablecloth, heavy silverware and beautiful china.

"This is our salon, even you wouldn't mind to eat here. It's for special guests only, but since you are staying in our hotel…"

I assured her that we wouldn't mind at all. As a matter fact, we'd be honored. We had a delicious, unhurried meal with plenty of calories and excellent beer. When we were finally ready to leave and went down to the restaurant, all the guests had left and the waitress was by herself, cleaning up.

"How are we going to pay?" Stuart, who was in charge of such necessities, wondered.

The waitress didn't know.

"We are closed already and we'll be closed tomorrow until evening. But don't worry, you'll get your breakfast in the morning. It will be on a tray in front of your rooms; only you'll have to heat your coffee on a small burner in the hall."

"When do we pay?" Stuart wanted to know this little detail. So far, our host hadn't seen a penny of our money. I asked the waitress. She shrugged her shoulders:

"I don't know. The proprietor isn't here now."

(After we returned home, it took Stuart a full month of negotiations to be able to pay the money we owed. There was a lot of red tape! I can only deduce that the restaurant and inn, "The Three Violins," didn't have a lot of American visitors!)

Stuart wasn't only in charge of money, most of the time anyway, but also in charge of driving. There are two kinds of drivers: those who get lost (I'm one of them) and those who don't, like Stuart. He finds his way even on poorly marked roads. He somehow takes the correct turn, where I would have done the opposite.

Since my daughters are like me, I guess that there must be a defective gene responsible! Anyway, the driving on our trip was remarkably uneventful, with one exception.

When we got to Cesky Krumlov, the walled city in the south of the Czech Republic that we'd wanted to visit, we couldn't find a place to park! No wonder: there were signs all over the town in Czech, German, and English: "World Convention of Fly Fishermen." The narrow streets were covered with men holding up signs telling the world from which particular fly fishing paradise they hailed. Since none of us was very much into the sport, our only reaction, correct as it turned out, was that it would be difficult to find hotel rooms.

We drove to the town center and asked for help at the information booth, which can be found in any Central European city that has even a little tourist traffic.

"You can't stop here," a well-fed lady barked at us. "You can't even drive in our town without a blue card!"

"How do we get a blue card?" we wondered.

"Only at the hotel after you've signed in," she said.

Oh, the spirit of Franz Kafka, you must be active here. After unauthorized driving and stopping at various hotels (there were lots of them), only to be told that they were full, we nearly resigned ourselves to leaving town. But then we saw a small inn across a little brook; it was impossible to get there except on a narrow foot bridge.

They had lovely rooms for us, even gave us a "blue card," which we immediately affixed to our car window. But our difficulties, or rather Stuart's difficulties, were just beginning!

Stuart thought that we should have parked in our hotel's parking lot rather than across the brook, about two feet wide, where the van was standing at the moment. "You move into your rooms, I'm going to re-park our van," he said.

This sounded like a good idea. Half an hour went by, and then a whole hour. Still no Stuart. We started to worry. Finally, he came back, all flushed, together with a policeman who shouted in Czech that Stuart had driven the wrong way on a one-way street! Even worse: obviously, a foreigner, he didn't have his passport on him! I tried to mediate, but it isn't easy to argue with a policeman in a foreign language! Finally, after Stuart produced his passport, which the policeman, a young, ruddy chap, carefully studied, we thought we'd all be friends again. I suggested that.

"Yes, sure. But first you must pay a thousand crowns! You drove the wrong direction on a one-way street!"

Stuart denied this. Upon closer investigation, it turned out that, technically, he might have committed this violation. There was an arrow pointing the other direction, but so small that it was hard to see. Furthermore, Stuart had driven backward on the disputed street for only a few feet.

"A thousand crowns!" The man of the law sternly repeated.

"How much is that in American money?" Stuart, who really looked beaten by that time, wondered.

"About 35 dollars," I said. "I think we should pay it and forget it."

Agreed. There was only one small problem. Stuart had only 800 crowns; we usually paid with plastic money. I tried to explain and bargain with the law.

"A thousand crowns, or I have to arrest him!"

Well, searching through all our pockets we just barely came up with another 200 crowns. The policeman was satisfied.

"Now I will give you receipts (plural)."

I indicated that we didn't need them. Actually, we just wanted him to leave.

"There must be order!" he proclaimed and proceeded to tear off little pieces of paper from the book, each good for 100 crowns. "One, two, three," he counted slowly until he reached 10. "Now, all you have to do is to get your automobile where it belongs: I'm going to give you a map of the town. Just watch the arrows!"

I volunteered to accompany Stuart, he was still rather shaken up. The car was standing about 50 feet from the parking lot where it belonged. Stuart is a good driver. We had a map. But it took us one and a half hours to get back!

Why? As noted, Cesky Krumlov is a walled city and there are only a few gates. While it is fairly easy to get out of town, or into town, it's very difficult to get first OUT and then back IN! The Vltava River winds around the walls; the bridges don't seem to be where the gates are, and then you get to these curved one-way streets. Well, we finally made it. I've never seen Stuart as tired as he was that evening in Cesky Krumlov.

The next day after a lot of sightseeing, we drove towards the Austrian border. According to our map, there was a good secondary road leading straight to the main Austrian freeway connecting Vienna and Salzburg. But suddenly we came to a "Road Closed!" Sign. Must we drive all the way back, a good 20 miles, we wondered? A couple of bicyclists came along, they stopped at our car.

"D'you want to get to Austria?" one of them asked us in German. "Sure," I answered, pointing at the 'Road Closed' sign. "But how?"

"There is a little side road. We came that way. You won't find it on any map, but it'll lead you right to upper Austria. Be careful! You wouldn't have much room to pass if you meet somebody driving in the opposite direction!"

We decided to try it. Stuart drove very slowly (Stuart – slow driving – a contradiction!) on an unpaved country road along a little brook.

When one travels without quite knowing where they are, there's often an unexpected bonus.

We found ourselves in a deep forest with a small stream on our left side sometimes flowing quickly, sometimes widening to a pond. This must have been where the famous Czech composer Smetana got his inspiration for his tone poem *The Moldau* (indeed this small stream was the source of that river). The late morning sun didn't quite manage to penetrate down to us. We could easily imagine that we weren't driving in a Ford van but were in a carriage drawn by two horses. We got out once or twice, just to relax, to look. During the half hour we drove on that narrow dirt road, we didn't encounter anybody. We were sorry to reach the main road, just a couple of miles from the Austrian border.

A freeway in Austria looks no different from one in America. There are two lanes in each direction, limited access, bypasses around towns, speed limits either non-existent or not enforced. You simply keep up with the traffic. By early afternoon, after driving through the province of Upper Austria, bypassing the city of Linz, its capital, we reached the outskirts of the city of Salzburg. Close to any important town or tourist attraction in most of Europe, there's an "information" booth where one can get directed to hotels. Perfect English (or French or Italian for that matter) is spoken. After his experience in Cesky Krumlov, Stuart was mainly interested in one item:

"How's parking?"

"No problem," a nice lady who had obviously heard that question before, assured him.

"After checking into your rooms, you simply park in the mountain!"

"IN the mountain?"

"Of course. We made a hole in the mountain for a huge garage. You leave your car there as long as you stay in Salzburg. In our city, you walk or take public transportation. For five dollars, you can get a ticket good for all buses and trolleys, even on the cogwheel up to the Hohensalzburg Fortress!" With that ticket, you also get free admission to all museums."

We made reservations at a centrally located three-star hotel, the "Blaue Gans" (Blue Goose).

The star system works well in Europe: one knows exactly what to expect. Five-star, the highest rating, is for luxury travelers who "want to be seen." A huge lobby with all kinds of unnecessary amenities you pay for; bell captains dancing around you. The tourists who stay there are either very rich or, more often, have their companies pay for them, at least $350 per night in Vienna or Salzburg. Four-star hotels are still excellent; you expect to find a travel agency in the lobby as well as a multi-language staff. We stayed in a four-star hotel only once, in Hungary, a relatively inexpensive country. Our preference was the three-star hotels: no fancy lobby, but there is a switchboard; you'll get an absolutely clean room with a telephone and its own bath or shower. In a two-star hotel, frequently called a "pension," the rooms are still clean, but you may expect to find the bathroom across the hall. One-star hotels are usually for students.

When Stuart and I parked our van in the mountain we had an eerie feeling. We are used to underground garages, but in Salzburg one drives right into the mountain! Once inside, there's a huge cavern. I almost expected stalagmites and stalactites. Of course, to hike to the outside, to daylight, takes a little time.

The Salzburgers really have the tourist business well organized, but in a typical Austrian fashion, which can drive any red-blooded American, who is used to his individual rights, crazy. You buy your daily tourist pass, which is indeed good for all public transport and admissions. But every time you use this pass its number gets carefully recorded by an employee who is in no hurry. This means long waiting lines in the museums or for the cogwheel! Well, you get used to that.

Before Stuart and I picked up our van early in the morning, after we had stayed in Salzburg for two days, we went for a little stroll, a time to think of long ago.

"Stuart, you certainly have come far," I mused. "When you married Fran…"

"I may have been poor then, but, in a way, very rich: a master's degree in journalism from Northwestern University; a job with ABC News.

"I saw the apartment on the north side of Chicago where you grew up. Your mother must have had a hard time after your dad died so young. You know what you said to me, what your dream was when you were a teenager? To have your own desk in your own room. Maybe that's why you have such a big house now!"

"Actually, it wasn't so bad. My mom had a job as a legal secretary. I always made a little money, working at a drugstore from the age of 12. I never felt I was lacking for anything. Right now, I'm certainly enjoying this vacation. I like the sightseeing, the driving, especially when I don't have to look for somewhere to park."

The last leg of our journey would take us to Vienna, but first we wanted to stop for a few hours in Slovakia's capital.

"Where will we spend the night?" Stuart asked. "We could drive as far as Bratislava but then again we'd have to look for a hotel after dark.

"We can get to a famous spa about an hour earlier," I said. "I know of Americans who took 'the cure' there and swear by it."

We decided to stop at Piest'any. I had been there once, many years ago, and hardly remembered the place. It was already getting late when we reached the town, but in early June the sun had not yet set. Although my guidebook to Slovakia promised several good hotels, we were a little worried. What kind of buildings would the communist regime have put up here? We had seen samples of the dreadfully ugly block houses built between the 1950s and 1980s while we drove through the Czech and the Slovak Republics.

To our pleasant surprise we found a beautiful large hotel, quite modern but not all drab or gray. Signs above the reception desk were in Slovakian, Russian and German, but English was also spoken. Rooms were quite reasonable, perhaps half of what they would cost in Prague, less than a third of the price in Vienna.

"This hotel is about 10 years old," we were told. "The Russian big wheels used to spend the holidays here when they wanted to get away from it all. Now we have western guests here. We are proud of our hotel and keep it up."

Well, almost. The seat of the toilet in our room had several screws missing. One had to be careful while sitting down. One can't have it all.

After dinner, we walked through the quiet streets of the town, finding signs such as "Rooms for Rent, Including our Special Black Mud Bath!"

The next day we drove up to Bratislava. Stuart was lucky to find a parking place in the inner city.

Then it was onto Vienna where we unloaded our luggage at our hotel. Stuart and I returned the van to the Avis agency (no problems) and slowly walked back through the inner-city, a 20-minute stroll.

"Thanks for the excellent job of driving!" I said.

"I'm glad that we could spend so much time together," Stuart answered. In short, my daughter couldn't have married a nicer fellow.

V. A STRAIGHT LINE IS A GODLESS LINE

What a strange statement! Since we have been old enough to tell right from wrong, we've been told to stay on the <u>straight</u> and narrow path. Now, however, there is a voice, which seems to advocate the opposite: avoid the straight line; God is not in it.

Let's have a close look at the man who coined this phrase: Friedensreich Hundertwasser.

He was, in his time, a much-celebrated artist and builder of rather strange-looking houses: Hundertwasser, translated into English, means "hundred water," sounding uncommon, to say the least, in either language.

According to Mr. Hundertwasser, straight lines are against nature. In fact, there are no straight lines in the natural world.

There are several houses in Vienna, great tourist attractions, built by Mr. Hundertwasser according to his specifications. The outsides are decorated with the colors of the rainbow; there are no right angles and the foundations and large courtyards are curvy, as are most rooms. Some windows are large, other small. The roofs are green (Mr. Hundertwasser wanted grass on the roofs, with goats munching, but the building commission of the city of Vienna didn't go along).

As I was looking at these strange buildings, I couldn't help but wondering: could it be that Mr. Hundertwasser is right? At least in my own life, straight lines have definitely not prevailed, at least not past my high school years. I didn't stay in the place where I was born. I didn't continue to study what I had started out to study. I didn't keep the same friends for very long, not because I didn't like them, but because they either perished or had to move to distant places. After I finally reached America and settled down in a job, I soon found out that it would not be to my advantage to keep doing "the same thing" for too long. Mild changes of direction, curves occurred, chances had to be taken. I've seen employees who asked no questions, did exactly what they were told, and did it well, day in and day out, even getting periodic raises in pay. They may be good for the boss, until this same boss finds them overpaid and is "forced" to lay them off.

I preferred to make a nuisance of myself by asking for different assignments, even if I had to push a little once in a while.

But even Mr. Hundertwasser's fancy curved houses must have a firm foundation, or the wind will blow them away. I was, and still am, so very fortunate to have such a firm foundation, one that transcends space and time: my family.

While I was in Vienna, I had a chance to meet again with my cousin, Dr. Otto Weinmann.

He survived the Hitler years in France as a "submarine," a man who lives underground, surfaces rarely, and is always in great danger. As a young physician, he joined the French Resistance and had many, many close calls, but somehow lived to see the end of the war, only to be refused a license to practice medicine by the new Austrian government.

"We don't need foreign doctors," he was told.

Then a strange thing happened to him. He was helped by people who were not supposed to do anything for a Jew except to kill him: Nazis! Or more precisely ex-Nazis. When my cousin returned to Vienna (he had no other place to go) to prepare for possible emigration overseas, he was approached by a colleague, Fritz Mejer, a doctor who had been a Nazi even before Hitler came to Austria, when the Nazi party was illegal in Austria. I had known

Fritz as well. We went to high school together. As a matter of fact, we had been on excellent terms.

"Why don't you stay in Vienna?" Fritz asked my cousin. "I know people who can help you to establish yourself here."

My cousin Otto always had been, and still is, a committed Social Democrat, a member of a party that is, by American standards, rather far to the left. But he gladly accepted help from "the other side," right wingers in postwar Austria who denied any connection to their erstwhile hero, Adolf Hitler.

Otto had come to Vienna with a new wife whom he had found in Belgium during the last days of the war. Soon there was a baby daughter. Fifteen years later the marriage ended in divorce. "I can't blame her," Otto told me. "I'm not fit for marriage. I never had time for her. All I wanted to do was to practice medicine and to read. My wife led a lonely life in Vienna. After the divorce, I gave her all the money I had, and she and my daughter immigrated to Israel. I see them there frequently. Both are married, I've got grandchildren there. *(Editor's note: Otto's daughter, Dorit Knobel, lives in Israel, married to Avi Knobel. Their two children are Yishai and Efrat.)* Too bad I can't talk to them because they don't know German or French, and I don't speak Hebrew. But now there's hope: they are learning English in school, and I, like any doctor in Vienna who has some American patients, can make myself understood in this lingua franca."

I asked Otto, who is a year older than me, and now long retired, to take my family to a "Heurigan."

"What's that?" my family asked after I introduced them to Otto and his "lady friend," with whom he has been living, on and off, for the last 25 years.

"Heurigen" literally means 'this year.' But it's understood that we are talking about this year's WINE! Every vintner has the right to sell this wine directly to the public for only six weeks. They run wine gardens, sort of like pubs. Sometimes food is also served; rather fattening food, high in calories, because that encourages you to drink more. And most important, there's music, typical Viennese music."

We took the "U-Bahn" (Underground Train) from the center of the city, where our hotel was located, to the outskirts of town, then a bus to our destination. The whole trip took only twenty minutes or so on public transportation, which is unbelievably clean and efficient. We didn't arrive all that late, but we were barely able to find a table big enough for the eight of us: the six travelers in our family and Otto and his lady friend.

"This is Thursday, but it's a Catholic holiday and the weather is perfect," the host explained as we sat down on the wooden benches, at the wooden table. No plastics here, no tablecloth! A waitress with two pitchers of wine came immediately. She asked no questions about what we wanted to drink; obviously, the house wine!

The crowd was huge, filling the garden to overflowing! Everybody was talking, of course, but not loud enough to drown out the music, which consisted of an accordion, a violin and little drums. I asked the waitress about food.

"We only serve wine," she said. "If you want to eat, you've got to get your own food, you can buy it down there." She pointed to the bottom of the wine garden. Sure enough, there were tables set up with all kinds of meats and cheese, all at a good price. But our immediate task was to stand in line. The Viennese are hearty eaters anyway, and standing in line, looking at the delicious food, helps to increase the appetite.

Finally, we found our way back to our table, carrying mountains of cold beef, smoked tongue, headcheese, all delicious-smelling. I was sitting next to my cousin Otto. It was time for reminiscing.

"Please forgive me for speaking in German to Frank," Otto explain to my children and grandchildren. "I read English medical literature very well, but talking is difficult for me in your language."

I'm afraid his lady friend felt a little left out of the conversation, but she did her best to entertain my family in her rather basic English. Not that my children and grandchildren needed much outside help to keep themselves happy. There was enough wine to do that.

"I'm glad we're going to take public transportation back to our hotel, I don't have to worry about driving," my son-in-law said. My daughters, and especially my grandchildren, also liked the dry slightly sour wine. I'm not much of an expert but I knew enough to realize that the wine was, well, not bad, but also nothing special. At Trader Joe's, back home in California, it might have sold for $3.45 a bottle.

"Our fathers looked much alike," I said to Otto. "I look more like my mother's family, but you look like a true Weinmann."

"Thanks for the compliment," my cousin replied, "the Weinmanns are not exactly famous for their beauty."

"Women seem to like us. For instance, your lady friend. She's very good-looking, taller than you, at least 15 years younger."

"I don't know what she sees in me. But then, I never knew much about women."

"You know, Otto," I said, "when I was a boy I had quite a crush on your sister. She was a good singer, and excellent entertainer."

"A wonderful girl. She died a long time ago in South America."

"Well, you and I, we are some of the survivors. There's my brother and me in America, our cousin in Israel, and you here in Vienna, where we all grew up."

"But four of us are dead already," Otto said after a while. "My brother in North America, my sister in South America, a cousin in England and another in Italy. But at least Hitler killed none of us, except indirectly, our cousin in Italy."

"Let me ask you a direct question: are you happy in Vienna? Aren't there too many ghosts from the past? I remember what the Nazis did to the Jewish students at the university and the police didn't do a thing, and those were the Austrian Nazis, many years before Hitler took the country over."

"Of course I remember," Otto said. "One day, these hoodlums pushed all Jewish students out of the window, just for the fun of it! Luckily, it was a first-floor window; I only broke an arm. But that was 60 years ago. Let me answer your question. Yes, I'm happy in Vienna. I'm an old man now. Until I retired, not so long ago, I practiced medicine. That's what I wanted to do all my life. Even now, I'm often called to help out when my clinic is especially busy. I'm getting a decent pension."

"How about the 'ghosts from the past?'" as you call them.

"Well, Franz," (my cousin called me by the first name I haven't used for 55 years.)

"I've laid them to rest. I don't know what the future will bring, not here in Austria nor in America. I understand that you've got some Nazis there too, or the religious right, whatever. I trust nobody. My only child and my grandchildren are in Israel and they are in charge of their own destiny. But I'm happy in Vienna."

While we were talking and eating and drinking, the musicians were moving from table to table. My children and grandchildren had a good time entertaining themselves. I was always happy to see them getting along so well. But now the musicians came to our table. I guess I was the guest of honor so it was up to me to tell them what to sing. Several hundred guests, most of them a little drunk, were looking at me. Luckily, I was prepared. I whispered to Otto:

"I wonder whether they know the song your sister used to sing so well, *De Gusta san Verschieden*?

The musicians must have heard me. Immediately they started to play and sing this old song.

It's about two Viennese neighborhoods: one is rich, the other one is poor, the latter obviously favored by the writer of the song. It is where "real people" live. I must admit, perhaps to my shame, that I joined the musicians with a loud voice. Many of the guests obviously knew the song too, which I hadn't heard or even thought of for well over 60 years.

Just what makes such old songs survive? One of the two neighborhoods mentioned hasn't existed in Vienna in 100 years. But through the "Kaiser Zeit" (the Emperor's Time), World War I, revolution, the short-lived Austrian democracy, the Nazi years and World War II, the good citizens of Vienna have drunk their new wine and sung their old songs. Politics and politicians come and go, great ideas are thought and discarded, but songs survive. Whoever hasn't got them in his background is lacking something important. As for me, Heine's poems and Goethe's "Faust" are still my home base.

Such were the thoughts that went through my mind as I wandered through familiar streets of Vienna. I was by myself, having sent my family to see Schoenbrunn Castle, a much-admired tourist attraction of Vienna, which didn't interest me enough to spend a whole morning there. The day before, all of us had visited our apartment at Bartensteingasse Number 8, my parents' address from 1924, when I was ten years old, until 1938. So, I didn't have to do that again. But I started out in my "old neighborhood," only to find out how little had changed. The coffee house, a short block's walk from my parents' apartment, where they had spent a lot of time, wasn't there anymore.

But the "Konditorei" (sweet shop, a fancy bakery where one can only "eat in") next door was still there.

Neither the name of the place nor the layout had changed. Our family had eaten there frequently. My late wife Frances and I had stuffed ourselves with the high calorie Viennese sweets when we visited in 1985.

I thought of doing the same but changed my mind just before sitting down at one of their fancy tables. No, not alone, not by myself. One doesn't do that in a Konditorei. I walked on into the park where I had often played as a child. The trees are much taller now, there's less sunshine, but I had no difficulty finding the monuments I remembered so well: Johann Strauss (the father, famous for the "Radetsky March," not his better-known son) as well as statues of assorted Austrian politicians.

Some of them had been Jews. No doubt the Nazis had removed the statues and the Austrians put them back after World War II. Then I looked at the two theaters, both within five minutes walking time, that I had so often visited. During my high school years, there was hardly a week when I didn't casually walk to one or the other, often meeting friends there. We always went "stephplatz," standing room, of course.

The opera was just a little farther away, but still not more than 20 minutes on foot or three stops by streetcar.

Just around the corner from our apartment lived my friend Teddy, apart from relatives, the only human being I had known before I came to America that I'm still in touch with. In many ways, we were opposites. I was the nice little boy who never caused trouble in school, with the reputation so good that I rarely had to do my homework because I knew I wouldn't be checked. I had an excellent memory then (now I can't even remember where I parked my car) and, being the auditory type, I only had to listen to the teachers' lectures to know all the answers. I agreed with Teddy's judgment about most of our teachers: they were idiots, of course.

"But Teddy," I often said to my friend, "we can learn a lot even from idiots. They are stupid, but they know their stuff. We have to be in school whether we like it or not. While we are here, why not listen to what we hear?"

Teddy didn't think so. "I want to show them as the idiots they are. They shouldn't have become teachers if they don't know how to teach. I never disturb the math class or the Latin class because these two professors are alright."

But he did disturb most other classes. Once, he brought a frog to biology class. When the teacher turned his back, Teddy put the luckless amphibian on his desk just in time for the frog to jump on the teacher's head. Another time, when a teacher asked us to concentrate in order to grasp a difficult concept, Teddy threw a paper airplane across the class.

I had to think of Teddy's antics while I passed by the house where he had lived, where we had often played together and, on rare occasions, also studied together. Now, Teddy is living in a small town in Israel, the retired owner of an automobile repair shop. His first wife kept the family together, but after she died, Teddy managed to quarrel with his four sons and several grandchildren to the point where they are not on speaking terms. Although he fought in Israel's 1948 War of Independence and was severely wounded, he hates his country. He hates the Arabs and doesn't like the Jews.

"All crooks and cowards," he says. "the only good ones are dead."

But Teddy loves his dogs, his second wife (in that order) and writes excellent, sensitive poetry and short stories in English, his fourth language after German, French and Hebrew. He glorifies Europe, the continent that he left when he was barely out of his teens, long before the Nazis invaded Austria.

"I saw the disaster coming," he wrote to me recently. "Nobody believed me then, you don't believe me now when I'm telling you that both your country and my country are going to the dogs."

I offered to mediate somehow between Teddy and his children. I'm getting so much joy from my family, it pains me to see this bitter old man suffer because, as he says, his children are persecuting him. Teddy wouldn't hear about it.

Walking through the inner city, I passed an old building in a narrow street where I had spent every Wednesday evening during my late teens: The Freemasons House. The Masons were a highly secretive organization in Austria. There's no outward sign on the building. My brother and I were much too young to be Masons, but since our father was a member, we could belong to the youth organization.

That made me think of the many hours I had spent in coffee houses. You were sure to find some of your friends there as you selected your "stamm café" (steamed coffee). And the newspapers! As soon as one sat down, a waiter would bring a selection of magazines or papers, and to a steady customer the ones he or she usually read. Somehow the waiters remembered.

Some of us played chess or bridge, some just read the papers (including *La Vie Parisienne*, much appreciated for its pictures). Others just talked. There was much table-hopping, much noise, unfortunately also much smoke.

Memories! Where are you, all my coffee house friends from Vienna, from Bratislava, from Prague? I looked in the local telephone books but couldn't find the name of a single friend I remembered, be they Gentile or Jew. All gone away or, more likely, dead. Hitler got many of us, including the Gentile boys who, having high school diplomas, were made junior officers and sent to the Russian front, never to come back.

I asked myself every survivor's quintessential question: Why me? WHY DID I SURVIVE?

I, ONLY I?

There is no explanation, of course. The question stands alone. If I expected to find an answer (and maybe I did) from the sentimental journey my family and I enjoyed together, the trip was a failure, at least for me. Reflecting on our trip now, several months later, I must admit that while I had spent much time thinking about what we could see in two weeks, where we would stay, even how best to balance our time, I neglected to prepare myself... for myself.

Before I was able to leave Hitler's Central Europe in 1941, when I was 27 years old, I had lived in five cities: Vienna, Bratislava, Prague, Kosice and Budapest. We visited all five of them on our trip; not a coincidence since my family wanted to know where I came from.

Vienna: Although I had spent more time there than anywhere else, Vienna was least important as far as my immigration is concerned. When I saw the Nazis march down the beautiful Ringstrasse on March 11, 1938 (the same street we all admired so much for its beauty in 1996), I knew that this wasn't my city anymore. All memories I have of Vienna pre-date March 1938: a happy childhood as one of a well-integrated family, twelve pleasant school years (four in grammar school, eight in high school). But I didn't take the time to visit my schools! I did see the Wienerwald (Vienna Woods) again.

I was first introduced by my father to the beautiful forests and hills surrounding the city. I had spent countless Sundays there with the Boy Scouts, my friends from the Masons and later with other young people. I had been one of them. It was on a small, secluded meadow in the forest where I first learned to kiss a girl; I never found this meadow. But on our trip, I only invested enough time for a short bus trip and lunch.

Bratislava: We were there only a few hours on our trip. Most of the time we spent in a museum and later, overlooking the city from the Castle Hill, we could see that my father's factory wasn't there anymore, not even the street. During the city's Communist time, the ugliest accumulation of smoking factories and square, bleak houses had been built there. I did right in not wasting time to go there.

But I should have looked up some of the coffee houses where I had spent so much happy time with Teri, where we had first decided to get married. And I should have walked on the "Corso," a group of streets in the inner city where one promenaded up and down on Sunday mornings, to see and to be seen; an integral part of life! Finally, I should have taken the time to visit the Jewish Community Center. Maybe, just maybe I might have found a name I could recognize.

Prague: We spent serval days there and took in many of the tourist attractions and Jewish museums, all certainly well worth seeing. And we walked through some of the ancient streets, heard good music, and we ate and drank well. But I didn't take time to look up the tiny apartment where my parents had lived from 1939 to 1941, and I with them until spring of 1940. Teri and I spent the worst time of our lives in Prague when we found out about her being pregnant. I should have retraced the way the taxicab took when it brought us, after the abortion, "home" to the small room she had rented.

And in spite of being aware of the danger of living under the Nazis, we experienced much happiness because we were so in love.

Kosice: This was the place I failed so miserably because I couldn't think of my parents- in-law's address. Yet, we had come to the small town only for the purpose of remembering; my daughters wanted to know so badly where their mother had grown up. My mind was a blank. Again, as in Bratislava, a visit to the local Jewish Community Center might have been all that was needed. I didn't think of that.

Budapest: All the time we spent in this beautiful city we were busy, like any tourists, enjoying the sights, eating good food, listening to good music. But it was in Budapest where Teri and I finally got our American visas, but thought they had come too late for us. There didn't seem to be any chance to get out! We were completely surrounded by war. Hungary had no common border with any neutral country. We resigned ourselves to our fate, resolved to live one day at a time. Then, suddenly, we learned that the "HAPAG," a German shipping agency with an office in Budapest, was now in the business of procuring transit visas as well as transportation to Spain (by airplane, no less!) for Jews who had overseas visas. A turning point in our lives!

I should have visited that office where Teri and I were first humiliated, cursed, screamed at by a woman who looked like a witch, but who later helped us enormously, refusing our thanks by saying: "This is the least I can do as a German woman."

In Prague, we visited the *Magic Lantern*, a typical Czech establishment. You think at first that you are in a rather large, conventional movie theater. A circus scene is projected onto the screen; there are animals, a clown, sparsely dressed ladies, and you wonder what this is all about? Why did you pay the rather high price of admission to see this? Then, suddenly, the clown, who seemed to be just a figure in a movie, lifts up the screen, which is only a white cloth, and comes out of the picture onto the stage, very much a live actor. He performs some acrobatics, then motions to one of the ladies to "come out" too. He gallantly lifts the screen for her, she appears on the stage. Later, the actors all go back to the make-believe world of a movie.

I wonder whether the Czechs haven't hit on something. Maybe life is just a mixture of "Sein" and "Schein," (German words for "reality" and "make-believe," what is and what only seems to be). And there are no straight lines, only curves. For instance: wanting to escape to the West in 1940 and 1941, we had to go East first. Fate throws curves at you, bad ones more often than good ones, but there are sometimes turning points.

A straight line is a Godless line.

<u>MY 90TH BIRTHDAY CRUISE</u>
<u>JUNE, 2004</u>

Editor's Note: on the occasion of Grandpa Frank Weinman's 90th birthday, his family organized a celebratory cruise from Los Angeles, down the Pacific Coast to Mexico with as many of Frank's family members as could make it along for the ride. It was a wonderful cruise that lasted a week and enabled the Schwartz, Gelber, Bash, Lichterman, Miller and Alt families to be with Grandpa Frank for his milestone birthday. Along the way, the ship stopped in San Diego. John and Rodica Weinman, Charles's son and daughter-in-law, hosted us at their home. The following are Frank's reflections on that cruise and his family:

Well, to tell the truth, my birthday was still one month away when 26 members of my family went on a cruise in June, 2004. I'm back home in Rossmoor, Walnut Creek, California now, a little tired, a little sunburned.

A good friend once told me: "There are two kinds of autobiographical stories: dull ones and lies."

He may well be right, but I still want to record a few highlights of the cruise my family gave me as a birthday present. They didn't even let me pay for my share and provided all transportation to and from the port of Los Angeles. But their mere presence, coming as they did from New York, Philadelphia, Chicago, Washington D.C. and California was the greatest gift.

But, on second thought, there were no highlights because every day, every hour, was a delight!

So, may I start with regrets: Teri, my first wife, who died in 1975 after 35 years of happy marriage, was not present and Frances, my second wife to whom I was married for 26 years, had passed away in February, 2003.

**I'm dedicating this report to these
ladies and their descendants.**

Well, am I a two-time loser? BUT NO! Perhaps a two-time winner? At this point, I can't resist the temptation, thinking back to my marriages, to describe how I met Teri, the mother of my daughters.

No, it was NOT a "love at first sight." None of that business of "seeing a stranger across a crowded room" and "suddenly." I guess I'm not, never was, a romantic soul. No, when I first met Teri (short for Teresa), what I admired about her was not her face, pretty but not beautiful, nor her figure, excellent although too slim and a little too tall for me, but rather her skill in freely conversing in four languages! I wanted to practice my poor Slovakian (needed for business while working in Bratislava, Slovakia's capital). So, I thought, why not start a friendship with this girl who could teach me?

Well, friendship slowly turned to love, a deep love only made stronger by the awful experiences we shared together, but somehow survived. Our love never cooled. And I consider myself a lucky winner because two clans (my children with their descendants and my second wife Frances's children and all their decendants) melded so seamlessly that I am not only a father and a grandfather several times over, but also a great-grandfather.

I met my second wife, Frances (short for Francesca) half a year after Teri's death, because I realized that I couldn't live by myself. So, I asked three happily married ladies to find somebody for me. And I gave them SPECIFICATIONS: she should be a widow who had had a happy married life, who must get along with her children (I didn't want to inherit family problems), who was neither very rich (I had no intention of getting used to a lifestyle I couldn't support myself) nor very poor (who would marry me for a meal ticket). Finally, if at all possible, she should have a background similar to mine. That might be too much to ask for, but it didn't take long until I was "invited to dinner." I might meet someone whom my friends had met at the Chicago Symphony.

Well, it certainly doesn't sound like a romantic beginning, but it worked! Frances and I liked each other instantly and soon the liking turned to loving.

A funny incident happened a month or two after we met: in a restaurant, we ran into another of the ladies I had charged with "finding somebody for me." This lady said to me in front of Frances:

"What was your hurry? I had THREE women lined up for you." Needless to say, she and Frances did NOT become best friends.

At this time, I should really start to describe my recent trip on the worthy cruise ship called *Monarch of the Seas*. If you have been on one of these giant vessels (ours had 11 decks, two swimming pools, three huge restaurants, etc.), then you know what to expect.

Our itinerary included three stops in California and one in Mexico; all very interesting, to be sure, but the purpose of our trip was for the whole extended clan to get together. Judy (Frances's daughter) had given us special green T-shirts with huge yellow letters made for our party, telling everybody that this was FRANK'S 90TH BIRTHDAY CRUISE. There may have been close to 3,000 people aboard, and many of them stopped me in order to inform me that I really didn't look "quite" that old.

I must interrupt my tale about the family get-together to explain the difference between just old (simply meaning not young) and REALLY OLD. You see, when you are really old you don't try to make yourself younger (not that you could anyway) but rather you start bragging about your age.

"Just look at me, see what I can still do in spite of having been around so long already." And you start remembering, thinking! Yes, thinking. Maybe this thinking defines you. Remember what the philosopher Descartes said a few hundred years ago: "I think, therefore I am." So, I remember! I am still around, thinking, not as sharp as in years gone by, but maybe just remembering.

Well, the real purpose of this exercise is to remember, to talk about my extended family. I might as well start with the youngest generation: three babies, two of them only six months old (the cutest ever, so all agreed). But I must confess that while all babies are wonderful, beautiful, smart and special to me, a prospective nonagenarian, they look much like. So, Jacob (*the son of Yvette and Jeremy Miller, Frances's granddaughter and husband*), already over two and a half years old, stole the show for the fourth generation. Here is why: I could show him something he'd never seen before: I can wiggle my ears. True, so can a donkey, but among people, especially great-grandfathers, the facility for ear wiggling is rare. Jacob was fascinated. He tried to do it too but couldn't do it yet. Well, Jacob, soon enough you'll learn more important things. What you already know is how to be an escape artist. In a split-second you could get out of the confinement of your highchair and give your parents a good chase around the ship. There was no danger; how far can one get running on the ship? And it was great fun for all to watch. When you got caught, your reward was a big hug!

Now to the third generation, the grandchildren. There's quite a spread in ages, from 16 years to 34. Jennine (*the daughter of Frances's daughter Judy and her husband Maynard Lichterman*) is the youngest, born more than 20 years after her parents married. There were some early concerns about Jennine as a baby. It took her a while to learn how to crawl on her hands and knees. When she wanted to get across the room, she rolled there, using her hands to help her turn over, but did nothing with her legs. Her grandmother put herself in what she thought was the correct baby-crawling position and urged Jennine on. The baby just looked at her and merrily rolled away.

That went on for a few weeks until one day Jennine raised herself up, made sure that we watched what she was doing, and walked on her beautiful legs across the room. She didn't fall, not even stumble as most babies do.

Luckily, my wife lived long enough to see her granddaughter become the best player on her high school basketball team, the fastest runner on the field, the star! But in one respect, Jennine hasn't changed much: she does what she wants, on her own time, and does it very well. I wish you all the luck in the world, my beloved step-granddaughter. But I think you won't even need my best wishes, you make your own good luck!

About Jonathan Gelber, the second youngest of the third generation, my youngest grandson. (There is also Jonathan Alt, my wife Frances's grandson; more about him later.) I admit that I sometimes worry about him. Not because of the crazy acrobatics he performs on his skateboard, but because he is so successful at everything he does. (Well, there may have been a disappointment here and there, but very few.) Just having finished his sophomore year in high school, his report cards never have included any grade lower than "A." Not that he spends an awful lot of time studying; he doesn't seem to bother with that. He has too many other things to do: hanging out with his many friends, seeing his girlfriend (he isn't even 17 yet!). And of course, music. He plays the saxophone, he's the drummer in a band, and recently he taught himself to play guitar. His self-confidence is enormous.

A few years ago, the family conversation got around to SAT scores, a subject dreaded by every high school student and so important for admission to a good university.

"Nothing to it," he said. "All I have to do is to answer all of the questions correctly, and of course I will." Well, Jonathan is too intelligent for such hubris now, but he still casually says: "I'll get a good education wherever I go."

When there was only room for one saxophone player in the junior high school band and they would hold tryouts, he said, "It's coming down to my friend Billy and me (everybody is his friend, no enemies). I know that Billy is a better player, but I will win the spot."

"How come if he's the better player?" I asked.

"Because I can improvise better. Part of the contest is to join in while a tape is being played which includes all voices except the sax. I'm the best improviser."

He won. Yes, to be a good improviser is certainly important, and so is hard work! Recently he won a contest in a science fair for high school students and he and his partner were sent to Portland, Oregon to represent California!

"All expenses paid!" he said proudly.

"It did not come easily," his mother, my daughter Linda told me. "The two boys spent many hours on the computer, got all the information available and then worked from morning to night to get everything just right."

"What did you learn?" I asked innocently. I guess a grandfather's questions can be so stupid.

"Essentially, that when you're sitting in a chlorinated hot tub your nose should be more than two inches above the water. It has something to do with chlorine gas killing fruit flies if they are closer than that. But you see Grandpa, the purpose of the science fair was to show how to best set up an experiment."

But, my dear Jonathan, you won't always be allowed to set up your own experiments. Life won't be that kind to you. And you certainly won't be able to answer all questions! I wish for you that when your first major defeat comes, and it will, it should not hurt you too much, and that you'll easily get over it. *(Editor's note: Jonathan is now a physician, like his parents.)*

The next youngest of my grandchildren is Ricky, a very good-looking man.

Nineteen years old, Jonathan's older brother Ricky. You are a gifted writer, ever since you composed your story about the "TIME BANK" at age seven. Why, you wrote, since they say time is money, can't we borrow a few minutes from such a bank, for instance when late for school, and repay those minutes by skipping the droning lecture of a dull teacher? You were disappointed when your daddy said that there is no such bank! Later, in your high school paper, you wrote an article about an auto accident that caused the death of your best friend.

Ricky, you were a little moody sometimes, retiring to your room, lying on your back and playing chords on your bass guitar. Then maybe you worried too much about getting into a good university although you had excellent grades. Well, you are at New York University now, the school of your choice, although George Washington University, where you attended your freshman year, obviously wanted you badly to stay. You are a success story; maybe you'll be a lawyer someday *(Editor's note: Ricky is, in fact, a lawyer)* or a politician, or a writer. At this time, you're sure you won't be a doctor like your dad, Alex, and mom, Linda, or a scientist like your brother. You split up with your girlfriend in California, but let me assure you, many mothers have beautiful daughters who will find you, unless you find them first. Only, Ricky, let an old man who loves you and wishes you well, assure you that while there is an awful lot of shit in this world, there is also sunshine. Look for it.

David, the next youngest of the third-generation of my direct descendants, is already 30 years old. As they say in New York, he's been around the block. He had been the shortest boy in his class (well, neither his father, Stuart, nor his mother, my daughter Frances, are exactly giants). But David knew what to do! In high school he became a weightlifter and wrestler. He may still be not exactly tall, measuring about five feet six or seven inches, but he's so good-looking and muscular that a magazine put his picture in among other "eligible bachelors." Well, bachelor he still is, to my and his mother's chagrin, after he has had some of the nicest of girlfriends.

"I'll only marry when I really love the girl," he said recently. I hope he'll find her soon!

What he did find is an interesting job, after a few false starts. His job has something to do with sports commercials; he travels to important events and may go to the Olympics in Athens.

(Editor's note: David did go to the Athens Olympics; he later became founder and owner of "Pressure," a video production company.)

I remember the incident that first made David so special to me. He may have been about four years old; his parents were on vacation (as were my wife and I, and babysitting). I was driving. David and his sister, two and a half years older than him, were also with us in the car. Our goal: the village swimming pool. My daughter had given me instructions how to get there. A drive of five minutes, she assured me.

"We should be there by now!" big sister said.

"I'm afraid we are lost!" my wife, not always the optimist, complained.

But David knew otherwise. "We are NOT lost! We are on the right way. It is a five-minute drive in daddy's car. Grandpa drives slower than daddy. We'll be there right away!" He was right; good, logical thinking!

A few years ago, I took my extended family on a "sentimental journey" through much of Central Europe, where I grew up. We rented a big van. Stuart, my son-in-law, was driving. David, the strongest of us, was in charge of managing the suitcases. He handled them by carrying three in one hand and two in the other. My job was planning the trip. Vienna, of course, Prague, Salzburg and Budapest, among other cities. On our last day, we had a discussion as to what each of us had liked best.

"Perhaps Prague?" I wondered. "Now that the Communists are gone, the mixture of the old romantic buildings and the new vibrant economy is fascinating."

"Budapest! Especially the gypsy music!" my younger daughter said.

"It must be Vienna, with its beautiful old buildings, modern transportation, prosperity," my older daughter insisted.

David kept quiet for a long time and then he said:

"Of course, all the cities. And don't forget Salzburg, nestled in the Alps, is a beautiful city. But what I liked best was still nature, like near Hallstatt. The towering mountains around the deep, blue lake where we rented a boat. Yes, there is nature, unspoiled nature. They don't even allow cars in the little town."

David had proved me right in including a day of "only" looking at nature into the crowded itinerary of our trip. Well, David, you now insist on living in Manhattan, but still, you know that what we call civilization isn't everything. Maybe you are really a romantic soul? I hope you'll find your romantic love soon! I'd like to meet her! *(Editor's note: In 2012, David married Juliana Alonso de Oliveiera. They live in New York with their two children, Teodoro and Stella.)*

Only a few months older than David, the next youngest of my grandchildren's generation is Jonathan Alt, 30 years old, my second wife Frances's only grandson. He's tall, slim, extremely handsome, usually smiling, and why shouldn't he be? He's married to a lovely wife and is the father of the youngest baby on board the ship where my 90th birthday was celebrated. Jonathan, with the same name as my youngest grandson (well, Jonathan is a good biblical Hebrew name, meaning "God's Gift") is one of those human beings who are just right! I first met him in Chicago when he was about four years old, being introduced to his future "grandpa." He had never known his real one, my wife's first husband who had died many years earlier.

"You have a beautiful car!" He said, pointing at my old, rusty Plymouth. A line, of course, but what can a four-year-old boy say to an old man who seems to belong with his beloved grandma. Everybody laughed and was happy. And we haven't stopped loving each other since.

Looking at him now, one may find it hard to believe that he had been a somewhat timid little boy. His grandmother and I were babysitting once (his parents had taken a well-deserved vacation). But as soon as his parents left, Jonathan said that he felt very, very sick. His head hurt badly. But even worse was his throat. A trip to the doctor, whose address we had been given, ended in a diagnosis that he had a strep throat. We bought the prescribed medicine. As soon as we got home, the phone rang.

"How are the children?"

Jonathan: "Let me talk to mom. Oh, I'm fine. The doctor said I'm not. But I really just wanted to talk to you." And, lo and behold, there was no sick child anymore.

One year later, same thing, a very sick Jonathan; only this time we called his parents, and as soon as he talked to his daddy and his mummy all the symptoms disappeared.

But "Jon," as his parents called him, soon changed! He became very self-confident. He may have been no more than 10 or 12 years old when he discovered that he could earn money! Lawn mowing, babysitting, snow removal, whatever. He was never afraid of hard work. He was still in high school when he got himself a permanent weekend job: carrying a camera and otherwise helping a photographer at parties. That necessitated buying his own tuxedo ("my boss paid half of it!" he beamed).

He went to the University of Illinois ("same as my dad, it was good for him"), studied business administration (what else?), was very good at sports, especially lacrosse, and became captain of the university's team. That helped in getting him his first job! There were several applicants for a desirable position at a prominent bank, all qualified, but when Jonathan pulled out a photo showing that he had been the captain of the lacrosse team, the job was his. "A tough sport," the interviewer said. "If you can handle it, you can handle the job with us. It's hard work."

So it was. There were special projects necessitating long hours. And, by the way, he got a handsome bonus at years' end. So, together with cash accumulated earlier, there was enough money for a down payment on a condo in a first-class location in Chicago. Of course, there was a good-sized mortgage and, furthermore, much work had to be done to bring the somewhat neglected apartment to first-class condition. But, what are daddies for? Jonathan has just the right kind of father, George (more about him later), who is a man who can do everything: not only give good advice but also help his son, no slouch either, with his hands.

So, aided by a general upswing in Chicago real estate, the value of the condo doubled within a year! A good time to sell! Jonathan, now having some "real money," quit his job and went into business for himself. It's a little complicated to describe just what he does: essentially buying and managing businesses whose owners want to retire. More important, he married Debbie, a wonderful girl (a biologist with a Ph.D.) and beautiful too. They have a daughter, Jordyn, now a beautiful baby, also a passenger on our cruise. *(Editor's note: Jonathan and Debbie also have a second daughter, Hailey.)* I love you; you have it made. I don't even have to wish you luck. You're making it yourself!

The second oldest member of the third generation is my granddaughter Dana. (I consider myself to be a survivor of the first generation and my children and stepchildren are the second generation on our FRANK'S 90TH BIRTHDAY CRUISE.)

She's easy to find in this country and in much of the world. You can see her on TV, working as a reporter covering the White House for CNN. I must tell how I bask in the sunshine of her career.

At services in our synagogue we have a short interruption, dedicated to "nachas" (good news) when members are asked to tell the congregation about joyful events. A couple may get up and say, "We are celebrating our 50th wedding anniversary," or a proud young mother: "My son just graduated from kindergarten." Well, there were more graduations, all the way to high school. But that's not all!

Here is a proud father: "My daughter is receiving her bachelor's degree at UC Berkeley."

Who can top that? Well, I could.

Frank Weinman

"MY GRANDDAUGHTER DANA IS THE COMMENCEMENT SPEAKER AT THE GRADUATION AT BERKELEY!"

Please forgive the "one-upmanship" of a proud grandfather. By the way, her speech was for the political science majors, not the entire student body at Berkeley (the school is much too large to hold a single ceremony for all graduates). Still, there were probably more than a thousand political science graduates, probably all anxious to get the speeches over with.

So, Dana had her job cut out for her to hold the graduates' attention! She certainly succeeded. Her opening sentence:

"You want to know what you can do with your degree? Perhaps open a political science store?"

Remember, she was talking to students just getting that very degree. Of course, she soon turned around, explaining how valuable this degree was; how much her studies helped her in her job; how important it was to know what's going on in the real world. She really had the students and the audience eating out of her hand, especially since she was not so many years older than the graduates and already a success at her job. She had an excellent ending for her (not too long) speech:

"Always be a skeptic. Don't believe half of what they tell you. But never be a cynic, thinking that there is nothing you can do about it."

"How about the ending, 'be a skeptic but not a cynic?' I wondered.

"My idea. I really believe that!" she said.

I asked Dana: "Is there a formula for your successful career at CNN?

"Perhaps. Push a little, but not too hard. Always cover for your boss. Be good to your co-workers. Don't ever say bad things about anybody." She added: Don't even *think* badly about them."

Maybe that's why everybody loves you so much, Dana.

The oldest of my grandchildren's generation is my wife's oldest granddaughter, Yvette.

I beg your pardon: *Dr.* Yvette Alt (Miller), mother of two babies on our trip, Jacob and Simone.

Yvette, I remember so well the delicious discussions you and I had when you were a teenager. They were about religion, politics, whatever, and we agreed on nothing! And as the arguments got hot, and hotter, we screamed at each other. Your poor grandmother started to cry until we both burst out laughing. The arguments were only for arguments sake! We both loved them!

I remember how you cried when you read the story about the spider and the pig; the spider had to die at the end, but you still didn't like spiders. Well, after high school came Wellesley, a women's college. I guess you were a feminist for a while, but changed your mind and transferred to Harvard. Then you attended the prestigious London School of Economics. You earned a Master's degree and finally your Ph.D. Obviously, you enjoyed your long years as a student, getting to interview some of the most important economists in Europe. I'm only sorry that your grandmother didn't live long enough to see you getting your formal Ph.D. degree. But luckily, she could still pose for a photo with you and your son Jacob, your father George, and herself. FOUR GENERATIONS! On her deathbed, this picture was the last thing she saw.

Yvette, you have the sunny disposition of the Alts. You are already a successful student, wife, twice a mother (*Editor's note: Yvette and her husband Jeremy now have four children: Jacob, Simone, Gideon and Natan*), and you still have far to go! I love you very much!

And now, the second generation: my children and stepchildren. Let me, an old man who has been in lots of places, seen lots of things, experienced some suffering and also much joy, tell you the age you're in (middle 50s to early 60s) is probably the best of your lives.

In your jobs, you are probably as far as you will go. You know what you're doing. No anxiety. Your children are either out of the house or soon will be. You know that they can take care of themselves. No babysitting required (a little financial help, perhaps, but you can afford it). ENJOY YOURSELVES! Build up a horde of souvenirs you'll remember later. All of you "have made it." I'm so proud of you, as your mothers would be. You honor their memories by being who you are!

As before, I'll start with the youngest, my daughter Linda. You have such a wonderful family now (true there was a false start but that was a long time ago). You and your husband are working hard but are successful in your profession; honored and loved. I wonder if I really influenced you in choosing your career as a doctor. Somehow you always knew what was right for you (well, almost always) and you got what you wanted without fighting. You inherited the common sense of your mother! That's so important! Less important, you also inherited my facility to get good grades on tests in high school and later without having to "sweat it." Maybe you also got the capacity for logical thinking that I had when I was younger.

You were so easy to bring up (except that you didn't like fruit; as a matter of fact, you still don't). You didn't have any temper tantrums. You got along with other kids (exception: you allowed your "best girlfriend" to bully you for a while). When you were in junior high school there was a sweet relationship you had with a handsome boy of your age. Everybody, including his parents, adored the two of you, holding hands, the picture of innocence.

A few years later you told me that your pre-teen and early teenage years were not all that happy; that some of your classmates wouldn't connect with you because you were too smart and your grades too good. I guess you never tolerated fools gladly, and you still don't. But maybe you secretly longed to be friends with the trashy cashmere sweater crowd you despised.

Some of this was probably my fault. Maybe I pushed you too hard as soon as I recognized your tremendous intellectual abilities. Not that either your mother or I ever asked you to have good grades in school; there was never any conversation about that; you did so well anyway without much effort (much like your son Jonathan). No, it was in a somewhat subtler way. For instance, I asked you to take Latin in junior high. When I was in Rome in 1961, I even sent you a Latin picture-postcard to summer camp (you must have been embarrassed). And there was our conversation at the dinner table, conversations about your schoolwork in mathematics or Latin, thus excluding your mother and your sister. So maybe I did my best to make you a little snobby or at least acting like one in school. I don't know, and I apologize if I did. I guess parents too often want to make their children in their image.

Now to Judy, my stepdaughter, my guardian who always looks out for me.

Judy, do you remember the first words you said to me when your mother and I showed up at your house in Lafayette in 1976?

"Frank, my mother wrote me much about you, but you are also good looking!" Well, that was a long time ago.

Judy, what would I do without you? As busy as your life is, you always have time for me! You (or maybe it was your wonderful husband Maynard) once said to me:

"Frank, you were so good to my mother, even when she was sick, so of course we…"

But Judy, if I was good to Frances, it was because I loved her. What your family is doing for me now cannot be, and should not be explained. You are just good people. Judy, if you add to that goodness your almost unbelievable efficiency, the result is what you are: always there when you are needed, doing what should be done without needing much coaxing. At the same time, you are nobody's fool. Nobody should try to take advantage of you! And your family will always come first, that's how it should be, always, always! That's why you are such a good mother and wife. Judy, there is so much I could add. But let me summarize: you are good and efficient.

Francie, my older daughter, do you know why I always called you "Fran," not "Frances?" Not because your name was too long, but because I was always, since my childhood, inflicted with "LISPING." I can't pronounce the "S" consonant correctly and was afraid you wouldn't be able to either.

I was so unsure of myself, afraid of doing things wrong; maybe most new fathers are. But luckily, your mother's common sense saved all three of us because she was always the steadfast pillar of our family. Luckily, you as well as your sister inherited so much from her, although not her tall stature. You always liked to look just right and well-dressed. Your first complete sentence was "Mommy, make me pretty!" I guess your perfect taste came early and never changed.

Not that you were all that easy to bring up. You were never a good eater (maybe that's why you have kept your slim, perfect figure to this day), and you had your temper tantrums as a small child. Well, you had to assert yourself, what's wrong with that? I only wish you had asserted yourself more and told me how wrong I was when I made fun of you when you used big words, when you tried to write like Shakespeare.

Unfortunately, some of your English teachers did as badly as I did. "Why doesn't she write like others do?" one of them said. How stupid can a teacher be? I always feel (although you deny it) that I helped in squelching a great gift you had, the talent to be the great poet our family never had. You have certainly got the necessary sensitivity. I'll never forget when, during your sophomore year in college, you wanted to participate in the freedom march in Alabama. Luckily, your mother, with her common sense, talked you out of it: "You, a pretty Jewish girl, would only put yourself in great danger without helping your cause!"

We (your mother and I) tried hard to instill in you what we thought to be the right values. Maybe we tried too hard, succeeded too well? I remember when the mother of one of your girlfriends called your mother: "Teri, are you going to allow Francie to go to THAT party? If you do, I'll let my daughter go too because YOU know what's right." Well, the answer was yes, but to have the reputation of always doing the right thing may not be a good way to make a girl popular!

Of course, I'll never forget when you screamed at us at the top of your excellent voice:

"It's All Your Fault!"

Here's what happened:

There was a big party at your junior high school, at the end of your summer semester. You were 13 years old. The school was just two blocks from us, so no need to pick you up. You promised to be home by 11 o'clock. But you came home running at 9 o'clock, screaming, and screaming. When you finally caught your breath, you explained why "it was our fault." It was her "bad upbringing." She was with her best girlfriend when "these two cute boys asked us to leave this stupid school party and go for a drive in the car one of them had 'borrowed' from his father." Her girlfriend was to sit in the back seat with one of the boys. Fran was to sit next to the driver.

"I was just about to get into the car when I remembered that 'YOU' wouldn't approve, so I ran home. Your stupid way of upbringing. I would have had such a good time!"

Well, my dear daughter, I still think YOU did the right thing.

Francie, you always do the right thing. You always dress right; you certainly married right. You have the right children. I LOVE YOU SO MUCH!

George Alt, my stepson, you are the oldest of the second generation. I think there was nothing but good feeling between us from the moment we first met.

It must've been difficult for you to meet a man who was supposed to become your mother's husband. True, your father had been dead for 16 years, but I think that you never stopped loving him. You had been in high school when this terrible accident happened; his laboratory blew up, there was a fire. You studied chemistry, possibly thinking that you might work in your dad's business sometime. You would have become an excellent chemical engineer. And since you inherited not only your father's optimism but also your mothers skeptical caution, you would have turned your father's business into a big success. But I can well understand that, after the accident, you didn't want to have anything to do with industrial chemistry and, from then on, studied accounting.

As we all know, you became a big success as a CPA. Besides, it seems that you can fix anything: in your home, on your computer I think that you are one of the few people who really understands how these damn things work. And I'm greatly impressed by how you put those gadgets together that come in boxes marked "easy assembly." Most people (me included) are afraid. You don't even need to read the instructions.

"The designers knew what they were doing," you would say. "But the writers of the instructions don't even know English!" So, you did what came naturally. As busy as you are, you always find time to do my taxes now as you did your mother's before. Your mother was very proud of you, her big son. She often talked about you and nobody was happier than she was to see you so successful in your work. You know that, of course.

George, you and your lovely wife Maureen brought up a splendid family, helping out when help was needed. You are grandparents now, three times (*Editor's note: now six times*); and that makes me a proud step-grandfather. I'm happy that I belong to your family.

Now a P.S. <u>MY APOLOGIES</u>.

I didn't write about so many of all you lovely people who made this trip such a success. In no particular order: Maureen, Maynard, Alex, Stuart, Jeremy Bash, Debbie Alt, and Jeremy Miller.

The reason: I want to dedicate this exercise to my two late beloved wives: Teri Vidor Weinman and Frances Dubsky Alt Weinman, and thus I only wrote about their DIRECT descendants, their children, grandchildren, and great-grandchildren. And now I have to make an exception. I refer to myself as "THE FIRST GENERATION." But I know that I was not the only one of this generation on this trip.

There is Anda Gelber, mother of Alex, mother-in-law of my daughter Linda.

This is not the place to write about her truly heroic act, how she saved her future husband, Dr. George Gelber, Alex's father, by getting him out of the Lvov Ghetto in Poland in 1942. I had the good fortune to meet him and talk to him extensively in California. There's more to it. But what I want to do now is to salute a great lady, Anda, like me, a member of the "FIRST" generation.

Now, may I say it again and again:

THANK YOU, THANK ALL OF YOU!

ADDENDA

Editor's Note: In 2009, a resolution honoring Frank Weinman on his 95th birthday was placed into the record of the U.S. House of Representatives by Congresswoman Nancy Pelosi of California. This resolution is reproduced here.

Also included in these addenda are translations of letters written over the course of 1941 to 1944 from Teri Vidor Weinman's family in Kassa, Hungary to Frank and Teri in Chicago. Many are signed "Apu" (Teri's father Rudolf), "Apuka (Teri's mother Mathilde) and Magda (Teri's sister), all of whom perished in the Holocaust. They reflect the daily lives of the family in the uncertain and no doubt terrifying years of Nazi rule in Hungary, after Frank and Teri had successfully emigrated to America. They write of their desire for Frank and Teri's happy and peaceful future in America and their ultimate wish, unfulfilled, to be reunited someday.

The following tribute was read into the Congressional Record in the United States House of Representatives by the Honorable Nancy Pelosi of California on Thursday, July 9, 2009 *(the day of Frank's 95th Birthday; the following day, Frank Weinman passed away in Walnut Creek, California).*

IN HONOR OF THE 95TH BIRTHDAY OF FRANK WEINMAN. SPEECH OF HON. NANCY PEOLOSI OF CALIFORNIA IN THE HOUSE OF REPRESENTATIVES, THURSDAY JULY 9, 2009.

Ms. Pelosi: Mr. Speaker, I rise today to pay tribute to a great American, Frank Weinman, on the occasion of his 95th birthday.

Born in Vienna, Austria, Frank has overcome great hardships and adversity on life's path, escaping the terror of Hitler's Europe to settle with his family in the United States.

Working in his father's paint factory in Bratislava, Czechoslovakia, Frank fell in love with his future wife, Teri, a Hungarian citizen. When the Germans occupied Austria, Frank was left stateless, because, as a Jew, he could not return to Vienna and was forced to flee to Prague. In Prague, Frank assisted Jews immigrating illegally to Palestine, undoubtedly saving many lives.

On the run from the Nazis, Frank and Teri were secretly married on October 25, 1939 in Prague. Separated often over the next 18 months, Frank received word that his brother Charles, who had immigrated to America, had procured visas for them, and Frank made a daring journey by foot over mountainous terrain to Hungary, where Teri was staying with her family. While waiting for exit visas in Kosice, Hungary, Frank and Teri were arrested and sent to Hungarian concentration camps, before being released due to their American visas.

Forced to leave behind family, Frank and Teri made a harrowing journey across Austria and Germany to Spain, where they found passage across the Atlantic on a small Spanish ship. They arrived to the New World, free from the fear of oppression they had narrowly escaped, on October 12, 1941, Columbus Day.

Frank and Teri lived together until Teri's passing in 1975, having raised a family of two daughters in Illinois. Frank married Frances Alt in 1977 and they moved to the Great State of California in 1988.

Though Frances has since passed away, Frank Weinman celebrates his 95th birthday in Walnut Creek, California today with daughters Francie and Linda, and their husbands Stuart and Alex, along with their four loving grandchildren.

He is also blessed to have a devoted step-daughter, Judy, and her husband Maynard, and stepson George and his wife Maureen. Thanks to them, Frank has three more adoring grandchildren and six great-grandchildren.

Frank's story is an inspiration to us all, and we are reminded of the importance of family, perseverance and faith. I encourage all Members of Congress to join me in wishing Frank a happy birthday and may he celebrate many more.

<u>LETTERS FROM KASSA</u>
<u>1941 TO 1944</u>

Editor's Note: The following are letters sent from the Vidor family in Kassa, Hungary to Frank and Teri after they had arrived in Chicago in late 1941. These letters were kept by Frank. It is unknown if they constitute all correspondence over the years, or just those that were saved. They span the years 1941 to 1943, during which time conditions under Nazi rule throughout Europe were becoming more and more dire, especially for Jews.

It was not until 1944 that the Jews of Hungary felt the full wrath of the Nazis. Until then, the government of Hungary, though collaborating with the Germans, had managed to protect many Jews from deportation to labor or death camps. The Vidor family, other than Teri, had decided to stay in Hungary.

These letters reflect day-to-day goings-on in Kassa involving the family, with intimations of how their circumstances were increasingly dictated by the political environment around them. There seemed to be an unstated hope that eventually the family in Hungary and Frank and Teri in Chicago might one day see each other again.

But that was not to be, as evidenced by the Vidor's final letter, documented earlier in this book. As far as is known, Teri's mother and father (who signed the letters

Frank Weinman

as _"Anjuka" and "Apu" or "Apuka") and her sister Magda
perished in the Holocaust._

The records of Holocaust victims at Yad Vashem in
Israel lists Magda Bettelheim (her married name) the
following way:

**"Magda Bettelheim nee Vidor was born in
Ujszeged in 1920 to Rudolf and Matild nee Stein.
She was married to Istvan. Prior to WWII
she lived in Satoraljaujhely, Hungary. During
the war, she was in Auschwitz, Poland.
Magda was murdered in the Shoah."
Source: Card catalogue of those who perished
from the labor battalions and deportees
from Hungary. Item ID: 6508191"**

_No records at Yad Vashem can be found for either
Rudolf or Mathilde Vidor._

_Note: some Hungarian names are written last name
first in the Hungarian manner. Some of the references to
people and events are unclear, as these letters, uncovered
only after Frank's death, did not have the benefit of his
interpretations._

1. Date Unknown. _(Presumably written in late 1941 or
early 1942 after the Vidors received Teri and Frank's first
detailed letter from Chicago)_

Precious children!

We experienced such inexpressible joy with the arrival of your first detailed report. We were particularly touched that the letter was almost entirely written by you, dear Franzl (*Frank*). Hopefully Tererka (*Teri*) has been able to rest and been able to settle in a bit into the new surroundings. I would appreciate receiving a detailed report from you, Terikém, about your daily activities and what you are doing (while) Franzl is busy at the factory. Terikém, please write about all the details that relate to you. You, dearest Franzl, I wish you so much luck and God's blessing as you begin your activities in your new line of work. That you may work undisturbed towards prosperity. You and your employer Karli (*Charles*) will surely enjoy working together. Have you heard the news of the dear parents? I can imagine your joy regarding the grandparents in Cuba. Have they got prospects to be with you? Terikém, our neighbors Grossman were asking whether you had sent the photos of their siblings? You didn't write a word about your big silver suitcase. Last Wednesday was satisfactory; however, today we haven't seen a soul. It is rainy and foggy, disagreeable weather. What do you think of my German concept?

All the relatives send their best wishes. Nothing of concern here.

I kiss you with all my heart,

Your dearly loving, Anjuka

2. Kassa, 23rd October, 1941.

My precious children!

In a few days, you will already be a "long standing" couple, and we thank the Almighty each day that for this reason, our ardent congratulations can be brought to you via Karli! May the dear Lord grant that your marriage for the next 75 years flourish in uninterrupted happiness, contentment and the best of health, and that it unfolds in the circle of your grandchildren, who shall hold you both in good remembrance, as very loving parents.

And so that someone may experience a tangible delight on your wedding day, we are sending you a care package to Skipper Ila, whose return home is still quite uncertain.

Juliska had procured two rooms for Aladár (*presumably* Aladár *Vidor, Francie's great-uncle*), which he cancelled and then contacted Hedka. But the former could only provide the same thing from the former hunch-backed office girl—in the conceivable primitive manner, and that is why Aladár is very upset with Hedka. In this case, Aladár is fundamentally in the wrong, something that doesn't need to be stated. This would have been a good time for Juliska's proposal, whose implementation is already delayed. What he will do now, I'm truly in the dark. I think that he will need to leave his present home by the end of the year. (*This may be a reference for plans to move residences or even to get out of the area, but it's unclear*)

Gyurka has been home since yesterday. He is negotiating with Gomboser farmers about the Anbau von Szina and next week is driving to Budapest. Magda is thinking about driving along and this, under the naïve pretext, that she hasn't, since your departure to Budapest, been there, and she wishes to undertake a tour of the manufacturers. These, indeed, are behaving in quite a mean manner, which doesn't bother me too much, since Franzl, for this reason, must now follow up and restrict the inventory—which, after all, is also a position to take, isn't it? Anyuska (*Teri's mother*) is continuing with her walking, her Wednesday miles, and won't be stopped even in the worst of weather. We often wonder about how she manages to do this.

Erzi wrote that her sister Sarí is learning to weave and asked that I send her a loom frame. I responded by asking diverse questions and am now waiting for her answer. In the meantime, we sold a loom frame to Mrs. Grünfeld, friend of Hexner Malvin. Frau Spira was also downstairs (*presumably in the Vidor's shop*), as Laci, who is now in Budapest and owns a fashion store, would like to play with weaving. As you can see, a true bull market in loom frame inquiries. I myself completed the coat fabric for Anyuska, which was, in fact, quite beautiful, and now Magda wishes that I might also weave her suit material, out of pure Khedive cross twill. I have already tried a test piece with Anyu's coat, and it will turn out magnificently beautiful. Sunday, I will start with the trees. If we only had news from you! About the loss of the suitcase, please provide a forthright clarification. Many, many best wishes and kiss from your, very, very, very loving and loyal

Apu

My most precious children!

I join in with Apu's sweet wishes.

With impatience, we await your news.

I kiss you with immense love,

Yours, Apuka

3. Kassa, 6th November 1941

My precious children!

Yesterday the postal carrier Haluska had another good day. This time Anyuska was the charitable one and, although it wasn't usual, gave him a pengó (*currency*) while I gave him a jigger of very special Slivovitz (*fruit brandy*). However, I am furious with Gyula, who received your letter already on October 25th and carried it about for ten whole days!

Franzl! You were, this time, so singularly sweet and kind and in order to express my appreciation, I hurried to confirm telegraphically the arrival of this letter, as I don't know how it is with receiving my correspondence and I don't wish that you have, on our account, even one single moment of worry! It hardly needs mentioning that Anyuska, whilst reading and then again reading aloud your letters after supper, fed the little mice. May the Almighty grant her similar causes for there to be tears in her sky-blue eyes!

We were so sorry to hear that during the duration of your cruise you slept in separate beds. What a ridiculous affair. Was it worthwhile to upgrade from second to first class? I imagine that in regards to the meal service and the comforts, it must have been! Fairly recently we saw a film with Marlene Dietrich starring as "Bijou," and therein the class differences were clearly to be seen. Truly, you were fortunate to have been helped by such a decent Dutch agent rather than be duped by the corpse robber.

Erzi will be informed about the special mention of her care package (in your letter). You do know that she appreciates such endearments, and deserves them, especially in regards to you, Franzl. She should receive recompense! Should you "at some point" have a little bit of extra time, please write to her.

So, it seems that Teri was one of the bravest passengers at sea? How was it that you, dear Franzl, were so often seasick? Teri has also had other notable achievements, or rather, successes.

On Tuesday Mme Dr. Balázs Miczi was here and told us that she was in S.A. Ujhely to see the senior physician Dr. Skékely Lázlo, who said the following about Mrs. Therese: "olyan bájos, megnyeró, intelligenciától sugárzo egyéniséggel talán még nem is találkoztam!" which means "that she has never met such a sweet, likeable, bursting-with-intelligence individual." This recognition, as Mizzi (Miczi) emphasizes, is no trifling matter as it is the opinion of a senior hospital doctor who consults with thousands of people. Thereupon M. mentioned that she knew this woman since the age of six and was a welcome friend in her home. However, this does not provide grounds for vanity, as the old Vidor and the young Weinmann don't necessarily have to share the same view!

We were particularly thrilled to hear in your telegram that you could speak with the parents in Havana. Though it was disappointing that you weren't able to lobby for a transit visa, with which you could have disembarked. To be three days in Havana and the entire time stuck on the ship is more than frustrating.

No signature.

4. Kassa, (Monday) 17th November, 1941

My precious children.

My eleventh letter will be concluded only today, in part because we have been waiting each day for your letter to arrive. As well, we were told that it is better to always write on Mondays as the mail leaves Budapest every Thursday, and so there is no purpose in our choosing that particular day as our correspondence day. Furthermore, it was such a busy week that I had my hands full – making sales preparations, repricing the entire stock, 15% off the evenly-colored artificial silk (rayon or viscose) and 20% off the multicolored ones. Every piece must be carefully marked with the inscription of origin, the date of purchase and sales price, whereby the date of purchase must be used as the basis for the calculation. As a result, it happened that two pieces of the same type, color and design were marked with considerably different prices and that we sold older stock at a much lower price than their current purchase price.

On Saturday, we received from Aladár the news that he will henceforth definitely move in with Juliska and occupy two rooms there. You can imagine that I was doubly thrilled by this news.

Most importantly, they have a roof over their heads, and in all cases, isn't it more favorable to have a good number of family members together—Hedka is housing her two daughters, including Katinkas' in-laws, Bözsi is living equally so with Manya, whereby Bálint is still a tradesman.

Anyuska is now standing next to me and is unraveling her work of three days—the Pinguin "drappen" (*this reference in later letters suggest this is a brand of wool*) from which Anyus had knitted a dress. "You made the front part, Terikém, so she should knit a skirt—Kabátka." That was Atlasz Jolly's instruction. She wrote: 20 rows instead of 20 centimeters for the sleeve. When Anyus had completed the piece, it turned out that the sleeve was half the length it should be, and thus Anyus is beginning anew. (You are using the same yarn to make a sweater for Franzl. Is it already finished?)

I've not been in Budapest since the 11th of September and should have traveled there, but now Magda is going instead of me to surprise Gyuri in her wildcat fur coat! You see, Gyuri has been in Budapest for the past four weeks and is working as the construction manager of the Adlerpalast (Adler Palace). The loom frames, which I had previously mentioned as sold are all still here. At first there was a big rush and then no one came for them. Such is the state of affairs.

We are terribly curious to learn what happened to your suitcase and we worry (since I haven't broached this subject) that it must be hopelessly lost. Should this be the case, wouldn't it be worthwhile to pursue a claim with the insurance company? Children! Please write regularly, as although we know that you are well, we would like to hear this confirmed firsthand from you.

Many thousand kisses and good wishes from your loyal parents, who love you beyond all measure.

Apu

Anjuka

5. Kassa, 12th March 1942

My precious Terinkóm, dearest Franzl!

On the 16th of January and the 17th of February, I wrote to you by way of the brother-in-law of von Ackersman Anci, and yet don't have any idea whether these letters were conveyed. It's thanks to Uncle Aladár that I have the address of Mr. Curt Kaiser, Zurich 1, Löwenstrasse 11, and that I write now to this address with greater hope.

In the previous letters, I wrote you that (Magda's relationship) ended with Adler Gyuri in mid-December and that shortly thereafter Dr. Bettelheim (already now your brand-new brother-in-law) came to visit Magda. Early January Magda went to Sátoraljaújhely, (*a town in northern Hungary near the Slovak border*) quickly won the heart of Márti's mother, took charge of the situation by speaking with her spouse and arranged that he, in the company of his son, arrive here on February 1st to retain the hand of your lovely sister. The wedding should have taken place Easter Monday, but when Magda again went to S.A. Ujhely, she began again to help Márti's mother, who then asked Magda why they would wait so long and that she could ask for "the wedding" as a birthday present! Magda didn't need to be told twice. They freed themselves from their respective duties and on the 1st of March, Magda, in the name of God and the civic laws, became the wife of Dr. Bettelheim Márton István. Still on that same evening they took the fast train to Budapest, where they are expected to stay until early next week.

Terezka may recall that Márti received his medical degree in Torino, and as a result, for the time being, cannot yet serve as a doctor. We thought that he might practice completely without pay at the Jewish Hospital but Márti shows little inclination in this regard and is thinking of learning dentistry to possibly make himself useful to you.

Dear children! Dr. Friedmann Heinrich received news from his son by way of the Red Cross! You haven't tried this route? Dr. Pollatsek received from Zsuzsi news through Switzerland. Just we are waiting to no avail for letters from you.

Hopefully, the dear parents have been with you for a long time already, and that they have been with you since then! It would be of interest to us to know if Marilee has married.

I believe that I have already informed you that Uncle Aladár, along with family, moved from Pressburg to Sillein and that, in addition, family Dr. Bálint went to Manyus in Sillein. Fritz Reismann is the only one, as the last Mohican, who came to Budapest on business for two weeks. He said that Ungár wasn't willing to pay a cent, meaning this can be offset from the money he advanced to you, dear Franzl.

Family Stark has relocated and the Philipps are living together with Katinka. Jenó is probably working in the office but is receiving a very small wage, for which reason Katinka is going to train to be a modiste (*dressmaker*).

Attending Magda's wedding were the Bettelheim parents, along with an uncle and cousin, and from our side Erzsi néni, Fedrit Zoli along with spouse and Vidor Gyula. Although we didn't invite anyone, my entire circle of friends, some with their wives, appeared. Last not least, even Adler Gyuri came directly from Budapest and brought, as a wedding present, a silver cup.

Stay out of mischief! We are! Even Ayuska is very, very well-behaved, though mentions you very, very often! Many, many good wishes and kisses. Your very, very loving parents,

Apu Anyuka

Please ask Mr. Kaiser to include international return postage.

6. Kassa, 9th April 1942

My precious Terinkóm, most dearest Franzl!

I wrote to you on the 22nd of M. (*March*) and would hope that you are already in possession of my news. Over the last two weeks I have become a little more anxious and would be necessary and have—after 14 years of abstinence—taken up smoking again. The reason thereof concerns not so much uncle Aladár, as his daughter Klárinka! On the 25th of March Aladár wrote that Klári, who is learning gardening, is languishing at home with her parents. To the contrary, today we received news from Gyula that Klári from now on will be engaged at the Bratislava Factory.

Furthermore, Gyula wrote that he had received news from Margit as well as Rozsi; it seems that it is just us who are waiting in vain for the mail. We ourselves are following our customary routines and are all, thank God, healthy and content. Magda and Márti moved into the third room as you did, with the difference that the recliner was also moved in for Magda's comfort.

Over the Easter holidays we were in Sátoraljaújhely though returned home after five days.

Anyuska started to knit for herself a dress from the black "khedive" but is not making much progress. Magda gave the blue Pinguin-wool, the very wool from which Anjuska already has a dress, to her mother-in-law as a gift. I myself have been massively lazy and haven't produced anything since Anyus' last dress, though I took apart the loom and am having a local carpenter fabricate an identical one for Vidor Pista. When Pista was here before Christmas, he took a great liking to it. The woodwork alone comes to 70 Pengó; nevertheless, I'm having two made. One loom—one of yours, Terikém—we gave to Magda's mother-in-law, and in return Magda received homespun angora wood.

Marti can't do anything with his Italian doctor's degree (*the rest of this sentence is unclear*)

Building an association with his brother-in-law from the Decalomania. And now the possibility no longer exists that, even if working without pay, he would find placement as a trainee. We received only sparse news from Hedka néni and Katinka; the latter live with the in-laws at the periphery of the town. Where exactly Klemka is puttering about we don't know. Likewise, we don't know whether in fact or from where Klárika (*Aladár's daughter, Teri's cousin)* was able to write to Aladár.

From amongst your mutual acquaintances, only family Nyulas moved back to S.A. Ujhely; otherwise everyone is feeling fairly good. On the business front, there is not much to report. Regarding consumer spending, we haven't fallen back, barely (quantitatively) just more than half, but this is not a reason to grumble; would be overjoyed to maintain the same levels.

Anyuska is still well-behaved and her sky-blue eyes desire as always to read from her Terezka a detailed letter. We hope you will, now with Uncle Kaiser's help, please include return postage.

We kiss you millions of times, with the best wishes to the dear grandparents, parents, Karli and spouse. From your loving and loyal,

Apu

Anyuka

7. Kassa, 16th May 1942

My precious Terinkóm, dearest Franzl!

Since my latest letter to you, enough has occurred which, to some degree, kept me from writing earlier to you, my dearest ones. In the final days of April, Klárika, rather than accept the invitation from Elsa—or Franzl's—drove to Lengyel's and since then hasn't written a syllable! On April 25th, Uncle Aladár wrote that on the previous day, Klárika, along with Malvinka and Miki, should have followed, but at the last minute his doctor intervened and he was not permitted to go on account of a heart condition. Since then I have been without any news from them. Is Aladár's health condition forcing her to stay put? Juliska's husband is working, as he was doing, in the textile mill.

And now for our news. Magda spent eight heavenly weeks with Márti. Since the 11th, Márti has been in a town near Budapest where he and several friends will remain until the 28th, at which time they will depart. After the well-used Liebig suitcase, an item that is part of my collection, became inconvenient, he demanded a knapsack, which Magda personally brought to him last night. But today we learned that Magda will have to wait until Sunday afternoon before she is able to be with Márti. We have the Pentecost holidays prior to the 28th, and so Magda will have occasion to visit Márti again before he can begin his new—medical (we hope)—posting. Soon I hope to be able to provide you with detailed answers to all previous questions.

Anyuska is, praise the Lord, doing well and is quite well-behaved, apart from her grumblings about what her Terinko and Franzl are doing, whether they are healthy and feel happy. Only the well-being of Aladár, Malvinka, as well as her own sisters and their children, are causing her, as well as myself, great concern. I will write to you on a regular basis and would be pleased to receive a sign of life from you!

On the business front, I have nothing new to report. We are finding our livelihood as erstwhile, unchanged, for which we are grateful to God, as He thereby allows us to also contribute sufficiently in charitable areas. Anyuska is making only slow advances on the dress she is knitting. Terike isn't here to spur her on! From the blue Thibet/ Lenclosstoff (*textile*) she had a coat fashioned, which is apparently going to be gorgeous. Magda's mother-in-law—almost as sweet and beautiful as our Anyuska— received, along with a dress, Pinguin-wool (*a type of yarn*) as a present.

Continue to behave yourselves; be good and healthy! Write also about the parents, grandparents and Karli, to whom we send our regards. We hug and kiss you millions of times.

Your very, very loving and loyal,

Apu

I kiss you affectionately many times!

Anyuska

8. 19th August 1942

My precious Terinkóm, most dearest Franzl!

This day has truly been a splendid day in that at the same time as your dear letter from June 28th arrived that Magda received the very first card (presumably from Márti) after four weeks since they said their goodbyes. From your letter, Terikém, I can conclude with joy, that you received my letters in a timely manner. In contrast, your above-referenced letter is the first news of yours since you announced your start at the textile factory. You can well-imagine how much your letter, which we received today, means to us and that, as a consequence, our dear Anyuska's nose turned purple, this time due to tears of joy! It was high time, at last, to have cause for such joy!

Family Aladár, Ellka and Klementine followed Klárika on July 10th; since then we have heard nothing more. We sent Klári money three times since June 4th, yet without the faintest hint whether she received it, because ever since May, at which time she wrote for the first time and shared her parents' address, she has not communicated even a syllable. From Hedka we heard the news last week that sometimes they are all together, though this won't last for too long. In regards to my smoking, Terinkóm, don't worry; I'm careful that it doesn't slip into the not permitted. Furthermore, I have learned to ride a bicycle and when there is no wind, I ride almost daily for half an hour. Magda is learning as well.

Anyuska is following your advice and, along with Magda, uses every possible opportunity to go to the cinema. Also, Anyuska enjoyed three weeks of holidays at Erzsi's and then visited Magda's mother-in-law. We have, in turn, invited her for the holidays. As you can see, Terikém, Anyuska is a truly good and courageous child!

Now – as for your age! This is a matter of course, isn't it? Anyuska was deeply touched by the account of your "cooking art" and is enormously happy that you get on so well with Marila (*Marilee, Charles' wife*). Franzerl! I'm so terribly proud of you and have a great hope that I will one day hold Karli, because he has become so fond of my Tertschike (*Teri*). Hopefully you have had the chance to deliver to family Marianne my kiss on the hand. What happened to the checked suitcase? Did your belongings make an appearance? Hereof you continue to remain silent.

It doesn't matter, children, if you sometimes repeat yourself in your letters. As you can see, there are great gaps in letter exchanges and, as stated earlier, there is a passage of time between your two letters, where you reported that on the third day of your new post you proofed 120 jackets. Between the letter received earlier and the letter received today lies a big vacuum, except for Rozsi's news that Franzl received a raise, which then prompted him to further elevate your status, Terikém, as a housewife.

Just so that you are informed about all the gossip, the primary reason that Anyuska visited Erzsi for such a long time is that Márti was awful. In the end, discipline must be kept; but the priority should be given to Terezka; Anyuska also wants to help with this. Would you agree with the handling of this? Further to the gossip…I bought a pigeonry and we aren't shy at all to sometimes sit for hours at a time, to marvel at the loveliness of these little creatures. It gives us great pleasure and we have a lot of fun with it.

Continue to keep out of mischief and be good. We are—word of honor! I hope that now we will hear—or rather read—more of each other!

We wish you the best and kiss you many, many millions of times, in expressible love, your always-thinking-of-you,

Apu

I greet and kiss you many times.
Your loving,
Anyuska.

9. 3rd of September, 1942

My precious Terinkóm, dearest Franzl!

Confirming your dear letter from June 28th and my response from the 19th of last month, and hope that you have been together with the dear parents and grandparents. We have still not heard anything more from Aladár, Ellkas and Klárika; only the Almighty knows if we shall ever see them again in this lifetime. Márti wrote already twice to Magda, each time a postcard; she writes daily. What's upsetting about the whole thing is that Márti is not employed in his area of expertise. It was our hope that he would practice medicine. But they are eight colleagues altogether and, as such, each only has a turn to provide medical services once a week. Magda will go to the in-laws next Monday and will remain with them during the holidays. She is in good company, which includes the pharmacist Hoffman, whom you know from the home on Fishergasse (*Fisher Alley*), and whose wife is Márti's schoolmate and best friend.

My precious Terinkóm! I will take the opportunity to wish you, my dearest child, on the occasion of your birthday, from all my heart, congratulations. May our Almighty Protector granted that you, on your path of life, alongside our good and kind Franzl, continue to be a happy wife and remain our noble-minded Terinko, upon whom we can gaze with calm, knowing that you are, in every way, content and surrounded by genuine love.

We have thought and spoken of you so often in the bygone days. Our conversations have been imbued with a unique retrospection, with there being a different theme almost each day and with Anyuska reconstructing in detail and speaking of each phase of the previous days. For me, however, the moment of your departure was the most terrible of my experiences, as I stood there at the railway station entirely numbed and reeling, unable to do more than wave wordlessly; much more difficult than the never-to-be-forgotten night, which the two of us spent together, Franzl, after Dr. Hausmann's despicable brother said his goodbyes. And afterwards, my visits with Terike and everything else. God grant that we may, for many years to come, recount all these memories with joy, together in cozy gatherings.

Since for weeks now it has continued to be exceedingly hot, Anyuska had a blue small-patterned sports dress made. As you know, blue is Anyuska's favorite color. Magda is working "diligently" on her white angora jacket, which might be completed in the fall. Magda hasn't changed much in this regard; when she asked her mother-in-law to teach her to cook, she postponed this until the winter, when it isn't so hot in the kitchen. But as you know, our kitchen in the winter is unbearably cold.

We'd very much like to have news of you. We send our best wishes—also to Karli and partner. Be hugged and kissed a million times.

Your always-thinking-of-you,
Apu

My most dearest children!
What should I wish you Terikóm—above all health.

10. 26th September 1942

My precious Terinkóm, dearest Franzl!
On Tuesday, I left to make purchases; on the following day at noon I called home to find out if my absence at the farmer's market hadn't disturbed Anyuska and not tired her out. At that moment, she didn't know yet to tell me as your dear letter from the 18th of last month only arrived in the afternoon; however, on Thursday evening Anyuska could

rejoice in your first report and when I arrived at home at noon I was delighted with the sweet "Teri-letter"! You complained that I'm not writing enough about personal matters. I reviewed the duplicates of the letters and find that the things I've written about are exclusively personal in nature. As regards to business matters, we are maintaining the levels of earlier consumption and are finding, thank the Lord, our livelihood herewith as always, though Bözsi and the considerable higher demands of the general charities must largely still be fulfilled. For instance, the membership fee c/o Dr. Enten has increased almost fivefold.

Apropos Aladár, all research has proven unfruitful; Juliaska and Hedka wrote similarly regarding Ella. On the occasion of your birthday, Terinkóm, we congratulated you in 25 words and repeat it again in the way: May the Almighty continue to help and protect you; and may He help us so that Márti – who has already written five times to Magda – be appointed medical doctor at his company. I wrote him to see if he could not possibly, in regards to his uncle, start to make inquiries. Karli wrote just once; since then we haven't heard anything. We were very, very pleased that the grandparents have achieved their aim and hope now that from now on Marianne can be a support for you in housekeeping matters. You describe your housekeeping virtue in such a spirited way that Anyuska, who is much like you, could not get enough of your writing.

The wife of your Superintendent must truly be a splendid person. What age difference is there between you that you get on so well together? What is the actual division? Is this gentleman Karli's superior or is Karli the general director of the entire factory (*company*)? We would be so happy to hear more about Franzl's sphere, so that we can, at the very least, have an approximate idea of his tasks. But I object—as if "only" Karli could be proud of his brother; where then is the old Vidor (*referring to himself*) and doesn't he also have this right?

Yesterday we made the acquaintance of Márti's best friend and university colleagues; the friend who is occasionally active at the hospital, was quite surprised to see how youthful Magda's parents are. He officially fell in love with Anyuska! We wrote a joint card to Márti; he was worried whether Márti's feelings might be hurt, since he is still able to be employed privately, whereas all the other colleagues, including Márti, are performing the same work, as when Franzl visited you both at the Bettelheim's.

Magda has, as a bicyclist, made a fool of herself; whereas I've become a capable rider; Magda couldn't manage getting onto the seat independently and has now given up the whole thing. It is the same with her intention to learn to cook, despite this being her mother-in-law's earnest wish.

Many millions of greetings and kisses.

Your very, very loving,

Apuka

My precious children! Most of all, I congratulate you on your wedding day. Magda has become more serious. She's doing beautiful knitted work. I kiss you both with much love.

Yours,

Anyuska

11. 26th October 1942

My precious Terinkóm, most dearest Franzl!

Yesterday was your third wedding anniversary and, thank God for that; that you may henceforth be together in joyful harmony. Two years ago, that wasn't the case and in the previous year, you were just then en route traveling. May the Almighty grant that we will celebrate your silver wedding anniversary with all your loved ones in happy, healthy and in good spirits.

Tomorrow is a second anniversary: Aladár's 56th birthday. God alone knows where and in what kind of living conditions he and his family are spending this day. We continue to be completely in the dark, and my queries with Goth & Co. have, as yet, brought no response at all.

This time I have good reason to complain about Anyuska! She had the flu but didn't look after herself and became bedridden. Actually, it happened like this: when she was washing herself in the morning, she leaned over the tub and couldn't stand up straight and was not able, even in bed, to move. For four weeks Jancsi came and treated her with vitamin B injections. As we have had a steady rain (which ended only today) and as today is a fairly warm sunny day, Anyus went out for the very first time. Her outing was to the dentist, since four cavities had fallen out in the last while; Dr. Grünstein is fashioning them.

Magda had quite a difficulty; namely, she tried to send Márti some warmer underwear, since the boy had taken nothing other than light summer clothing. The situation was much like your suitcase scenario. Not many people have such bad luck as Márti has. For example, Adler Guyri was just then departing from his parents' house. At the same time Erzsinéni became widow and in order that she not be home alone, her parents moved in with her.

Last week we had Márti's parents here; I truly don't know whether it is possible to love a daughter-in-law more, as is the case with Stefi Bettelheim. The father is also a good person, but Stefi can only be compared to Anyuska, in regards to her loveliness and other apparent character traits. All three mothers-in-law are quite similar in nature and we are happy about this; may Marianne delight Terike equally so. Given the tenor of your last report from the 18th of August, is this possible to assume?

At the moment, Magda is knitting herself, under direction from Atlas Joly, a fabulously beautiful "Schoss" (*possibly a shawl or skirt of some kind*) from the leftover Pinguin-wool, with green and red squares and she is, for once (but only as regards this isolated case) very industrious. Previously she worked for eight months on a "lumberjack" (*jacket*)—using white angora given to her by her mother-in-law—which was also very beautiful and which was, according to Magda, well-liked by all, both men and women. Otherwise she is also a good girl in that she plays "Römi" (*a card game*) with Anyuska night after night, starting after the evening meal and lasting until bedtime.

Márti wrote in his last card that Magda should act in a way becoming of a doctor's wife, from which we can assume that he now has an opportunity to further himself professionally. How is Franzl doing with the chemistry, and his wife in her honorable role as housewife? Please send new reports on these matters.

Many, many millions of greetings and kisses to you and all of your precious ones.

Apu

12. 19th April 1943

My precious Terinkóm, most dearest Franzl!

Today I ran into Director Mandl, who knew how to boast about having received news. I take it that this could also be the case with you and therefore hasten to take initiative and write. Your last letter was the one in which you wrote about your nice birthday present and I, amongst other things, wrote that we hadn't received your previous letter.

It's likely that all the misfortune is now behind us; since my last report Anyuska and I have gone through difficult days. On the occasion of my birthday, Anyuska surprised me by undergoing a serious operation, whose side effects she felt for a full four weeks. We were under the impression that it would be a matter of stitching ligaments. But it turned out that during the operation itself –as prompted by the discovery of an alleged myeloma – the professor preferred to remove the entire womb (*hysterectomy*). This didn't happen, however, with the help of an incision in the abdomen; rather it was made vaginally. You can imagine my surprise when Anyuska emerged from the operating room and the professor announced this news. I stayed at Anyuska's bedside for the full two weeks and then we went through another difficult week at home; hereafter the stitches were removed and now there is a noticeable improvement. After another two weeks had elapsed, Anyuska promptly forgot what great anxiety she had caused me! Now she is again beautiful, smart-looking, and as vibrant as before.

In our absence, Magda was both homemaker and business chief, however, when her cold didn't go away and her fever kept returning, we had an x-ray made – confirmed by both the specialist as well as the hospital's senior lung specialist – which showed that during our absence our young lady managed to contract pneumonia, which didn't stop her from smoking for even an hour! At the time of the x-ray, or rather the follow up visit, it was determined that it was already post-festum (*too late*). According to the senior lung specialist, her case was a miracle; things could have turned out much differently, and with dire consequences. How does one say, "In Nessel schlägt kein Blitz ein" (*Lightning doesn't strike untreated cotton*).

At the present time, she has gone to see her in-laws to spend the Easter holidays with them. Apart from that, she is busy knitting and has already finished some smart-looking pieces. Márti is writing, as he has been, once a month and according to the report received the day before yesterday he is, thank the Lord, doing well. Next month it will be already a full year that he hasn't seen Magda; the dear Lord alone knows when they can be together again; at this time, there do not appear to be any prospects.

How are you, dear children, spending your time? Hopefully Marianne can help you, Terinkóm, with your work as venerable homemaker. How is it going with you, Franzerl, with your studies? Do you plan on doing a Ph.D.? I wrote to Klárika last month; the letter was returned to me, minus the money. In regards to her parents, I am equally without any sign of life. As regards our business, there is little to say; Magda hardly ever comes downstairs; Anyuska only between 10 and 12 noon—mainly not to be bored at home. Usually Anyuska works on Magda's bed linen. The old staff is all present, but mostly without work assignments. At present, I am still in the position to honor the charitable duties, whose demands are increasing by the day. Please give everyone our best. We kiss and hug you many millions of times and we always think of you.

Your loyal and very, very loving,
Apuka

I am confirming everything that Apuka shared. Hopefully you will receive this letter. I kiss you many times!
Yours, Anyuka

Editor's note: As posted earlier in this book, the final letter from Teri's family arrived in Chicago in late 1945, a year and a half after it was written. It was the last time the family was heard from:

13. April 23 1944

RUDOLF VIDOR, Kassa (Kosice)
My beloved Teri, my dearest Frank!

Until this moment at least I could hold myself together, but now that I have to write a farewell letter to my dearest children, my heart is getting very heavy. I must stop after every word and collect myself in order to continue writing. Well, we are about there! When Frank filled his rucksack, he could at least hope to be with his Teri soon. But when we fill this rucksack, which he bought in Prague, for ourselves, we are confronted with utmost uncertainty. Will we ever find an anchor to sink into secure soil?

My Teri!

I left my last will with Dr. Joseph Pilat, attorney. Be sure to visit our Ilus (*a former employee*) who knows all about the content of this last will. We placed Ilus with Mrs. Steven Palcso, textile shop, Szent Isvan korut 6, next to Hausmann's shop, Szepsi korut. By talking to Ilus, you will know how we spent the last five days of excitement and where our life insurance is. You will find your mother's very good photograph with Janos Papcun (address: Srobarova 23, Kosice, this is the Czechoslovakian address). We sent you this picture through Curt Kaiser *(a Swiss intermediary, who was kind enough to receive and forward letters, even during the first years of the war).* (We hope) that you receive it. Both in January and in February we sent you long letters through him, but we must assume that you never received them. Teri! Find out all about two of my best Christian friends, who will receive you, as former corresponding secretary, with open arms! *(This is probably a hint that these two friends are Freemasons.)* They will not let you go empty-handed! *(Frank's Note: This is probably a hint that some of his valuables are with some of the above-named Christian friends)* One of them was your good friend; in spite of the fact that he would not marry his beloved, the pharmacist's daughter, he did not forsake her in her different religion.

The bravest of the three of us *(Rudolf Vidor, Teri's father; Matilde Vidor nee Stein, Teri's mother, and Magda Bettelheim nee Vidor, Teri's sister)* is Magda, who is of course 30 years younger and this is important. Her husband, Dr. Martin Steven Bettelheim, from Satoraljaujhely, was sent to the front after a marriage of only two months, as a non-armed and not-fighting Jewish member of a special working battalion. Imre, now in Israel, was in a similar unit. *(Frank's Note: The lives of many thousand Jewish young men were thus saved by the Hungarian government. Martin Bettelheim survived and went back to Hungary or Czechoslovakia. He is not in Israel. Teri could not find him.)* The poor boy, a graduate physician, works in the mud, chopped wood, makes bunkers, everything except as a doctor. He loves Magda since early and, like our dearly loved mother, enjoyed few good things. It is a miracle that he is still alive!

We are praying to the Almighty that the three of us will stay together and not, like the Aladárs, whom we hardly can hope to be alive anymore, were torn from each other! We can bear all suffering if we can just stay with our dear mother!

(Frank's Note: Rudolf Vidor's brother and Teri's uncle, Aladár, along with his wife Malvinka, daughter Hana Klara (referred to in the letters as Klárika) and son Miklos, lived in Bratislava. None survived. Editor's note: The letters make numerous references to the fact that the Vidors (Teri's parents) lost touch with Rudolf's brother Aladar and his family, and as of the last letters written, had not been able to contact them for what appeared to be a number of years).

We are often talking about you, dear Teri, what you are doing now, if you are hearing anything about our fate? Frank, my dear son, continue to be good to our often-obstinate Teri and love each other always. Always fervently and sincerely.

Be well, my dear children. Be happy with each other. Give our regards to your parents and to Charles' family. I kiss you many millions of times. I love you very, very much.

Your Father *(written in Hungarian as Apuca).*

The following lines were written by Matilde Vidor, Teri's mother

My dearest Children!

I hope with great confidence to our dear God that we will see each other again in gladness and will spend many happy hours together. I kiss you, dear children, with great love.

Your loving mother *(written in Hungarian as Anyuka).*

The following line is written by Magda Bettelheim, Teri's sister.

I kiss you.

Your loving Magda.

(Frank's note: we were later told that Magda survived in a concentration camp but died a few days after its liberation).

A Final Editor's Note:

Since Frank Weinman passed away in 2009, his descendants have multiplied.

In June of 2011, another great grandson, Jonah Frank King, was born to Frank's granddaughter Dana Bash and her then husband John King.

In addition, Frank's grandson David married Juliana Alonso de Oliveira in 2012 and they now have two children, two more great grandchildren of Frank: Teodoro de Oliveira Schwartz and Stella de Oliveira Schwartz.

This record of Frank's writings and his life experiences is a gift to all of these descendants and all others that may follow.

Stuart Schwartz (Frank's Son-in-Law)
Potomac, Maryland
June, 2017

Printed in the United States
By Bookmasters